The Recipe Project

A collaborative effort

TotalRecall Publications, Inc.
1103 Middlecreek
Friendswood, Texas 77546
281-992-3131 TEL
www.totalrecallpress.com
Published in Canada by First Class Press

All rights reserved, except as permitted under the United States Copyright Act of 1976. No part of this publication may be reproduced, stored in a retrieval system, or transmitted in any form or by any means electronic or mechanical or by photocopying, recording, or otherwise, without prior permission of the publisher. Exclusive worldwide content publication/distribution by TotalRecall Publications, Inc.

Copyright © 2018 by: The Authors
Cover Design by: Larry Cavanagh
Contents compiled by: Liane Desmarais-Cavanagh
All rights reserved

ISBN: 978-1-55323-711-2
UPC: 6-43977-47112-3
Library of Congress Control Number: 2018948969

Printed in the United States of America with simultaneous printing in Australia, Canada, and United Kingdom.

FIRST EDITION
1   2   3   4   5   6   7   8   9   10

The scanning, uploading and distribution of this book via the internet or via any other means without the permission of the publisher is illegal and punishable by law. Please purchase only authorized electronic editions, and do not participate in or encourage electronic piracy of copyrighted materials. Your support of the author's rights is appreciated.

This book is dedicated with love and gratitude

to the memory of

Christina Henderson.

She instilled in us, her children and grandchildren, an appreciation for family and good food.

For many of us, happy memories are triggered by the smells and tastes that came from a kitchen in Richmond, Quebec. That kitchen belonged to Christina Henderson.

The idea for *The Recipe Project* was born from a desire to preserve her culinary legacy, and ensure that future generations could experience those same smells and tastes.

The original plan had been to collect Christina's recipes, organize and share them. When I started receiving contributions, I noticed that I was receiving her recipes as well as many others that have become individual family favourites.

What a treasure trove! If the 'flavour' of a family is measured by its recipes…we are indeed a diverse group.

It is with deep gratitude that I acknowledge the contributions of:

Ellen Desmarais,
Mireille Desmarais,
Valerie Healy,
Heather Ross, and
Judy Ross,

without whom this book would never have been realized.

Table of Contents

Chapter	Page
~ Breads ~	0
~ Breakfast / Brunch ~	16
~ Hors d'œuvres ~	24
~ Lunch / First Course ~	44
~ Soups & Chowders ~	66
~ Salads ~	78
~ Starch ~	98
~ Veggies ~	114
~ Main Course (meat) ~	130
~ Desserts & Sweets ~	178
~ Preserves ~	264
~ Drinks ~	286

~Breads~

All-Year Blueberry Corn Muffins

Contributed by: Heather Ross
Source: Bon Appétit, December 1992 (via Epicurious.com)
Yield: 12 muffins
Note: These muffins are sophisticated and substantial, not cake-like.

Ingredients

1 cup	Butter milk (or 1 cup milk plus 1 tbsp lemon juice or vinegar)
2	Eggs
¼ cup	Butter, melted & cooled
1 cup	Cornmeal
1 cup	Flour
½ cup	Brown sugar, packed
1½ teaspoons	Baking powder
½ teaspoon	Baking soda
¼ teaspoon	Salt
12 oz	Blueberries, frozen

Directions

Preheat oven to 400°F.

Whisk buttermilk, eggs and butter together in small bowl.

Sift cornmeal, flour, brown sugar, baking powder, baking soda and salt in a large bowl. Add blueberries and toss to coat thoroughly.

Add buttermilk mixture and stir just until dry ingredients are moist.

Spoon batter into prepared muffin pan.
Bake about 27 minutes.

Transfer to a rack and let stand for 15 minutes before serving.

Apple Bread

Contributed by: Liane Desmarais-Cavanagh
Source: Lynn Normand, October 2010
Yield: 2 loaf pans
Note: A tasty treat, great with peanut butter.

Ingredients

3 cups	all-purpose Flour
2 teaspoons	Cinnamon
1 teaspoon	Baking Soda
½ teaspoon	Baking Powder
½ teaspoon	Salt
½ cup	Vegetable Oil (not Olive)
2 cups	Sugar
2	Eggs, beaten
½ teaspoon	Vanilla
2 cups	Apples - peeled, cored, and coarsely chopped
1 cup	broken Walnuts (I like Pecans)

Directions

Preheat oven to 350°F
Grease two loaf pans

In bowl, combine flour, cinnamon, baking soda, baking powder and salt; set aside.

In large mixing bowl, place oil, sugar, eggs, vanilla and apples

Stir into flour mixture

Add nuts and mix

Divided mixture between two greased 8-in. x 4-in. bread pans

Bake at 350°F for 40-45 minutes or until bread test done.

Cool for 10 minutes on wire rack before removing from pan

Biscuit Dough (Tea Biscuits)

Contributed by:	Mireille Desmarais
Source:	*A Guide to Good Cooking,* Five Roses Cook Book, 1938
Yield:	6 biscuits
Note:	I always have good results with this recipe.

Ingredients

2 cups	All-purpose flour
4 teaspoons	Baking Powder
½ teaspoon	Salt
3 tablespoons	Shortening - you can use margarine
1 cup	Milk.

Directions

Mix together flour, baking powder, and salt.
Cut shortening with 2 knives or a pastry blender, until mixture is the consistency of coarse cornmeal.

Make a well in centre of these ingredients; add liquid slowly.
When all the liquid has been added, stir down rather vigorously until it comes freely from the side of the bowl.

Turn dough onto lightly floured board and knead lightly for a few minutes.
Roll or pat out to desired thickness – about ½".
Cut dough with 2" floured biscuit cutter and place on an ungreased baking sheet.

Bake at 450°F for 12 to 15 minutes.

Note: If baked in a round cake tin, the biscuits rise higher and look nicer.

Variations for tea biscuits:

Cheese:	Decrease shortening to 3 tbsp. and salt to ¾ teaspoon
	Cut in ½ cup grated cheddar cheese with shortening
Buttermilk:	Decrease baking powder to 2 teaspoon; add ½ teaspoon baking soda
	Substitute 1 cup buttermilk (or sour milk) milk
Fruit or Nuts:	Add ¼ cup granulated sugar and decrease milk to ¾ cup
	Add ¾ cup raisins, currants or nuts with milk
Sweet Cream:	Use ½ cup skim milk and ½ cup whipping cream
Whole Wheat:	Use 1 cup Whole Wheat Flour and 1 cup all-purpose Flour

Bread Stuffing for Meat

Contributed by: Mireille Desmarais
Source: Ellen Desmarais
Yield: Enough for a large chicken or a small turkey.
Note: This is an "adapt as you go" recipe. Make it to your taste.

Ingredients

4 cups	torn bread, should be old
½ cup	Onions
½ cup	Celery
½ cup	Apple
To taste	Herb de Provence
To taste	Poultry seasoning
To taste	Salt & Pepper
1 tablespoon	Olive oil
½ cup (ish)	Chicken broth

Directions

Tear the bread. (The bread should be one (or more) days old. Use white, brown, multigrain or light rye. You may also add a few slices of raisin bread too.)

Chop ½ cup each of the following: onions, celery and apple.
Add to the torn bread.

Season with: Herbs de Provence or poultry seasoning, salt and pepper.

Add chicken broth to moisten the mixture so it will stick together, but not too wet.
Add 1 tablespoon of olive oil.
Mix well with a spoon.

Rinse out the chicken and dry the inside with a paper towel.
Fill the cavity with the stuffing.
Whatever is left, put into a pan to cook in the oven.

Put the bird on a rack, uncovered, into the oven for about 20 minutes per pound.
Baste frequently with the drippings in the pan so the bird will be a nice golden brown.

Note:
The dressing can be cooked outside the bird in a pan in the oven, covered with aluminum foil. Bake at 350° F, 45 minutes.
Cranberries can also be added. Use whole cranberries, not the dried ones.

Bunratty Brown Oatmeal Soda Bread

Contributed by: Liane Desmarais-Cavanagh
Source: Ladies @ Bunratty Folk Park, Ireland (May 3, 2005)
Yield: 2 big loaves
Note: A lovely, hearty bread with no yeast, that can be prepared in 45 minutes or less.

Ingredients

2¼ to 2½ cups	all-purpose Flour
2 teaspoons	Baking soda
1 teaspoon	Baking powder
2 teaspoons	Salt
2 cups	Whole-Wheat Flour
1 cup	old-fashioned rolled Oats (plus additional for sprinkling the bread)
2 cups	Buttermilk
1 large	Egg, beaten lightly

Directions

Preheat oven to 350°F. (175°C.)

Into a large bowl sift together:
- 2¼ cups of the all-purpose flour
- the baking soda,
- the baking powder, and
- the salt.

Stir in the whole-wheat flour and 1 cup of the oats.

Add the buttermilk and the egg and stir the mixture until it forms a dough.

Turn the dough out onto a floured surface and knead it (kneading in as much of the remaining ¼ cup all-purpose flour as necessary) until it forms a manageable but sticky dough.

Halve the dough, form the halves into round loaves, and put them on a greased baking sheet.

Sprinkle the loaves lightly with the additional oats, dust them with flour.

Bake them in the middle of the oven for 30 to 35 minutes (or until they are browned lightly).

Let the loaves cool on a rack.

Corn Bread

Contributed by: Liane Desmarais-Cavanagh
Source: Christina Henderson
Yield: Makes 2 loaves
Note: I have no idea how I came to have a photocopy of this recipe, but it's in Grama H's handwriting and I have used it many times.

Ingredients

2 cups	all-purpose Flour
2 tablespoons	Baking Powder
1 teaspoon	Salt
2 cups	Yellow Cornmeal
1 can	Corn kernels, drained and patted dry (see**)
½ cup	Sugar (does not work with Splenda)
2 cups	Milk **
2 large	Eggs
1 cup	unsalted Butter, softened to room temperature

Directions

Preheat oven to 400° F.
Generously butter two 9" x 5" loaf pans.

Into a large bowl sift together flour, baking powder, and salt and whisk in cornmeal and sugar until combined well.

Add butter to flour mixture and with an electric mixer beat until mixture resembles coarse meal.

In separate bowl whisk together milk and eggs until just combined.

Beat egg mixture into flour mixture until just combined (batter will be thin).
(If you're adding the corn kernels, fold them in now)

Pour batter into pans and bake in middle of oven until golden and a tester comes out clean, about 50 minutes.

Cool corn bread in pans on a rack 10 minutes then turn out onto rack to cool completely.

Corn bread may be wrapped in plastic wrap and kept in a cool, dry place 2 days or frozen 2 weeks.

** I like to add canned sweet corn niblets, if you are doing that then drain the liquid from the can into the measuring cup and top with milk to make the 2 cups of liquid (this juice intensifies the corn flavor)

Double Chocolate Banana Muffins

Contributed by: Valerie Healy
Source: Nancy Willey-Smith
Note: This came from Nancy Willey Smith. If you would like a change from plain Banana Muffins this is a good replacement.

Ingredients

1½ cup	Flour
1 cup	Sugar
¼ cup	Baking Cocoa
1 teaspoon	Baking Soda
½ teaspoon	Salt
¼ teaspoon	Baking Powder
1 1/3 cups	Bananas, mashed
1/3 cup	Vegetable oil
1	Egg
1 cup	Chocolate Chips (miniature)

Directions

Preheat oven to 350°F

Combine first 6 ingredients in large bowl

Combine bananas, oil & egg

Stir into dry ingredients unil moistened

Fold in chocolate chips

Fill muffin cups ¾ full

Bake at 350°F for 20 – 25 minutes

Hobo Bread

Contributed by: Valerie Healy
Source: Charlotte Griffith
Yield: 2 loaves
Note: The only bread easier to make is to use a bread maker. This is similar to Mum's Oatmeal bread, not as good but a good substitute if time is a problem. My boys love it. The two loaves never last long.

Ingredients and Directions:

Grease 2 48 oz Juice tins

Combine and set for 10 minutes
2 tablespoons	Yeast
½ cup	Warm Water
1 teaspoon	Sugar

In another bowl combine:
¾ cup	Rolled Oats
2 tablespoons	Brown Sugar
½ cup	Molasses
1 teaspoon	Salt
1½ cups	boiling Water

Cool till lukewarm
Add yeast
Stir in 4 cups Flour
Knead

Divide into 2 portions and put in cans
Let rise for 90 minutes (or until bread reaches top of tins

Bake at 350° F for 45 minutes

Mildred's Pineapple Loaf

Contributed by: Ellen Desmarais
Source: Christina Henderson
Note: This recipe is handwritten by Mum in the back of my copy of the <u>1954 Personal Recipes of the Ladies Auxiliary to the Canadian Legion</u>, Richmond, Quebec. I presume Mildred is Mildred Stevens

Ingredients

2¼ cups	Bread Flour, Sifted
¾ cup	Brown Sugar
3 level teaspoon	Baking powder
½ teaspoon	Baking Soda
½ teaspoon	Salt
1½ cups	Bran flakes
¾ cup	Walnuts
1½ cups	Pineapple, crushed
1	Egg
¼ cup	Butter, melted

Directions

Preheat oven to 350°F

Mix the flour, brown sugar, baking powder, soda, and salt together and sift.
Add to this the bran flakes and walnuts.
Add the pineapple with juice to one egg and mix; add this to the dry ingredients and add the melted butter and mix altogether.

Bake at 350°F for 1 hour + 10 minutes.

Monkey Bread

Contributed by: Liane Desmarais-Cavanagh
Source: EzraPoundCake.com
Yield: enough for 10 people
Note: Biscuits are best if made from scratch, but in case of emergency 'Mr. Pillsbury' is a life-saver

Ingredients

16 ounces	Biscuits (uncooked) or 2 large cans {16.3 oz.} refrigerated Pillsbury biscuits
1 cup	Butter, unsalted & melted
1½ cups	Sugar
2 tablespoons	Cinnamon (I prefer Nutmeg)
½ cup	Pecan halves
½ cup	Raisins/Currents (optional)

Directions

Preheat the oven to 350 degrees F.

Grease a Bundt pan or tube pan with butter (or non-stick spray)

In a small bowl, combine the sugar and cinnamon
Set aside.

Roll your biscuits into golf-ball sized rounds (or cut the Pillsbury's into quarters)

Dip each biscuit bite in melted butter, roll it in cinnamon sugar, and place it in the pan (try to keep them random).

Sprinkle pecans (and raisins/currents) onto the biscuit pieces at random.

Pour any remaining butter evenly over the biscuit pieces in the pan.

Bake for about 40 minutes or until the top springs back when touched.

Cool in the pan on a wire rack for 10 minutes.

Invert onto a plate, and serve immediately.

Old Fashioned Soda Biscuits

Contributed by: Valerie Healy
Source: Christina Henderson

Ingredients

2 cups	Flour
1 tablespoon	Sugar
1 teaspoon	Baking Soda
2 teaspoons	Cream of Tartar
S cup	Shortening
1 cup	Milk

Directions

Preheat oven to 425°F

Cut Shortening into flour, sugar, salt, soda & cream of tartar mixture

Add Milk

Knead dough a few turns

Roll out and cut biscuits

Bake at 425°F for 20 min

Penny Puffs

Contributed by: Ellen Desmarais
Source: Mrs. Herbie Stevens (Lorraine, who played the piano for teen dances in the 1950's). *Personal Recipes of the Ladies Auxiliary to the Canadian Legion, Richmond, Quebec, 1954.*

Ingredients
2 tablespoons	Shortening
1	Egg
3 tablespoons	Sugar
Pinch	Salt
½ cup	hot Water
1	Yeast cake, dissolved in a little warm water (¼ cup)
½ cup	cold Water
3½ cups	Flour

Directions
Set * and let rise for 2 hours.

Put in small cup tins (cupcake tins) and let rise for 1 hour.

Bake 12 minutes in a hot oven, 350-400 ° F.

*Set means to dissolve the yeast and gradually mix the other ingredients into the yeast then put the dough into a greased bowl to rise.

Refrigerator Rolls

Contributed by: Valerie Healy
Source: Christina Henderson

Ingredients and Directions

½ cup	Shortening
½ cup	boiling Water
¼ cup	Sugar

Stir (above ingredients) well and let cool 'till lukewarm

Dissolve 1 pkg yeast (about 1 tablespoon) in ½ cup warm water
Add 1 teaspoon sugar, leave 20 minutes

Then add:
1	Egg, well beaten
1 teaspoon	Salt
2 cups	Flour

Mix well, put in greased bowl put in fridge overnight
Three hours before required make into small rolls in greased muffin tins

Stand in warm place until double in bulk
I just cut pieces off and drop in the tins

Bake 15 – 20 minutes at 325°F

Splenda Muffin (or Cake)

Contributed by: Ellen Desmarais
Source: From a Splenda pamphlet
Yield: 12 muffins
Note: Muffins can be frozen (once cooked) if desired, in zip-top freezer bag, and kept frozen up to 3 months.
Can also be made in a cake pan for a single layer cake.

Ingredients

2 cups	all-purpose Flour (500 ml)
2 teaspoons	Baking powder (100 ml)
¼ teaspoons	Salt (4 ml)
½ cup	light Margarine, softened (125 ml)
1 cup	Splenda (250 ml)
¼ cup	Honey (60 ml)
2 large	Eggs
1 teaspoon	Vanilla (5 ml)
½ cup	low-fat Milk (125 ml)
1 cup	Blueberries or Raspberries, fresh (or frozen berries, thawed) (250 ml)

Directions

Place oven rack in top 1/3 of oven.
Preheat oven to 400°F (200°C.)
Lightly spray liners with non-stick spray.

Sift together flour, baking powder and salt.
Beat margarine at medium speed with an electric mixer until creamy.
Gradually add Splenda and honey, beating until light and fluffy.
Add eggs one at a time, beating until blended after each addition.
Stir in Vanilla.
Alternately add flour mixture and milk, to the egg mixture, beginning and ending with flour mixture.
Beat at low speed until blended after each addition.
Fold in berries.

Spoon batter evenly into paper-lined muffin cups.

Bake 20 to 22 minutes or until golden.

Remove from pan immediately and cool on wire rack.

~Breakfast/Brunch~

Brie & Apple French Toast

Contributed by:	Liane Desmarais-Cavanagh
Source:	(I don't remember)
Yield:	Makes 12 "sandwiches"
Note:	The ultimate winter Sunday morning treat

Ingredients

6	Eggs
2 cups	Milk
[teaspoon	Nutmeg
¼ teaspoon	Cinnamon
1	French baguette
½	Golden Delicious apple
1 medium wedge	Brie cheese (or Caprice des Dieux)
1 knob	Butter

Directions

Slice French bread into 24 ¼" slices and place 12 slices in a large baking dish.
Set the other 12 pieces aside.
Core apple and thinly slice into 12 pieces.
Place 1 apple slice on each piece of French bread in baking dish.
Cut 12 [slices of brie and place 1 slice on each apple-topped piece of bread.
Place remaining 12 bread slices on top of brie.
In blender mix: eggs, milk, nutmeg and cinnamon well.
Pour egg mixture over brie and apple "sandwiches" turning the "sandwiches" to insure coating well on both sides.
Allow bread to soak up all the egg mixture evenly.

Warm griddle (or frying pan)
Melt some of the butter
Put your sandwiches in the pan (brie side closest to the heat) Don't crowd them as you will need to flip them and they're floppy)
Turn after cheese has begun to melt.
When they are golden brown they are done.

Serve immediately with fresh berries, bacon and warm maple syrup.

Dad's Cereal Salad

Contributed by: Mireille Desmarais
Source: Denise Cloutier, Dietitian, Elizabeth Bruyère Family Health Centre
Yield: Makes 12 servings
Note: Sometimes known as "Meow-Mix".

Ingredients

3 cups	Bran Flakes
1½ cups	Natural Wheat Bran
1½ cups	100% Bran Cereal (by Post)
1 cup	Almonds, sliced
½ cup	Raisins
8	dried Apricots, chopped (or 8 dried cranberries)

Directions

Mix all ingredients together
Store in a covered container

French Toast (Make Ahead)

Contributed by:	Ellen Desmarais
Source:	A B&B in Stratford
Yield:	Serves 6 [1 serving: 418 calories]
Note:	This is a brunch treat given to us by the owner of a B&B in Stratford. It can be prepared the night before, stored in the refrigerator then cooked just before serving."

Ingredients

¼ cup	Margarine (or butter)
½ cup	Brown Sugar, packed
1 loaf	"French", "Italian" or Sourdough Bread, cut into 1" slices for a total of about 12 slices. (Do not use a baguette)
4 large	Eggs
1½ cups	Milk
½ teaspoon	Cinnamon, ground
½ teaspoon	Vanilla
A sprinkle	Confectioner's sugar

Directions

Melt margarine (or butter) in small saucepan on medium heat.
Add brown sugar.
Stir until well combined.
Pour into greased 9" x 13" pan.
Spread evenly.
Place bread slices in tight single layer on top of brown sugar mixture.

Beat next 4 ingredients in medium bowl.
Pour over bread.
Cover.
Chill for at least 3 hours.

Preheat oven to 400°F

Remove cover.
Bake in 400°F oven for 20 to 25 minutes until edges are browned and knife inserted in center comes out clean.

Can be served sprinkled with berries, icing sugar or maple syrup

Pancakes

Contributed by: Valerie Healy
Source: Un-named Kids Cookbook
Yield: enough for 2 – 3 people
Note: Many Christmas' ago Judy gave me a kids cookbook. To this day this is the recipe I use for pancakes.
Marshall makes them every Sunday, Taylor is his helper.

Ingredients

1¼ cups	Flour, sifted
2½ teaspoons	Baking Powder
2 tablespoons	Sugar
¾ teaspoon	Salt
1	Egg
1¼ cups	cold Milk
1 tablespoon	Butter, melted

Directions

There are only two simple mixtures that go into homemade pancakes:

Sift together: flour, baking soda, salt and sugar

Lightly beat the egg, then add milk and melted butter

Slowly pour the liquid mixture into the flour mixture and stir just until mixed. Batter will be a little lumpy.

Heat your frying pan until hot but not smoking, and spoon out 1 tablespoonful of batter for each pancake.

When bubbles appear in pancakes turn them over to brown the other side.

You can keep pancakes hot in a warm oven until you've cooked enough for everyone.
Serve with butter and syrup (preferably from the Eastern Townships!)

Quick Broccoli & Cheddar Quiche

Contributed by: Valerie Healy
Source: The Milk Calendar
Yield: 4 servings
Note: Crushed Crackers mimic a crust in this fresh, easy egg dish.
It makes a satisfying meatless main dish with a fresh salad on the side.

Ingredients

5	Eggs
¼ cup	Flour (all purpose)
1¼ cups	Milk
1 tablespoon	Dijon Mustard
¼ teaspoon	each, Salt & Pepper
1 cup	Finely crushed whole wheat crackers (e.g. Wheat thins, Breton, Stoned Wheat)
2 cups	frozen Broccoli florets, thawed, drained and chopped
1 cup	Cheddar Cheese, shredded & divided
½ cup	Cherry or Grape Tomatoes, halved

Directions

Preheat oven to 400°F (200°C)

Lightly butter a 9" deep dish glass pie plate

In a large bowl, whisk eggs until blended
Whisk in flour, Milk, Mustard, Salt and Pepper
Stir in Crackers and ¾ cup of Cheese and pour into prepared plate
Sprinkle broccoli into filling, pressing to submerge
Arrange tomatoes, cut side up on top, and sprinkle with remaining cheese

Bake for about 30 minutes or until puffed, golden and knife inserted in centre comes out clean

Let stand for 5 minutes before cutting into wedges

Cooking tips: To crush crackers, place in a sealable plastic bag and crush with a rolling pin, meat mallet or bottom of a saucepan.
For the Adventurous: Replace broccoli with chopped thawed frozen or blanched asparagus and add ¼ cup chopped smoked salmon. Use Swiss or cubed brie in place of Cheddar.
Healthy Eating Tip: This recipe is an excellent source of calcium and vitamin D, two very important nutrients for bone health. Even adult bones need attention – they're not growing in length but they are alive and changing every day. Too little calcium and vitamin D even in adulthood can cause your bones to weaken. Aim for at least 2-3 Milk products daily.

Salmon and Asparagus Frittata

Contributed by: Liane Desmarais-Cavanagh
Source: Self Magazine, April 2011
Yield: 6 people

Ingredients

¾ pound	Red Potatoes, cut into 1/2-inch cubes
6	whole Eggs, lightly beaten
3	Egg whites, lightly beaten
½ teaspoon	Salt
1/8 teaspoon	Pepper
2 teaspoons	Olive Oil
1 cup	Onion, chopped
½ cup	Red Bell Pepper
1 teaspoon	Oregano, dried
8 ounces	Asparagus, trimmed and cut into 3/4-inch pieces
12 ounces	Salmon fillet, skin removed, cut into bite-size pieces

Directions

Bring lightly salted water to a boil in a medium saucepan.
Boil potatoes until just tender, about 7 minutes; drain.

Heat broiler to low.

Combine eggs, egg whites, salt and pepper in a bowl.

Heat oil in a 12" ovenproof nonstick skillet over medium-high heat.
In skillet cook onion, bell pepper and oregano, stirring occasionally, until vegetables are somewhat soft, about 3 minutes.
Add asparagus and potatoes; cook 3 minutes.
Add salmon and cook until opaque, 3 minutes.
Pour egg mixture into skillet; reduce heat to low.

Cook, stirring occasionally, until egg begins to set but is still wet on top, 5 minutes.

Cook, without stirring, 5 minutes.

Transfer skillet to broiler; broil until golden, 2 to 3 minutes.
Remove from broiler and slice into 4 wedges; serve.

~ Hors d'œuvres ~

Aïoli

Contributed by:	Liane Desmarais-Cavanagh
Source:	Mireille Groseiller, 2008 (Ste-Cécile-les-Vignes)
Yield:	12 people as a dip
Note:	Mireille G shared this recipe with me and we love it. It's best if made the day before, as it gives the flavours a chance to mellow. For a taste variation try adding a few stamens of Saffron a few hours before serving.

Ingredients
2 cloves	Garlic
1 large	Egg yolk
2 teaspoons	Lemon juice, fresh
½ teaspoon	Dijon mustard
¼ cup	Extra-virgin Olive Oil
3 tablespoons	Vegetable oil (I like Grapeseed)

Directions
Peel, cut in half and remove core if it's green)
Mince and mash garlic to a paste with a pinch of salt using a large heavy knife.

Whisk together yolk, lemon juice, and mustard in a bowl.

Combine oils and add, a few drops at a time, to yolk mixture, whisking constantly, until all oil is incorporated and mixture is emulsified. (If mixture separates, stop adding oil and continue whisking until mixture comes together, then resume adding oil.)

Whisk in the garlic paste and season with salt and pepper.
If aïoli is too thick, whisk in 1 or 2 drops of water.

Chill, covered, until ready to use.

Asian Triangles

Contributed by:	Liane Desmarais-Cavanagh
Source:	*The Diabetes Snack, Munch, Nibble, Nosh Book*
Yield:	Serves 6 people 4 pieces each
Note:	Admittedly these take time to make, but we think they are worth the effort. Keeps well in an air-tight container, and are great snacks when friends drop in.

Ingredients

1 tablespoon	Peanut butter (smooth)
½ tablespoon	lite Soy sauce
1 teaspoon	Water
½ teaspoon	Asian sesame oil
4 teaspoons	Rice vinegar
¼ teaspoon	Ginger
2 to 3 drops	hot pepper sauce (or more if you like them spicy)
12	wonton wrappers, cut in half to form triangles

Directions

Preheat oven to 400°F.

Spray a large baking sheet with non-stick spray.
Set aside

In a small microwave-safe bowl combine:
peanut butter, soy sauce, water, oil, vinegar, ginger and hot sauce.
Microwave for 20ish seconds to warm mixture so that the peanut butter will easily combine with the other ingredients.
With a small wire whisk, mix until well combined.

Arrange wonton wrappers on the baking sheet in a single layer.
Brush the peanut butter mixture over the top of the wonton triangles
Bake for 3 to 5 minutes, or until the triangles have crisped.

Asian triangles can be served fresh from the oven or they can be cooled on a wire rack and stored in an airtight container for up to a week.

Asian-Style Pickled Shrimp

Contributed by:	Liane Desmarais-Cavanagh
Source:	Bon Appétit magazine via May Hum 1995
Yield:	Makes 8 servings
Note:	These can be made the day before you need them and sit in the brine until you are ready to serve them. I have been known to sever this as a first course at dinner with a dollop of hot Creamy Artichoke Dip on each plate.

Ingredients
2¼ cups	Water
3 tablespoons	Rice vinegar
2 tablespoons	Lemongrass, fresh and minced
1½ tablespoons	Pickling spice
1 tablespoon	Salt
1 teaspoon	whole black Peppercorns
2 pounds	medium Shrimp, uncooked, unpeeled, & rinsed
½ cup+2 tablespoons	Cilantro, fresh & chopped (I omit this because I don't like the taste)
4 small	Scallions, chopped (about ½ cup)
3 tablespoons	Pickled Ginger, minced
2 tablespoons	Pickled Ginger brine reserved

Directions
Place first 6 ingredients in medium pot.
Add shrimp.
Cover; bring to boil.
Uncover and cook until shrimp are just cooked through, about 2 minutes.

Remove from heat.

Stir in ½ cup chopped cilantro, scallions, pickled ginger, and ginger brine.
Cool 1 hour.

Put entire mixture in plastic container, cover and chill at least 4 hours and up to 1 day.

The morning of the day you are going to serve them remove all the shrimp from the brine and peel them (leaving the tails on) and put the peeled shrimp back in the brine.

To serve remove shrimp from brine, dab off excess moisture, and arrange on a plate.
Sprinkle lightly with chopped cilantro

Bacon Dip (Warm and Creamy)

Contributed by:	Liane Desmarais-Cavanagh
Source:	Daisy Dairy advertisement, December 2011
Yield:	15 people
Note:	Interesting counterpoint to Asia-style Pickled Shrimp…also wonderful on baked potatoes, or as a decadent dip for raw veggies.

Ingredients

8 ounces	Cream cheese, softened
2 cups	Daisy Brand Sour Cream
3 ounces	Bacon bits (make sure they are crispy)
2 cups	Cheddar cheese, shredded
1 cup	Scallions, chopped

Directions

Preheat the oven to 400°F.

In a bowl, combine all ingredients.

Place the mixture in a 1-quart baking dish.
Cover and put in oven (I put it on a cookie tray in case it bubbles over).

Heat the dip for 25-30 minutes or until hot.

*Serving option:
Dip may also be placed in hollowed round sourdough loaf, wrapped in foil and heated in 400°F oven for 30 minutes.

Cake with two (2) Olives (Cake aux deux olives)

Contributed by: Ellen Desmarais
Source: Mireille Groseiller (2009)
Yield :   1 Loaf pan
Note :   In France a "cake" is a savoury dish, made in a loaf pan, and served with a glass of wine as an appetizer.

Ingredients
¾ cup	Flour
3 teaspoons	Baking powder
3	Eggs
¾ cup	Gruyere cheese, grated
2 teaspoons	Olive Oil
2 teaspoons	Milk
½ cup	Smoked bacon
½ cup	Green Olives, pitted
½ cup	Black olives, pitted
	Salt & Pepper

Directions

Preheat oven to 325° F.

In a bowl, mix the baking powder and flour.

In a second, beat the eggs, oil and milk.
Salt and Pepper this preparation and mix with the flour.
Mix carefully to get a smooth batter.

Cut the bacon and mix as well as the olives and the gruyere. [In Canada, lightly cook the bacon before.]

Grease and flour (or line with parchment paper), a loaf pan and pour in the batter.

Cook for 50 minutes; check doneness by inserting a knife blade; it should come out clean.

Cool before removing from pan.

Crab Dip (hot)

Contributed by:	Liane Desmarais-Cavanagh
Source:	colleague of Larry's @ Algonquin College
Yield :	3½ cups
Note :	Yummm

Ingredients

1¼ cups	Low fat (1%) Cottage Cheese
3 oz	Light Cream Cheese, softened
½ cup	Sharp Cheddar Cheese, shredded
2 tablespoons	Onions, minced
1 tablespoon	Lemon juice
1 teaspoon	light Worcestershire sauce
1 teaspoon	dry Mustard
1 clove	Garlic, minced
3 – 4 dashes	hot Pepper Sauce
1 pound	lump Crabmeat, chopped and broken up (imitation crab meat works as well)

Directions

Preheat oven to 350°F

In a food processor (or blender) whirl cottage cheese and cream cheese until smooth
Transfer to a large bowl and stir in remaining ingredients

Spray a medium casserole dish with non-stick spray.
Spoon crabmeat mixture into casserole dish.
Cover and bake for 25 minutes
Remove from oven,
Stir
Let cool uncovered, for 5 minutes before serving.

Serve as a spread for crackers or as a dip for veggies

Eggplant Caviar (Caviar Aubergine)

Contributed by: Ellen Desmarais
Source: *Homemakers Magazine*
Yield: 1 cup (dependant on the size of the eggplant)
Note: I have had this recipe for many years, so I was surprised and pleased to learn that it is a very popular item as an appetizer in France. Serves well with tapenade.

Ingredients
1	Eggplant
2 tablespoons	Lemon juice
½ teaspoon	Salt
2 tablespoons	Scallion, finely chopped
¼ teaspoon	Pepper
2 tablespoons	Parsley
2 tablespoons	Olive oil
1 clove	Garlic, finely chopped.

Directions
Preheat oven to 450°F

Bake the eggplant whole & unpeeled in the oven for 1 hour or more if needed.
Remove from the oven and peel.
Discard the skin.

Place eggplant in a bowl.
Chop or mash and add all of the other ingredients.
Mix well.

Chill
Serve with French bread or crackers or as a canapé.

Fig, Pear & Boursin Crostini

Contributed by: Liane Desmarais-Cavanagh
Source: Provence, October 2004
Yield: 8 people
Note: I love the creamy and crunchy contrast of the cheese and fig. Great with a glass of bubbly.

Ingredients

1 cup	dried Figs, chopped
½ cup	Port or Marsala
2 tablespoons	Sugar
5 slices	Ginger, fresh & peeled
1 small sprig	fresh Rosemary (or ½ teaspoon crumbled dried rosemary leaves)
1 firm ripe	Pear
½ thin	Baguette
1 round .	Garlic & Fine Herbs Boursin cheese (or 1 pkg. goat cheese).

Directions

For Fig & Pear Compote:
- in a small sauce pan over med heat place figs, port, sugar, ginger and rosemary.
- bring to a boil, uncovered, stirring occasionally.
- then reduce heat to medium and simmer, stirring occasionally, 3 minutes.

- meanwhile, peel and core pear, then chop.
- stir into fig mixture and continue simmering, stirring occasionally, until most of liquid isabsorbed, 2 to 4 minutes.

- refrigerate to cool quickly.
- discard ginger slices.
- (If making ahead, put in a jar or plastic container. Seal tightly and refrigerate up to 1 week.)

Make crostini:
- preheat oven to 400° F.
- slice baguette into ¼" thick rounds.
- spread out on a baking sheet.
- toast in oven until edges are golden tinged (5 to 6 min.) (If making ahead, store in an airtight container at room temperature up to several days.)

To serve;
Spread each toast with a heaping teaspoon of cheese.
Top with a generous dollop of fig mixture.

Green Goddess Dip

Contributed by: Liane Desmarais-Cavanagh
Source: Grama Desmarais
Yield: 1¾ cups (430 ml)
Note: I love how this looks (very 1950's) & how it tastes (unexpectedly fresh)

Ingredients

3 teaspoons	Anchovy paste (I added)
1	Scallion, finely chopped (including green part)
2 tablespoons	flat leaf Parsley, finely chopped
1 tablespoon	fresh Tarragon, finely chopped (I added)
1 cup	Mayonnaise (I used low fat)
½ cup	Sour Cream, (I used no fat)
1½ tablespoons	White Wine Vinegar or Champagne vinegar
2 tablespoons	Chives, finely chopped
	Salt and freshly ground pepper
	Top with a scattering of fresh chopped Scallion or Chives

Directions

In food processor (or bowl) combine:
- anchovy,
- green onion,
- parsley,
- tarragon,
- mayonnaise,
- sour cream,
- vinegar,
- chives
- salt and pepper

Mix until blended.
(Don't forget to scrape the sides of the bowl to get everything mixed well)

Transfer mixture to a serving bowl.
Cover and chill at least 1 hour (or up to 2 days)

Serve with:
sliced zucchini, carrot sticks, fennel sticks, celery, or any other veggie you fancy

Mushrooms - Greek Style (Champignons à la Grecque)

Contributed by:	Ellen Desmarais
Source:	Mireille Groseiller, 2000
Yield:	Appetizer servings for 4.
Note:	This is not Greek, but French. We used to buy this ready made, but when Mireille gave me the recipe we could eat as much as we wanted.

Ingredients

2 cups	small white Mushrooms
1/3 cup	White wine
¼ cup	Olive oil
juice	1 lemon
1 small can	Tomato concentrate
2 teaspoons	Coriander
1	"Bouquet Garnie" (thyme, rosemary and bay leaf tied together)
	Salt & pepper

Directions

Choose small mushrooms, clean them.
Heat the oil and add the mushrooms, add the juice of the lemon, white wine, the coriander, the tomato concentrate, the bouquet garnie, salt and pepper.

Cook over high heat, without covering, for 8 to 10 minutes.
Let it sit in the cooking juice until cool.
Serve very cold.

(If the sauce is a bit acid, add 2 teaspoons of sugar while it is still hot.)

Can be stored in the fridge about a week.

Mushrooms - Parisian

Contributed by: Ellen Desmarais
Source: I have had this recipe so long I don't remember its origins.
Note: It makes a lovely appetizer dish and goes well with cold meat or salads.

Ingredients

½ pound	small Mushrooms
1 tablespoon	Olive oil
juice	½ lemon
1 teaspoon	Mustard (Dijon)
½ teaspoon	Salt
1 tablespoon	Parsley, chopped
¼ teaspoon	freshly ground pepper

Directions

Wash and trim mushrooms.

In small saucepan, combine mushrooms, lemon juice, salt, pepper and oil. Cover.

Cook over brisk flame for 10 minutes.

Let cool in the cooking juice.

When cold, remove the mushrooms to a serving dish.

To cooking juice, add mustard and blend well.

Pour over mushrooms.

Sprinkle with parsley.

Potted Shrimp

Contributed by:	Liane Desmarais-Cavanagh
Source:	Ghrobnia @ Lissadell House, Drumcliff, Ireland, May 2005
Yield:	about 1 ½ cups (if you don't nibble while you cook!)
Note:	This is the single most successful hors d'oeuvre I have ever made. We even have had dinner guests call ahead to request it. Can be prepared in 45 minutes or less but requires additional unattended time. (I make it 2 days ahead, it stores beautifully in a sealed container in the fridge.)

Ingredients

½ cup	Shallots, chopped
1	Bay leaf
6 tablespoons	Butter (unsalted), softened to room temperature
½ pound	Shrimp, raw, shelled and cleaned
3 tablespoons	medium-dry Sherry (can add more if you like the taste)
4 oz	Cream Cheese (about ½ a pkg. of Philly), softened
1 tablespoon	Lemon juice, fresh squeezed is really best
2 tablespoons	fresh Chives, finely minced (optional)

Directions

In a large skillet cook shallots with bay leaf in 1 tablespoon butter over moderate heat, stirring, until soft and lightly caramelized.

Add shrimp and cook, stirring occasionally, until shrimp are pink and cooked through, about 3 minutes.

Add Sherry and simmer mixture gently until almost all liquid is evaporated.
Cool mixture and discard bay leaf.

Transfer shrimp to a cutting board, reserving shallot mixture, and chop to fine chunks.

In a bowl stir together remaining 5 tablespoons butter and cream cheese until smooth.

Stir in shrimp, shallot mixture, lemon juice, chives, and salt and pepper to taste

Transfer to a 1½-cup crock.

Chill potted shrimp, covered, at least 4 hours and up to 48.

Serve potted shrimp with crackers, celery, or it's really yummy with fresh soda bread.

Prosciutto and Gruyere Pastry Pinwheel

Contributed by: Liane Desmarais-Cavanagh
Yield: About 30
Note: The perfect appetizer with Champagne or a really cold beer.
Can easily substitute black forest ham and old cheddar

Ingredients
1 sheet	frozen Puff Pastry (half of 17.3-ounce package), thawed
12 pieces	Prosciutto, thinly sliced
3 tablespoons	Basil, fresh & chopped
¾ cup (packed)	finely grated Gruyère cheese (about 2½ ounces)
1 egg + 1 teaspoon	Water beaten to blend

Directions

Roll out puff pastry on a lightly floured surface.
Arrange one layer of prosciutto on the Puff Pastry, leaving ½" border along 1 side.

Sprinkle prosciutto with the basil, then top with the cheese.

Brush plain border with egg glaze.

Starting at long side opposite border, roll up pastry jelly-roll style, pressing gently to seal long edge.

Wrap well in Saran Wrap.

Refrigerate until firm, at least 3 hours and up to 2 days.

Position rack in centre of oven and preheat to 400°F.

Line 2 large baking sheets with parchment paper.
Cut logs crosswise into ½" to ¼" thick medallions.
Arrange rounds on prepared sheets, spacing 1 inch apart.

Bake until pastries are golden brown, about 16 minutes.
Using spatula, transfer pastries to racks and cool slightly.

Serve warm.

Roman Cheese

Contributed by:	Liane Desmarais-Cavanagh
Source:	Marcus Gavius Apicius: De Re Coquinaria
Yield:	Makes 1 cup
Note:	This is wonderful when paired with (Olive) Tapenade. My mother also adds pureed garlic but I find it a little overpowering. If Herbs de Provence are not available, use a mixture of finely chopped rosemary, parsley and thyme.

Ingredients

1 small log	plain Goat Cheese
2 teaspoons	Herbs de Provence, ground
1	Lemon, washed and zested
1 teaspoon	Olive Oil (extra virgin is best)
	Salt, preferably sea salt (or Fleur de sel if you have it)
	Pepper, preferably fresh ground

Directions

Remove goat cheese from fridge and bring to room temperature.

Using a fork break up the goat cheese in a medium bowl.

Sprinkle with 1 teaspoon ground Herbs de Provence.
Blend into goat cheese.

Sprinkle with ½ of the lemon zest.
Blend into goat cheese.

Add ½ teaspoon olive oil and blend until smooth.
Taste. (I would add remaining Herbs de Provence and lemon zest but you may like it milder)

Add remaining olive oil and blend.

Salt and Pepper to taste.

Put completed Roman cheese in a container and seal.
Store in the 'fridge.

Bring to room temperature before serving.

Swedish Nibbles

Contributed by: Liane Desmarais-Cavanagh
Yield: 12 people
Note: I had two recipes that were uninteresting individually, so I combined them. Make as close to the time you serve it as you can and throw out the left-overs…it does not keep!

Ingredients

¾ pound	Pickled Herring, peeled and cubed
1 tart	Apple (Granny Smith), cored and finely chopped
2 tablespoons	sweet Onion, minced
2 tablespoons	Mayonnaise (I use low fat)
3 tablespoons	Sour Cream/Crème Fraiche (I used no fat sour cream)
	Salt and Pepper
	cocktail sized pieces of Pumpernickel bread
1 small bunch	Chives, ½ inch length
	Paprika

Directions

In a bowl combine; the chopped herring, the sour cream, apple, onion, mayonnaise, ¼ teaspoon salt and white pepper.
Mix well.
Taste and adjust seasoning if required.

Chill for an hour.

Serving option:
Scoop 1 tablespoon of the herring "salad" onto the bread.
Sprinkle with paprika
Top with two pieces of chive (criss-crossed)

(I serve the herring "salad" in a bowl, sprinkled with paprika and the pumpernickel triangles on the side so guests can help themselves.)

Tapenade

Contributed by: Liane Desmarais-Cavanagh
Source: Mireille Groseiller, Ste. Cécile les Vignes, FR, May 1999
Yield:: 1 cup
Note: A Provençale staple. The quantities given for ingredients are from Mum's recipe, I've been known to play with the proportions.

Ingredients

1 cup	pitted black Olives*, salt-cured but unflavored
4 to 6	Anchovy fillets, or 1 Tbsp. Anchovy paste
¼ cup	drained Capers, mashed
2 tablespoons	Mild extra-virgin olive oil
2 cloves	Garlic, peeled (This from Mum's recipe.)
1 tablespoon	Lemon juice (This from Mum's recipe.)
	Herbs de Provence, ground
	Salt and pepper to taste

Directions

Mash the olives, anchovies, and capers together. (I use a 4:1 olive vs caper ratio)
Add herbs de Provence
Add very little salt and pepper.
Drizzle in the oil until creamy.
If you are looking for a little variety tapenade can be flavoured with:
- crushed fresh Garlic,
- ground Bay,
- ground or fresh Thyme leaves,
- Rum or Cognac
- Dijon Mustard

* Loblaws sells tubs of mashed black olives, it's a good base

Ellen's Directions

<u>Do not add salt if using anchovies.</u> In food processor or blender, process olives, anchovies with their oil, capers and garlic until well blended. With machine running, add olive oil and lemon juice; process until well combined. Spoon tapenade into serving bowl; garnish with lemon slices. Serve on thinly slices French Bread. (Toast the bread under the broiler on both sides.) Delicious with Roman Cheese (see recipe**)**.

Note: Keeps well in the fridge for several days.

Thai Guacamole

Contributed by: Liane Desmarais-Cavanagh
Source: Epicurious.com
Yield: enough to top 6 burgers
Note: I was looking for an interesting guacamole for a BBQ we were having and tried this. It's now my "go-to" recipe for hamburger topping.

Ingredients

4	Avocados, pitted and peeled
1 large	Red Pepper, seeded and diced (I omit)
5	Scallions (including the green part), chopped
¼ cup	fresh Mint, finely chopped
1 tablespoon	Ginger, peeled and grated
1 tablespoon	Lemongrass**, minced very finely (use only the 2" closest to the roots)
3 tablespoons	Lime Juice, fresh is best
1 tablespoon	Soya Sauce
1 tablespoon	Asian Fish sauce
¼ teaspoon	Chinese chile paste with garlic (I omit)
	Sea Salt

Directions

In a large bowl mash the avocados with a fork until mostly (but not completely) smooth.
Stir in the:
- bell pepper,
- scallions,
- mint,
- ginger,
- lemongrass,
- lime juice,
- soya sauce,
- fish sauce,
- chile paste.

Taste (adjust with salt and pepper accordingly)

Cover and refrigerate 1 hour.
Serve at once. (Will not keep)

Serving with:
- black, blue or red corn chips
- slices of bell pepper

** If Lemon grass is not available use 1 tablespoon Lemon balm or finely chopped Lemon zest.

Tzatziki

Contributed by: Liane Desmarais-Cavanagh
Source: Nikkos, Lake Vouliagmeni, Geece, July 1972
Yield: Serves 4 to 6.
Note: I have a very clear memory of eating this (with lamb) in Greece. Recipe was recreated from my memory of the flavours so may not be exact, but it works for me. (sometimes I add some chopped up mint too.)

Ingredients

8 oz.	Plain Yogurt (Greek Style)
1	Large Cucumber
6-8 cloves	Garlic, minced
1 teaspoon	Black Pepper (or to Taste)
1 tablespoon	Lemon Juice (fresh)
	Pinch of Kosher Salt

Directions

Peel and shred the cucumber, then press to get out most of the water let drain.

In a medium size bowl add the remaining ingredients and mix together.

Add the pressed cucumber stir to combine.

Taste and adjust the seasoning to your liking.

Chill 1 hr., better if chilled overnight

This is great as an appetizer or snack served with pita or flatbread, or served with grilled chicken or lamb.

Watermelon and Feta Appetizer

Contributed by: Liane Desmarais-Cavanagh
Source: Angelina Vanikiotisis, 1994
Yield: 12 people as an appetizer
Note: The contrast of sweet Watermelon and the salty Feta creates a real taste sensation! While the combination looks lovely in a bowl, I also like threading cubes of watermelon and feta on bamboo skewers and then sprinkling with the remaining ingredients. It's the perfect cold starter (or hors d'oeuvres) on a hot day. Don't let it sit too long or the watermelon gets mushy."

Ingredients

3	Watermelon, medium sized (seedless if possible)
2 cups	Feta (125 ml), crumbled
2	Limes, zested
12	Black Olives, pitted, finely chopped
1 tablespoon	Parsley (15 ml), finely chopped
Pepper	freshly ground
1 teaspoon	Extra Virgin Olive Oil (5 ml) (or you can use Balsamic Vinegar instead of oil)

Directions for serving in a bowl:
Into a large bowl cut wedges of watermelon so that the wedges are 2" thick and are bite sized
In a separate bowl combine:
- the feta
- lime zest
- olives
- Parsley
- fresh ground pepper and
- olive oil.

Add feta mixture to watermelon and fold to combine.
Cover with plastic and let sit in fridge until you're ready to serve.

Directions for serving on skewers:
Cut wedges of watermelon so that the wedges are 1" thick and are bite sized
Cut feta into cubes about the same size as the watermelon.
Thread the watermelon and feta onto skewers (alternating so start and end with feta)
Lay the skewers in a non-metallic baking dish
In a bowl combine:
- lime zest
- olives
- Parsley
- fresh ground pepper and
- olive oil.

Drizzle mixture over watermelon/feta skewers, cover with plastic wrap, and let sit in fridge until you're ready to serve.

~ Lunch / First Course ~

Asian Meatball Subs with Hoisin Sauce

Contributed by: Liane Desmarais-Cavanagh
Source: Karyn Kant, Nov. 2010

Ingredients

1 slice	white sandwich Bread
1½ tablespoons	Milk
1 teaspoon	Soy Sauce
5	Scallions, chopped (white and green parts separated)
1¼ pounds	Ground Pork
3 large cloves	Garlic, finely grated
1 tablespoon	Ginger (about a 2-inch piece), peeled and finely grated
½ cup	Water Chestnuts, drained, rinsed and chopped
1 large	Egg, lightly beaten
½ cup	Cilantro, chopped fresh (I use mint)
1½ teaspoons	toasted Sesame Oil
	Kosher salt and freshly ground pepper
½ cup	Hoisin sauce
¼ cup	Mayonnaise
2½ tablespoons	Lime juice, fresh
3 to 4 teaspoons	Asian Chili-garlic sauce
	Peanut or vegetable oil, for frying
1 cup	Bean Sprouts
4 pieces	Baguette (7-inch-long), split open

Directions

Tear the sandwich bread into small pieces, then toss with the milk and soy sauce in a large bowl.
Let stand 10 minutes.
Meanwhile, mince the scallion whites.
Cut the scallion greens into thin 2-inch-long strands.
Put the green strands in a bowl of ice water and refrigerate while you make the meatballs.
Add the scallion whites, pork, garlic, ginger, water chestnuts, egg, cilantro, 1 teaspoon sesame oil, 1¼ teaspoons salt and ½ teaspoon pepper to the bowl with the bread; mix until combined.
Gently form into 16 golf ball-size meatballs.
Put the meatballs on a baking sheet, cover with plastic wrap and refrigerate 1 to 4 hours.
Stir the hoisin sauce, mayonnaise, 1½ tablespoons lime juice, the chili-garlic sauce and the remaining ½ teaspoon sesame oil in a medium bowl.
Cover and refrigerate until ready to serve.
Heat about 1½ inches peanut oil in a large, wide saucepan over medium heat until a deep-fry thermometer registers 350º F.
Add the meatballs in batches and cook, turning occasionally, until browned and cooked through, 8 to 10 minutes.
Transfer to a paper towel-lined plate to drain.
Drain the scallion greens and toss with the bean sprouts, the remaining 1 tablespoon lime juice and a pinch of salt in a bowl.
Spread the hoisin mayonnaise on the inside of the baguette pieces, then fill with the meatballs and top with the scallion-sprout mixture.

Baby Endive Tarte Tatins

Contributed by: Liane Desmarais-Cavanagh
Source: Laura Calder
Yield: 6 people as a first course or great with salad for lunch
Background: "Yummmm."

Ingredients

2 tablespoons	Sugar
3 tablespoons	Red wine Vinegar
1 tablespoon	Olive Oil
2 tablespoons	Butter
1 handful	Rosemary, chopped fresh
6 heads	Endive, trimmed and halved lengthwise (quartered if large)
To taste	Salt and Pepper
Splash	Red wine, (about 3 Tablespoons)

1 sheet frozen puff pastry

Directions:

Melt the sugar over medium heat in a large sauté pan, about 5 minutes.
Add the vinegar, then the olive oil, butter, and rosemary.
Lay the endive in on top, cut side down.
Sprinkle with salt and pepper, cover with foil, and cook over medium-low heat, turning a few times, until very soft and darkly caramelized, about 45 minutes.
Uncover, and continue cooking 15 minutes to reduce the liquid.
Pour over the wine, and reduce the pan juices to a glaze, 3 to 5 minutes.

Heat the oven to 400ºF

Divide the caramelized endive among six non-stick muffin tins.
Roll out the pastry and cut out six rounds to fit the top of the muffin moulds.
Place a round on top of each mould, tucking the pastry down in around the endives, like a blanket.
Bake until the pastry is golden and puffed up, 20 minutes.

Flip out the baby tarts onto a cutting board. (Careful the caramelized sugar is very hot!)
Serve straight from the board at the table, along with an arugula or frisée salad.

Brie, Pear and Onion Strudel

Contributed by: Liane Desmarais-Cavanagh
Source: Ellen Desmarais (November 2005)

Ingredients

1 tablespoon	Vegetable oil
1	Onion, sliced
1 teaspoon	Granulated sugar (optional)
¼ cup	Chopped walnuts, toasted
2 tablespoon	Chopped dried cranberries
Half pkg	frozen puff pastry, thawed
2 teaspoons	Dijon Mustard
4 oz	Brie cheese, thinly sliced
1	Pear, peeled, cored and thinly sliced
1	Egg, beaten

Directions

In large skillet, heat oil over medium heat; cook onion and sugar, stirring occasionally, until onion is golden and softened, about 20 minutes.
Stir in walnuts and cranberries.
Set aside.

On lightly floured surface, roll out puff pastry into 12" x 9" rectangle; spread mustard lengthwise along middle third of pastry.
Spoon onion mixture over mustard; top with cheese and pear.

Starting at corner of 1 long edge of pastry, make diagonal cuts, 1" apart, almost to filling.
Repeat on other side in opposite direction.
Alternating strips from side to side, fold over filling to resemble braid, brushing each strip with some of the egg to secure.
Brush top with remaining egg.
Transfer to parchment paper-lined baking sheet.

Bake in 450°F (230°C) oven for about 25 minutes or until pastry is golden and pear is tender.
Let cool slightly.

(Make-ahead: Cover loosely with foil and let stand at room temperature for up to 4 hours; reheat to serve.)

Cut into 8 slices.

Butternut Squash, Ricotta, and Sage Crostini

Contributed by: Liane Desmarais-Cavanagh
Source: Anna Spadaccini (my landlady for 6 years)

Ingredients

1 to 2-pound	Butternut squash, peeled, seeded, cut into 1/2" cubes (about 4 cups)
3½ tablespoons	extra-virgin Olive Oil, divided, plus more for drizzling
1½ teaspoons	Light brown sugar, (packed)
	Coarse sea salt and freshly ground black pepper
24	Sage leaves, fresh
¾ cup	fresh Ricotta
½ teaspoon	finely grated lemon zest
12	Baguette slices (about ¼" tick), toasted
	Fresh lemon juice

Directions

Preheat oven to 425°F.
Toss squash, 2 tablespoons oil, and sugar in a large bowl.
Season with salt and pepper.
Arrange in a single layer on a rimmed baking sheet.
Roast, tossing occasionally, until squash is golden and tender, 25-30 minutes.
Let cool on sheet.

Heat 1½ tablespoons oil in a small skillet over medium-high heat.
Add sage; cook until edges begin to curl and turn dark green, 1-2 minutes.
Using a slotted spoon, carefully transfer to paper towels to drain.
Mix ricotta and lemon zest in a small bowl.
Season with salt and pepper.

DO AHEAD:
Butternut squash, sage leaves, and ricotta can be made 1 day ahead.
Cover and chill squash.
Store sage airtight at room temperature.
Cover and chill ricotta mixture. Bring squash to room temperature before serving.

Spread 1 tablespoon of ricotta mixture on each baguette slice.
Top each with a few squash cubes.
Drizzle crostini with lemon juice and olive oil.
Sprinkle with salt and pepper.
Top crostini with 2 fried sage leaves each.

Croque Monsieur

Contributed by: Liane Desmarais-Cavanagh
Source: chef at the café in the Luxembourg Garden
Yield: 4 sandwiches
Note: Yummy with a Tomato salad,

Ingredients

4 tablespoons	Butter (about), room temperature
8 thin	White Sandwich Bread, crusts removed
8 thin	Gruyère or Swiss cheese slices
4	Ham slices
½ cup	Béchamel Sauce

Directions

Butter the eight pieces of bread.

Place 4 pieces (buttered side down) in skillet.

On each piece of bread in the skillet place 1 piece of cheese, then 1 piece of ham, then 1 last piece of cheese.

Smear Bechamel sauce on under side of last piece of bread, and put it on the sandwich (buttered side up).

When the first side is browned flip sandwich.

Brown second side.

When second side is browned remove from skillet

Top with shredded cheese and grill (under broiler) until browned

Serve.

For a Croque Madame....
Complete as above and top the sandwich with a fried (or poached) egg.

Crèpes Forestiers (Crepes with Ham & Mushrooms)

Contributed by: Ellen Desmarais
Source: Michèle Filippi's mother, Aix-en-Provence 1965
Yield: 8 to 10 crèpes
Note: The first time we were served this, as a first course, was at Michèle Filippi's in Aix-en-Provence, it was made by her Mother. We enjoyed it so much that I asked her for the recipe.

Ingredients:

¾ cup + 4 tablespoons	Flour
2 whole	Eggs
	Salt
1 + 2 tablespoons	Butter
1 cup + 4 cups	Milk
1 cup	Water
1 cup	Mushrooms, chopped
¼ cup	Gruyère, grated
10 thin slices	Ham (Jambon de Paris)

Directions

Step 1 - Make 8 to 10 crepes:

¾ cup	Flour
2 whole	Eggs
1 pinch	Salt
1 cup	Milk
1 cup	Water

- Mix, until smooth, flour, eggs, salt, milk and water.
- Just befor pouring the batter on the griddle add about 1 tablespoon of melted butter.

Step 2 - Make the Béchamel sauce (3 cups)

5 tablespoons	Butter
4 tablespoons	Flour
4 cups	Milk

Salt and a little pepper

- In a medium saucepan, heat the butter over medium-low heat until melted.
- Add the flour and stir until smooth.
- Over medium heat, cook until the mixture turns a light, golden sandy colour, about 6 to 7 minutes.
- Meanwhile, heat the milk (in the microwave) and slowly add the hot milk to the butter mixture 1 cup at a time, whisking continuously until very smooth.
- Bring to a boil.
- Cook 10 minutes, stirring constantly, then remove from heat.
- Season with salt, pepper and nutmeg.

See over for step 3 & 4
Crèpes Forestiers (Crepes with Ham & Mushrooms) con't

Step 3 –
- Cook the chopped mushrooms in butter and add them to the Béchamel sauce.
- Add the grated gruyere to the sauce and stir.

Step 4 –
- Take each crepe and lay a piece of ham over the middle, drizzle with the Mushroom/Cheese sauce and roll up the crepe.
- Place the crepes on an oven proof plate and put them in the oven (on very low) to stay warm until serving.

(Be careful when you plate them as they are floppy.)

Curried Chicken Sandwich

Contributed by:	Liane Desmarais-Cavanagh
Source:	Bob Fenske
Yield:	6 sandwiches

Ingredients

20 whole	Peppercorns
2	Bay leaves
2	whole Cloves
½	Lemon
3 pounds	medium Chicken fillets
½ cup + 2 tablespoons	Spicy brown Mustard
½ cup	Honey
1 ¼ teaspoons	Curry powder
¾ teaspoon	Lemon pepper
	Salt
	Butter for spreading
1 loaf	Challah (or other rich egg bread), cut into 12 thick slices
½ cup	Carrots, shredded
½ cup	slivered Almonds
2 medium	Tomatoes, chopped
about 5 ounces	Mescaline salad greens
	Red grapes and assorted berries for garnish

Directions

In a large saucepan over high heat, add peppercorns, bay leaves, cloves, lemon and 14 cups water; cover and bring to a boil.
Add chicken and cook, uncovered and stirring occasionally, 7 to 10 minutes, or until cooked through; drain.

Once cool, quarter each tender crosswise.

In a large bowl, combine mustard, honey, curry powder, lemon pepper and salt; stir in chicken.

Cover and refrigerate at least 30 minutes, or up to 1 day.

Butter both sides of bread slices.

In a heated non-stick skillet over medium-high flame, cook bread in batches 3 to 5 minutes or until browned, turning once.

Combine carrots and almonds with chicken mixture.

Divide chicken curry among 6 bread slices.

Top with tomatoes, mesclun and remaining bread slices. Serve with fruit.

Grilled Cheese and Apple Sandwich

Contributed by: Liane Desmarais-Cavanagh
Source: SAQ magazine
Serve with: Pinto Gris from Alsace
Note: Should <u>not</u> be prepared ahead

Ingredients

8 slices	Cranberry and orange (or three-fruit bread)
2 oz.	Butter, softened
8 slices	Vacherin cheese, sliced
8 thin slices	Bayonne ham (preferable) or prosciutto
2 apples	Royal Gala or Granny Smith, peeled, seeded and thinly sliced

Directions

Preheat oven to 65 °C (150 °F).

Heat a skillet to medium heat.

Spread some butter on one side of each slice of bread.

In the skillet, place a slice of bread buttered side down.

Place 1 slice of cheese on the slice of bread, 1 slice of ham, a few slices of apple, another slice of cheese, and finally a slice of bread, buttered side face up.

Press lightly with a spatula.

Cover and cook for about 2 minutes, until nicely browned.

Flip the sandwich, press it again, cover and cook for another 2 minutes.
Put in the oven.

Repeat

Serve as soon as the 4 sandwiches are ready

Grilled Ham and Gouda Cheese Sandwich with Caramelized Onions

Contributed by: Liane Desmarais-Cavanagh
Source: Bobby Flay, Fall 2010

Ingredients

1	Spanish or sweet Vidalia Onion, halved and thinly sliced & caramelized

Roasted Tomato Mayonnaise:
1	Plum Tomato, halved & seeded or 2 sun-dried tomatoes, drained and patted dry
1 tablespoon	Canola oil (if roasting tomato)
	Salt and freshly ground black pepper
½ cup	Hellmann's mayonnaise
2 cloves	Garlic, chopped
2 teaspoons	fresh Thyme leaves (or ½ teaspoon dried thyme)

To make the Roasted Tomato Mayonnaise:

Preheat the oven to 375°F.
Place the tomato in a small dish or baking sheet, drizzle with oil and season with salt and pepper. Roast until the tomato is very soft and golden brown, about 20 minutes.
Remove from the oven and let cool slightly.
Put the mayonnaise, tomato, garlic and thyme in a food processor and process until smooth, season with salt and pepper.
Scrape into a bowl.

For the Sandwich:
6 slices	White Bread (Belgian or country loaf) cut into ¼" thick slices
1½ cups	grated Gouda cheese
	Caramelized onions
8 slices	Prosciutto, sliced about 1/8 inch thick
8 tablespoons	unsalted Butter, at room temperature

Assembling the Sandwich:

1. Place 4 slices of the bread on a flat surface.
2. Divide half the cheese among the slices.
3. Top the cheese with 2 slices of prosciutto, then top the prosciutto with some of the onions and the remaining cheese.
4. Place the 4 remaining slices of bread on top to make four sandwiches.
5. Butter the top of the bread using half the butter.
6. Preheat a cast-iron pan or cast iron griddle over medium heat.
7. Place the sandwiches in the pan, butter side down (may need to do in batches) and cook until lightly golden brown.
8. Spread the remaining butter on the bread facing up, then flip and continue cooking until the bottom is golden brown and the cheese has melted.
9. Serve with roasted tomato mayonnaise on the side.

Mushroom, Goat Cheese & Tomato Tart

Contributed by: Liane Desmarais-Cavanagh
Source: Marcus Samuelsson
Yield: 8 people
Note: This eggless tart is easy to make.

Ingredients

½ cup + 2 tablespoons	Olive Oil
1 cup	Button Mushrooms, sliced
½ cup	Portobello Mushrooms, sliced
½ cup	Shiitake Mushrooms, sliced
8 cloves	Garlic, halved lengthwise
¼ cup	Balsamic Vinegar
8 oil-packed	Sun-Dried Tomatoes, drained and halved lengthwise
6 to 12	Anchovy fillets, coarsely chopped
¼ cup	pitted Kalamata or Niçoise Olives, chopped
1 teaspoon	Thyme leaves, fresh
2 small-to-medium	Idaho russet or other baking potatoes, unpeeled
1 unbaked	10-inch tart shell
	Kosher salt and freshly ground black pepper
6 ounces	fresh Goat Cheese

Directions

In a large skillet, heat 2 tablespoons of the olive oil over medium-high heat.
When the oil is hot, add all of the mushrooms and the garlic and sauté for 10 to 15 minutes, or until the mushrooms are golden brown.
Remove from the heat.

In a bowl, combine the mushrooms and garlic, the remaining ½ cup olive oil, the vinegar, tomatoes, anchovies, olives, and thyme and mix well.
Cover and let stand at room temperature for 2 hours.
After the mushrooms have stood for about 1 hour, preheat the oven to 400°F.
Poke the potatoes in a few places with the tines of a fork and bake them for 40 minutes, or until they offer only a little resistance in the center when pierced with a thin-bladed knife.
Remove from the oven and let cool slightly.
Reduce the oven temperature to 375°F.
When the potatoes are cool enough to handle, peel them and slice into ½-inch-thick rounds.
Layer the potato slices in the bottom of the tart shell, seasoning them generously with salt and pepper as you go.
Drain the mushroom mixture in a sieve held over a bowl to capture the marinade.
Spread the mushroom mixture over the potatoes.
Crumble the goat cheese evenly over the top.
Bake the tart for 20 to 25 minutes, or until the cheese begins to turn golden.
Remove from the oven, let cool on a wire rack, and serve warm or at room temperature.
Drizzle with a few tablespoons of the reserved marinade just before serving.

Pissaladière (Traditional Provençal pizza)

Contributed by: Liane Desmarais-Cavanagh
Source: Michèle Filippi, Aix-en-Provence 1999
Yield: 12 servings
Background: Can be made up to 4 hours ahead; let stand at room temperature. If made 1 day ahead; cover when cooled then chill. Bring to room temp. before serving."

Ingredients
Topping
¼ cup	Butter
6 pounds	Onions, thinly sliced
6	fresh Thyme sprigs
4	fresh Rosemary sprigs
2	Bay leaves
6 tablespoons	extra-virgin Olive Oil
20 drained	Anchovy fillets
20	oil-cured Black Olives, pitted
1 tablespoon	chopped fresh Thyme
	Capers (optional)

Crust (You can use store bought pizza dough, but make sure to roll it out <u>very</u> thin)
1 cup	warm Water (105°F to 115°F)
1 tablespoon	dry Yeast (from 2 envelopes)
1 teaspoon	Sugar
2¾ cups (or more)	All-purpose Flour
1 teaspoon	Salt
3 tablespoons	extra-virgin Olive Oil
	Cornmeal (yellow)

Directions
For topping:
Preheat oven to 350°F.

Place butter on heavy large rimmed baking sheet; place in oven until butter melts, about 5 minutes. Spread half of onions on baking sheet; top with 3 thyme sprigs, 2 rosemary sprigs and 1 bay leaf. Drizzle with 3 tablespoons oil & sprinkle with salt and pepper.
Top with remaining onions, 3 thyme sprigs, 2 rosemary sprigs, and 1 bay leaf & Salt and pepper. Drizzle with 3 tablespoons oil (onion layer will be about 2½" thick but will settle during baking). Bake until onions are very tender and golden, stirring and turning every 30 minutes, about 2 hours total.

Cool & Discard herb sprigs and bay leaves.

For crust:
Pour 1 cup warm water into small bowl; sprinkle yeast and sugar over.
Stir to blend.
Let stand until foamy, about 10 minutes.

Blend 2¾ cups flour and salt in processor.

Add yeast mixture and 2 tablespoons oil; process until dough clumps together, adding more flour by tablespoonsful if dough is sticky.

Process until shiny ball forms, about 1 minute.

Turn dough out onto floured work surface and knead until smooth and elastic, about 5 minutes.

Coat large bowl with remaining 1 tablespoon oil.

Add dough to bowl; turn to coat with oil.

Cover with plastic wrap, then kitchen towel.

Let rise in warm draft-free area until doubled in volume, about 1½ hours.

Punch down dough; cover and let rise until puffed and almost doubled, about 1 hour.

Sprinkle heavy 17x11x1-inch baking sheet with cornmeal.

Roll out dough on lightly floured surface to 18x12-inch rectangle.

Transfer to prepared baking sheet; press edges of dough up along sides and corners of sheet.

Cover with dry kitchen towel; let rise until slightly puffed, 1 hour.

Preheat oven to 475°F.

Spread onions evenly over top of dough.
Arrange anchovies and olives atop.
Bake until crust is golden, about 15 minutes. Take out of oven and sprinkle with thyme. (I add capers too!)

Cut into 3-inch squares.

Serve warm (not hot) or at room temperature.

Quiche

Contributed by: Ellen Desmarais
Source: Mireille Groseiller, Ste. Cécile les Vignes
Yield: serves 6
Background: Quiche, or anything with a pastry crust is always a challenge. This recipe takes the anxiety away.

Ingredients

1 uncooked	Pie shell
6 to 8	Eggs
4 cups	Milk or heavy cream
	Salt & Pepper
1/8 teaspoon	Nutmeg

Additions: such as salmon, broccoli, spinach, onions, tomatoes

Directions

Preheat oven to 350°F

Prepare a bake a pie shell.

Prepare the garnishes and flavouring ingredients and add them to the pie shell.

Prepare the custard and add it to the pie shell. (Ratio of eggs to milk or heavy cream vary depending on the specific recipe, but 6-8 eggs to 1 liter of liquid is usually sufficient to bind the custard.)

Bake at 350°F the quiche until set (approximately 1 hour)

Allow it to cool slightly before cutting.

Shallot & Garlic Tart Tatin with Parmesan Pastry

Contributed by: Liane Desmarais-Cavanagh
Yield: 6 – 8 as first course
Note: A great way to start a meal, visually appealing and taste. Best if served right out of the oven!

Ingredients

11 oz	Puff Pastry, (store bought or homemade) thawed but still chilled
¼ cup	Butter
1 cup	Parmigiano-Reggiano cheese, freshly grated

for the topping:

3 tablespoons	Butter
1¼ pounds	Shallots, cleaned but left whole
15 - 16	Garlic cloves, peeled but left whole
1 tablespoon	Sugar, (superfine if possible) (do not substitute Splenda)
1 tablespoon	Balsamic Vinegar
3 tablespoons	Water
1 teaspoon	Fresh Thyme, chopped
	Thyme sprigs for decoration
	Salt
	Pepper

Directions

Pastry:

Roll out puff pastry into a rectangle.
Smear with butter leaving a 1" border around the outside
Sprinkle with chunks of Parmesan cheese
Fold the bottom ⅓ up to the middle
Fold the top ⅓ down to the bottom
Seal the edges, give a quarter turn and roll into a rectangle.
Fold again and rolled out one more time.
Wrap in wax paper and damp tea towel, and chill for 30 min.

Filling:

In a 9 - 10" oven proof skillet melt the butter
Add the shallots and garlic and cook until lightly browned.
Sprinkle with sugar and cook a little longer until the sugar begins to caramelize.
Make sure the shallots and the garlic are well covered in the syrup.
Cook partly covered for another 5 - 8 minutes(until garlic is tender).
Cool slightly

Preheat the oven to 375° F.
Roll out the pastry to the same diameter as the frying pan and lay it over the shallots to cover completely.
Prick the pastry with a sharp knife and bake for 25 - 35 minutes (until pastry is golden)
Set aside and cool for 5 - 10 min. then invert onto a serving platter
Sprinkle with thyme sprigs and serve.

Sherried Chicken Salad Sandwiches

Contributed by:	Liane Desmarais-Cavanagh
Source:	Eudora Garrison via Fern Radmore
Note:	Eudora was the editor of the *The Charlotte Observer*, and shared this recipe with Fern. Fern passed it on to me. I know it sounds dubious but I have eaten it and it is yummy

.

Ingredients

1 can	Cream of Mushroom soup (10.75oz.)
¼ cup	Dry sherry
½ teaspoon	Salt
2 pounds	Chicken thighs or breasts, Boneless & skinless, cut into ¾ dice
16 slices	White Bread, toasted
1 bunch	Watercress, washed and dried

Directions

Whisk soup and sherry in large sauté pan over medium heat.

When simmering, add chicken.
Cover and simmer, stirring occasionally, until chicken is cooked through and sauce has thickened, about 10 to 12 minutes.

Transfer to large bowl and chill 1 hour.

For each sandwich,
Toast bread
Place ½ cup of chicken and sauce on a piece of toast; spread mixture to corners of bread.
Top with watercress and another piece of toast and serve immediately.

Shrimp and Citrus Cocktail Salad

Contributed by:	Ellen Desmarais
Source:	Claude @ the Centre Artistique de Piégeon, 2006
Yield:	4 people as a starter
Note:	Guests are surprised and pleased with the taste and texture combination.

Ingredients

2	Oranges
¾ pound	Shrimp, cooked, chilled and peeled (400 g)
¼ cup	Cream (10 cl)
1	Grapefruit (pink)
1	Heart of Lettuce (can also use wild baby greens)
½ teaspoon	cider Vinegar
1 tablespoon	Ketchup
	Salt, pepper
½ teaspoon	Mustard (I prefer *not* hot Dijon)

Directions

Peel and cut sections of oranges and grapefruit into a bowl
Keep the juice

De-vein the shrimp and add to the citrus sections

Make dressing:
    Mix the mustard, vinegar, salt and pepper
    Add the ketchup
    Add the cream

Cut the heart of the lettuce into fine strips
Divide greens evenly between individual plates

Top Salad greens with Shrimp and Citrus pieces

Pour dressing over each salad

Serve chilled.

Shrimp and Devilled-Egg Salad Sandwiches

Contributed by: Liane Desmarais-Cavanagh
Source: Fairyland School PTA in Lookout Mountain, Georgia

Ingredients

1 tablespoon	Shellfish-boil seasoning, such as Old Bay
2 pounds	large Shrimp, heads off and shells on
12 large	Eggs
4 slices	thick Bacon
¾ cup	Mayonnaise
1 tablespoon + 2 teaspoons	Tabasco
1 tablespoon + 1 teaspoon	Dijon mustard
	Kosher salt and freshly ground black pepper
¼ cup	finely sliced Scallions
16 slices	white or whole wheat Bread
8 leaves	butter lettuce
4 vine-ripened	Tomatoes, cut into 16 slices

Directions

Fill a 6-quart pot with 2 quarts water, add the shellfish-boil seasoning, and bring to boil over high heat.
Turn off heat, add shrimp and cook for 1 to 2 minutes, until shrimp are pink-orange and slightly firm.

Transfer shrimp to a colander and rinse under cold water.
Return the shrimp water to a boil, then reduce heat to low and gently add eggs.
Simmer eggs for 14 minutes.

Meanwhile, peel and chop the cooked shrimp and place in a large bowl.
Transfer eggs to a strainer; rinse under cold water until cool.

Cook bacon in a skillet over medium-high heat until crispy.
Transfer to a small bowl and crumble.

Peel eggs; cut in half lengthwise.
Separate the whites from the yolks; coarsely chop the egg whites and add to the bowl with the chopped shrimp.
Press the yolks through a mesh strainer and into a large bowl.
Add mayonnaise, Tabasco, mustard, and 1 teaspoon salt; whisk until mixture is consistency of cake batter, about 1 minute.

Fold yolk mixture into shrimp mixture, add bacon and green onion; toss.

Season with salt and pepper; toss.

Use 1 cup per sandwich, along with sliced tomatoes and lettuce.
Serve immediately.

Spinach Wheel

Contributed by: Liane Desmarais-Cavanagh
Source: Laura Calder's TV show, February 2010
Yield: serves 4 - 6 people
Background: This is a great lunch (or as an hors d'oeuvres). We never have any left-overs!

Ingredients
Pastry
2¼ cups	Flour
½ teaspoon	Salt
1 cup	Butter, cut into pieces
S cup	ice-cold Water

Tart
2 teaspoons	Olive oil
1 clove	Garlic, peeled and halved (more is good too)
1 pound trimmed	Spinach, chopped (I used frozen spinach, that was thawed and drained)
½ cup grated	Parmigiano Reggiano cheese
3 tablespoons	Crème Fraiche (or really thick sour cream)
1	Egg, lightly beaten
	Salt and pepper to season
1 tablespoon	Sesame seeds (particularly good if toasted)
1 teaspoon	dried Oregano leaves, fresh
1 tablespoon	Thyme leaves, fresh
	Zest of one Lemon

Directions
Pastry
Put the flour and salt in a large bowl.
Add the butter pieces and pinch with the fingers to create a crumb texture.
Make a well in the middle and pour in the water.
Quickly work the mixture to create dough.
Divide into 2 disks, wrap in plastic, separately, and refrigerate 15 minutes before rolling out.

Tart
Heat the oven to 425°F/220°C.
Roll one disc of pastry into a rectangle and place on a pastry sheet.
Heat the oil in a large skillet.
Add the Garlic for one minute.
Add the Spinach, cover, and cook until soft, 5 minutes.
If there is a lot of liquid, cook uncovered until it evaporates.
Remove from the heat and stir in the Cheese.
In a small bowl mix together the Egg and the Crème Fraiche
Quickly stir the Egg/Crème mixture into the spinach (make sure it's well incorporated).
Season with S&P.
Spread over the tart base.
Scatter the sesame seeds, herbs, and lemon zest evenly over top.
Bake until the crust is crisp and the top very hot, about 20 minutes.
Slide the tart onto a large wooden cutting board, cut into diamonds, and serve straight from the board.

Warm Goat Cheese Salad with Pears, Nuts

Contributed by: Liane Desmarais-Cavanagh
Source: Chef in Cap Nez Gris, 2008
Yield: 4 people
Note: If you want omit breading & cooking the goat cheese and just crumble it on cold.

Ingredients

1¼ cup	Breadcrumbs, fresh white
2 tablespoons	Thyme, minced fresh
11 ounces	Goat Cheese (such as Montrachet), cut into 8 rounds
1	Egg, beaten to blend
2 tablespoons + ¾ teaspoon	White Wine Vinegar
1 tablespoon	Dijon mustard
½ cup + 3 tablespoons	Walnut Oil
8 cups	baby Greens
2 heads	Belgian Endive, cut crosswise into ½-inch pieces
2 large	Pears, (ripe) peeled, cored, cut into ¼-inch-thick slices
S cup	Walnuts, chopped (I use Pecans)

Directions

Mix breadcrumbs and thyme in glass pie dish.
Season goat cheese with salt and pepper.
Dip cheese into beaten egg, then into breadcrumbs, coating completely.
Cover and refrigerate until ready to use.
(Can be prepared 4 hours ahead.)

Whisk vinegar and mustard in small bowl to blend.
Gradually whisk in ½ cup oil.
Season to taste with salt and pepper.
Combine mixed greens, Belgian endive and pears in large bowl.

Heat remaining 3 tablespoons oil in heavy large skillet over medium-high heat.
Add nuts and sauté until lightly toasted, about 2 minutes.
Transfer to plate using slotted spoon.
Reduce heat to medium.
Working in batches, add cheese rounds to skillet and cook until crisp and brown on outside and soft on inside, about 2 minutes per side.

Toss salad with enough dressing to coat.
Divide among 4 plates.
Using metal spatula, place 2 cheese rounds in centre of each salad.
Sprinkle with nuts.

~Soups & Chowders~

Aljotta

Contributed by: Liane Desmarais-Cavanagh
Source: Chef Pat McBride, Papanni's Restaurant, Valetta, Malta, May 2011
Note :   Chef Pat shared this recipe with us because we liked it so much. I made it as soon as we were back in France and it was such a success it has become one of our favourite recipes. Don't be put off by the fish heads, you won't be eating them and they add huge flavour to the stock.

Ingredients
1	Fish head (white fish if possible)
1 or 2	fish collar(s)
1 cup	Mirepoix (chopped carrots, celery & onion - pre-sauted with butter if you desire)
1 or 2 cubes	Court Bouillion (like Oxo for fish)
	White fish meat (filet of Monk is best)
	Olive oil
	Onion, finely chopped
	Garlic, minced or puréed
	Oregano, fresh leaves
	Marjoram, fresh leaves
	Mint, chiffonade
	Tomato purée

Directions
In a very large pot put the fish head and collar(s)
Add 1 cup of Mirepoix
Add enough water to just cover the fish head
(Add Court Bouillion)
Bring liquid to a boil, then turn down temp to reduce to a simmer.
Leave pot partially uncovered and simmer for 1 hour.
While stock is cooking....
In a large fry pan sauté Onion and Garlic until lightly browned.
Add Oregano and Marjoram
Once you can start to smell the herbs, add the Tomato purée
Ensure tomato is well incorporated.
(If mixture too dry dilute with white wine)
Let simmer gently to incorporate all the flavours.
Rinse your fish fillet, and cut into "bite-sized" pieces. Reserve
Once your stock has finished cooking, drain liquid through a sieve into a clean pot.
Put liquid back on stove on low heat.
Make sure you pick through and keep all the pieces of fish meat (from the head and collar) that can now be added back to the fish stock.
To your fish stock add:
> the onion/garlic/tomato mixture, and
> the pieces of raw white fish.

Cook soup for a further 15 to 20 min
Add mint and then serve.

Avgolemono

Contributed by: Liane Desmarais-Cavanagh
Source: George Constantinis' Mum
Yield: About 3 cups (750 ml); or 4 first-course servings.
Note: My friend's mother taught me to make this. The tricky part is the smooth blending of the warm broth into the raw egg & lemon mixture. Just remember to temper your eggs before you add them into the broth.

Ingredients
4 cups	Chicken stock
6 tablespoons	long-grain white Rice
8	Egg yolks
¼ cup	Lemon juice, fresh
	coarse Salt, to taste
	freshly ground Pepper, to taste

Directions

In a medium saucepan, bring the stock to a boil.

Stir in the rice and cook until tender, about 8 to 10 minutes.

Meanwhile, beat the egg yolks and lemon juice together in a large bowl.

When the rice is tender, slowly drizzle half of the hot broth into the yolks to temper them, whisking constantly.

Now whisk the egg yolk mixture back into the broth and place over low heat.

Cook, stirring constantly, just long enough to thicken the soup.

Do not boil!

Season to taste with salt and pepper.

Cabbage Soup

Contributed by: Valerie Healy
Source: Laurel Gunter
Note: My family like this soup without the cabbage!

Ingredients

1 pound	Hamburger
1 medium	Onion diced
½ cup	Celery
½ teaspoon	ground Pepper (optional)
2 teaspoons	Salt
½ teaspoon	Paprika
1 – 28 ounce	can Tomatoes
4 cups hot	Water
2	Beef boullion cubes
2 tablespoons	Parsley, chopped
1 cup	diced Carrots
2 cups	diced Potatoes
6 – 7 cups	diced Cabbage

Directions

Cook hamburger, onion and celery.
Add spices and tomatoes
Put soup in pot, add veggies and simmer all day.
Add more water or any veggies left over in the fridge.
You can also add a small can of tomato sauce.

Carrot and Honey Soup (Chilled)

Contributed by: Liane Desmarais-Cavanagh
Source: Alison Fenske
Yield: 6 servings
Note: Soup can be made 3 days ahead and kept chilled, covered. For another flavour dimension try adding a little curry powder, or some grated ginger, and I've added a dollop of Greek yogurt before serving.

Ingredients

1 pound	Carrots, peeled and cut into ½-inch pieces (2¼ cups) (best if using frozen carrots)
2¾ cups	Water
2 cups	reduced-sodium fat-free Chicken broth
1 cup	chopped Onion
1 teaspoon	Salt (best if sea salt)
¼ teaspoon	ground Coriander
¼ teaspoon	ground Cumin (I omit - allergic)
¼ teaspoon	Paprika
[teaspoon	Cayenne (I omit – allergic)
2 tablespoons	mild Honey
2½ tablespoons	fresh Lemon juice

Garnish: 6 thin lemon slices and 1 tablespoon mild honey for drizzling

Directions:

Combine all ingredients except ½ tablespoon lemon juice in a 3-quart heavy saucepan and bring to a boil over moderate heat, stirring occasionally.
Reduce heat and simmer, covered, until carrots are tender, 30 to 40 minutes.

Purée soup in 2 batches in a blender (use caution when blending hot liquids) until very smooth, then chill soup quickly, stirring occasionally, in a metal bowl set in a larger bowl of ice and cold water, about 30 minutes.

(Alternatively, cool soup, uncovered, 30 to 40 minutes, then chill, covered, until cold, about 4 hours.)

Stir in remaining ½ tablespoon lemon juice and salt to taste.
Divide soup among 6 bowls with a ladle.
Float a lemon slice on top of each serving, then drizzle with honey and serve.

French Onion Soup/Soup à l'oignon (Julia Childs')

Contributed by: Liane Desmarais-Cavanagh
Source: Julia Childs
Note: *"The onions for an onion soup need a long, slow cooking in butter and oil, then a long, slow simmering in stock for them to develop the deep, rich flavour which characterizes a perfect brew. You should therefore count on 2½ hours at least from start to finish. Though the preliminary cooking in butter requires some watching, the actual simmering can proceed almost unattended. Julia Child"*
Easy and always successful. This improves with age, even better the next day.

Soup ingredients

1½ pounds	yellow Onions (I like Vidalia), thinly sliced (about 5 cups)
3 tablespoons	Butter
1 tablespoon	Oil
1 teaspoon	Salt
¼ teaspoon	Sugar (helps the onions to brown)
3 tablespoons	Flour
2 quarts	Beef bouillon, or 1 quart of boiling water and 1 quart of stock or bouillon
½ cup	dry White Wine or dry white Vermouth
	Salt and pepper to taste
2 tablespoons	Cognac
	Rounds of hard-toasted French bread (see below)
1 to 2 cups	grated Swiss or Parmigiano-Reggiano cheese

Garnishings for Onion Soup:

Plain Croûtes (Hard-Toasted French Bread)
• 12 slices of French bread cut ¾" to 1" thick
• Olive oil or beef drippings
• Garlic clove cut in ½
Pre-heat oven to 325°F.
Place the bread in one layer in a roasting pan and bake for about 15 min.
Remove from oven and brush with olive oil or beef drippings
Bake a further 15 minutes
After baking, each piece may be rubbed with cut garlic.

Croûtes au Fromage (Cheese Croûtes)
• 12 slices of French bread cut ¾" to 1" thick
• Olive oil or beef drippings
• Grated Swiss or Parmesan cheese
Pre-heat oven to 325°F.
Place the bread in one layer in a roasting pan and bake for about 15 min.
Remove & spread one side with grated cheese & sprinkle with drops of olive oil.
Turn broiler on to LOW and brown under broiler

See next page for directions to make soup

French Onion Soup/Soup à l'oignon (Julia Childs') con't

Directions for soup
Heat stock to a rolling simmer

In a deep covered saucepan (I use a heavy stock pot) cook onions slowly with the butter & oil for 15 min.

Uncover, raise heat to moderate, and stir in the salt and sugar.

Cook for 30 to 40 minutes stirring frequently, until the onions have turned an even, deep, golden brown.

Sprinkle in the flour and stir for 3 minutes.

Remove from heat and slowly blend in the boiling liquid.

Add the wine, and season to taste.

Simmer partially covered for 30 to 40 minutes or more, skimming occasionally as necessary.

Correct seasoning.

Set aside uncovered until ready to serve.

Just before serving gently reheat to a simmer, and stir in the Cognac.

Place the croûtes (bread) in individual bowls and pour soup into a soup tureen (or into the bowls) Pass the cheese separately.

Shrimp and Coconut Milk Soup with Lemongrass

Contributed by: Liane Desmarais-Cavanagh
Source: May Leung, Oct. 2005
Yield: Serves: 4 full bowls
Note: When my brother-in-law Pat told me that this was his favourite soup I had to learn how to make it. I asked around and discovered that a work colleague knew how to make it, so she shared her recipe with me. It's very easy to make, and you can even prepare the stock part the day ahead. Just don't add the shrimp until the last minute that way they stay tender. Cooked too long shrimp get tough.

Ingredients

4 stalks	Lemongrass
1 stalk	Celery
2 cloves	Garlic
¼ cup	Ginger, minced
¼ cup	fresh Cilantro, minced
1 large	Tomato, diced
6 tablespoons	fresh Lemon juice
5 cups	unsweetened Coconut milk
1 cup	dry white Wine
1 tablespoons	Olive Oil
1 medium	Onion, thinly sliced
1	Carrot, thinly sliced
½ pound	Shrimp, peeled and de-veined
2	Scallions, sliced for garnish
	Salt and pepper

Directions

Smash the 4 stalks lemongrass with a cleaver or side of a heavy knife.
Squeeze enough lemon juice to measure 6 Tbs.

In a 2 quart saucepan combine; lemongrass, celery, garlic, ginger, cilantro and lemon juice.
Add 5 cups coconut milk, white wine, and salt and pepper to taste.
Cover and bring to boil over high heat.
Strain the broth through a sieve and reserve.

In a 4 Qt. saucepan, heat olive oil over med. heat.
Add the strained coconut broth
Add the shrimp and cook 2 - 3 minutes (watch carefully!)
When the shrimp turns pink remove from heat.

Stir in the diced tomato.
Ladle into bowls and serve with a sprinkle of sliced scallions on top of each bowl.

Spicy Sweet Potato Soup

Contributed by:	Liane Desmarais-Cavanagh
Source:	LCBO Magazine, Winter 2012 (By: Marilyn Bentz-Crowley & Joan Mackie)
Yield:	Serves 6
Note:	The surprise ingredient is peanut butter in this delicious soup, which can be made a day or two ahead and refrigerated. We first had this soup at our friends Jord & Fran's New Year's Eve dinner party. It was smooth, subtle, and rich. I have made it since and while we couldn't really taste the peanut butter; it does add an unexpected richness.

Ingredients

½ cup	Sour Cream (I like crème fraîche)
1 teaspoon	grated Lime zest
1 large	Plum Tomato
1½ to 2 pounds	Sweet Potatoes (about 2 large)
1 tablespoon	Butter
1	Onion, sliced
2 large	Garlic cloves, sliced
4 cups	Chicken stock (or vegetable)
2 tablespoons	grated fresh Ginger
¼ cup	crunchy or creamy Peanut Butter
1	Lime

Directions

Stir Sour Cream (crème fraîche) with zest, then cover and refrigerate

Seed and dice Tomato; set aside to use as garnish
Peel Sweet Potatoes and cut into chunks

Melt Butter in a large pot over medium heat
Add Onion and Garlic
Cook 4 to 5 minutes or until softened

Add Sweet Potatoes, stock and Ginger
Bring to a boil, stirring frequently

Reduce heat and simmer 15 minutes, covered, or until potatoes are soft
Puree soup in batches in blender or food processor; return to pot

Using a whisk, stir peanut butter into soup
Heat until hot

Squeeze juice of lime into soup
Taste and add salt as needed
Ladle into warmed bowls and add a dollop of Sour Cream (crème fraîche)
Top with a few diced tomatoes.

Spicy Tomato Soup

Contributed by:　　Valerie Healy
Source:　　Charlotte Griffith, Richmond, QC

Ingredients

1½ cups	minced Onion
3 cloves	crushed Garlic
1 tablespoon	Butter
1 tablespoon	Olive Oil
1 teaspoon	Dill weed
½ teaspoon	Black Pepper
6 cups	chopped Tomatoes and the juice
1 tablespoon	Honey
1 tablespoon	Mayonnaise

Directions

Sauté onions and garlic with salt in olive oil and butter.

Cook 5 minutes, add dill pepper and tomatoes and honey.

Cover and simmer 45 minutes on low heat.

Five minutes before serving, whisk in mayonnaise.

Trout Chowder

Contributed by: Liane Desmarais-Cavanagh
Source: Saveur Magazine, February 2013

Ingredients

¼ pound	Salt Pork or Bacon, cut in small cubes
2	Onions, finely chopped
2	Potatoes
3 cups	whole Milk
2 cups	poached Trout (2 10-oz. trout), in chunks
	Salt and pepper
1 tablespoon	Butter

Directions

In a heavy medium-sized pot, brown salt pork or bacon over medium heat until crisp. Drain on paper towels.

Pour off all but 1 tablespoon of fat from pot.

In the same pot, cook onions over medium heat, stirring often until tender and translucent (about 20 minutes).

Peel and cut potatoes into ½" cubes.
Add potatoes and milk to pot and cook over medium heat for about 10–15 minutes or until potatoes are tender.

Add trout to the pot and continue cooking for 1 minute.

Stir carefully so trout doesn't break up.

Add salt and pepper to taste, then serve chowder in bowls garnished with a little butter and the reserved cubes of salt pork or bacon

Zuppa alla Pavese

Contributed by: Liane Desmarais-Cavanagh
Source: Chef at the Best Western Hotel, Mestre, Venice, May 2010
Yield: Serves: 6
Note: I had been talking to the Chef at the Best Western about the foods he had eaten as a child growing up in Venice. He told me this recipe (which I wrote on a napkin). The next day when we happened to meet he invited me to taste some he'd made. It is surprisingly light and has a more complex flavour component than you would expect. I don't like Kale so I substitute Spinach.

Ingredients

12	thick slices Country bread (Italian)
½ cup	Butter (can be garlic butter but not too much garlic)
12	Eggs
3 cups	Swiss Chard, steamed and chopped (I use Spinach),
½ cup	freshly grated Parmigano-Reggiano cheese
	Salt
8 to 9 cups	clear Stock (Veggie, Chicken or Beef - not veal!)

Directions

Liberally butter your bread

Fry the bread quickly until golden brown on both sides (but still soft in the middle)

Put 2 slices of bread in each soup bowl (If you are adding greens put ¼ cup on top of each slice of bread)

Warm stock (in pan on the stove) and bring to a soft boil

Break 2 eggs carefully onto greens/bread in each bowl
Sprinkle eggs with grated cheese & salt

As carefully as possible pour stock into each bowl.
The stock must be as hot as possible, without remaining on the boil when off the heat, so that it will poach the eggs. (I gently pour it down a spoon so that it doesn't touch the eggs directly.)
The point of pouring it slowly is so that it cooks the eggs without breaking them.

Serve immediately if you want the eggs to still be runny when the guest breaks into them.

Alternately, you can pre-poach the egg and add it to the soup, but the soup will have a different flavour and (in my opinion) won't be as good.

~Salads~

Apple, Dried Cherry & Walnut Salad with Maple Dressing

Contributed by: Liane Desmarais-Cavanagh
Source: Valerie Healy, Fall 2004
Yield: 6 people
Note: Larry loves this salad because it's sweet and salty. I usually serve it with BBQ Pork chops as the flavours marry well."

Ingredients
Maple Dressing:
¼ cup	Mayonnaise
¼ cup	pure Maple Syrup (preferably from the Eastern Townships)
3 tablespoons	Champagne vinegar (or other white wine vinegar)
2 teaspoons	Sugar (I use Splenda)
½ cup	Vegetable Oil (I use Grapeseed)

Salad:
1 5oz. bag	mixed Baby Greens (about 10 cups lightly packed)
2	Apples (Granny Smith), peeled, cored, cut into matchstick-size strips
½ cup	dried tart Cherries
½ cup	chopped Walnuts, toasted (I use Pecans)

Directions
Whisk mayonnaise, maple syrup, vinegar, and sugar in medium bowl to blend
Gradually whisk in oil until mixture thickens slightly
Season to taste with salt and pepper
(Dressing can be prepared 3 days ahead. Cover and refrigerate. Re-whisk before using.)

Toss greens, apples, cherries, and ¼ cup walnuts in large bowl to combine
Toss with enough dressing to coat
Divide salad equally among plates
Sprinkle with remaining ¼ cup nuts and serve

Asian Slaw

Contributed by: Heather Ross
Note: I used to enjoy Grammie's coleslaw, especially the raisins! These days, my go-to slaw is more west coast-inspired.

Ingredients

1 medium head	Napa or regular cabbage, shredded
1	Red Bell Pepper, sliced thin
2	Carrots, grated
2	Serrano Chili Peppers, sliced thin (optional)
1 bunch	Scallions, sliced thin
¼ cup	chopped Cilantro
¼ cup	chopped fresh Mint
2" knob	Ginger, grated
½ cup	Rice Wine Vinegar
1 tablespoon	Soy sauce
2 tablespoons	Sesame Oil

Directions

Toss the vegetables and chopped herbs together in a large bowl.

In a separate bowl whisk together ginger, rice wine vinegar, soy sauce and sesame oil.
Pour the dressing over the vegetables and allow them to marinate in the dressing for at least 20 minutes before serving.

FYI: Keep a chunk of ginger in the freezer. It will keep for months and grates very easily when frozen.

Beet Salad (Moura Auer's)

Contributed by: Ellen Desmarais
Source: Moura Auer,
Yield: Serves 4 to 6
Note: Moura babysat the children 2 or 3 afternoons a week when we lived in Paris. She called this her "Russian beet salad" because she was Russian.

Ingredients

2 – 3	Potatoes, cooked
1	Beet, cooked
1-2	Cucumbers
1 small	acidic Apple
1 hard-boiled	Egg
1	Onion

Directions

Mix together: salt, pepper, oil, lemon juice and mayonnaise.

Cut everything in pieces and mix all together.

Chill and serve.

Caesar Salad

Contributed by: Heather Ross

Source: Bobbie Farquhar
Yield: 6 servings
Note: I lived with Bobbie for two summers when I was a student working in Toronto. This was the salad we frequently ate with dinner, and we usually added fresh mushrooms and a red pepper, both chopped into big chunky pieces.

Ingredients

2 slices	Whole Wheat Bread, cubed
1 large head	Romaine lettuce
2 tablespoons	White Wine Vinegar
1 tablespoon	Dijon mustard
1 large clove	Garlic, minced
½ teaspoon	Lemon juice
	Worcestershire sauce
¼ cup	freshly grated Parmesan cheese
¼ cup	Mayonnaise
1 tablespoon	Water
1 tablespoon	Olive Oil
	Salt & Pepper
2 tablespoons	fresh Breadcrumbs (optional)

Directions

Bake bread cubes at 350°F 10-12 minutes or until golden, turning halfway through; set aside.

Meanwhile, in salad bowl, whisk together vinegar, mustard, garlic, lemon juice and Worcestershire sauce to taste.
Whisk in cheese, then mayonnaise.
Gradually whisk in water, then oil.
Season with salt and pepper to taste.
Stir in breadcrumbs.

Tear lettuce into bite-sized piece.
Toss with dressing.
Add croutons and toss again.

Carrot and Raisin Salad With Pineapple

Contributed by: Ellen Desmarais

Source: Doris Desmarais (aka Grandma D), Fall 1973
Yield   Serves: 4 to 6
Note: A favourite with kids because it's sweet

Ingredients

T cup	Raisins
2 cups	Carrots, coarsely grated
1 cup	crushed Pineapple, drained
S cup	Mayonnaise-type salad dressing (Coleslaw dressing)
1 tablespoon	Lemon juice
¼ teaspoon	Salt
1 tablespoon	Sugar (I omit)

Directions

Toss raisins, carrots, and pineapple together lightly;
Set aside.

Stir together mayonnaise, lemon juice, salt and sugar.

Add dressing to the raisin mixture.

Refrigerate until served.

Celeriac Remoulade

Contributed by:	Liane Desmarais-Cavanagh
Source:	Ellen Desmarais, January 2007
Yield:	Serves : 6
Note:	One of Larry's favourite recipes because he says it tastes like being on holiday. Celeriac is sometimes called the "frog prince of vegetables" because it's ugly but surprisingly tasty. Buy a larger root ball than you think you will need. The knobby root ball hides dirt very well, so you may lose a fair bit when cutting away the sections you can't clean.

Ingredients

1 pound	Celeriac
2 teaspoons	freshly squeezed Lemon juice
1½ teaspoons	Sea Salt
3 tablespoons	Boiling Water
¼ cup	Dijon mustard
2 tablespoons	Red Wine Vinegar
½ cup	extra-virgin Olive Oil
¼ cup	Sour Cream (in Canada I use no fat yogurt, in France I use Crème Fraîche)
	Sea salt
	Freshly ground pepper

Directions

Peel & wash the celeriac and make sure to get out all the grit.
Cut in half and remove the core if spongy.
Thinly slice, then stack up the slices and cut into thin, matchstick strips.
Toss with the lemon juice and salt. (This prevents discolouring.)
Let sit for 20 minutes

Slowly add boiling water to the Dijon mustard, whisking the whole time.
Dribble in vinegar and olive oil, again whisking constantly.
Stir in sour cream; season to taste with salt, pepper.

Rinse celeriac under cold water and drain well.
Pat dry and toss with the dressing.

Refrigerate at least 30 minutes.

This keeps well in the fridge a few days.

Cole Slaw

Contributed by: Ellen Desmarais
Source: Elizabeth McCauley
Yield: Serves 10 to 12
Note: John got this recipe from his secretary at the Senate, Elizabeth McCauley, in the 1970s, and it has been a favourite in our house ever since. While it never rests for 2 months in our house, it is very handy to have in the fridge and it keeps for up to 2 month.

Ingredients

Chop and mix:
- 1 Cabbage
- 1 Carrot
- 1 Onion

Boil:
- 1 cup Vinegar
- ¾ cup Sugar (or Splenda)
- 2/3 cup Salad Oil
- 2 teaspoons Salt

Remove from the heat and add ½ teaspoon Salad herbs (or dill and lemon).
Let this cool and then pour it over the cabbage etc.
And mix well.

Refrigerate 1 – 2 months (yes! 2 months) in Tupperware container.
Mix it occasionally.

Cream Coleslaw

Contributed by: Liane Desmarais-Cavanagh
Source: Doris Desmarais (aka Granma D)
Yield: Serves 6

Ingredients
Dressing:
1 tablespoon	Mustard (I use Dijon)
1 tablespoon	Vinegar (I use sherry vinegar)
1 tablespoon	Lemon juice, freshly squeezed
1 tablespoon	Sugar
1 teaspoon	Salt (I use fleur de sel)
½ cup	Mayonnaise (or Miracle Whip)
¼ cup	Sour Cream

Vegetables:
1 small green	Cabbage, (about 1¾ pounds), finely shredded
2 medium	Carrots, shredded (I cut into [thick matchsticks)
2	Apples (cored and chopped)
½ cup	Raisins
½ cup	Celery, chopped
1 small	Onion, coarsely grated (optional)

Directions
Whisk together mustard, vinegar, lemon juice, sugar, salt, mayonnaise, and sour cream in a small bowl. Refrigerate dressing, covered, until ready to use, or up to 2 days.

Put cabbage, carrots, and onion (if desired) in a large bowl.
Pour in dressing, and toss thoroughly.
Refrigerate, covered, until slaw begins to soften, 1 to 2 hours.

If not using immediately, refrigerate, covered, up to 2 days.

Just before serving, toss coleslaw again.

Fattoush Salad

Contributed by: Liane Desmarais-Cavanagh
Source: Ramlah Mohammed
Note: Ramlah shared this Moroccan specialty at a Diversity Day pic nic, it was so tasty I asked for the recipe (it's her mother's). The vegetables are cut into relatively large pieces as compared to tabbouleh which requires ingredients to be finely chopped. Sumac is usually used to give fattoush its sharp taste. This is very good with BBQ Chicken.

Ingredients

2 cups	Romaine Lettuce, torn
2	Tomatoes, chopped and de-seeded
2 small	Cucumbers, peeled, chopped and de-seeded
1	Green Pepper, chopped (I omit – allergic)
3	Scallions, minced
15	Mint leaves chopped (or 1 tablespoon dried mint)
¼ cup	chopped Parsley (curly)
2 tablespoons	chopped Purslane or chickweed (optional)
1 to 2 cups	Pita bread, torn into pieces

Classic Lemon Vinaigrette:
  ¼ cup   Lemon juice
  ¼ cup   Olive oil
        Salt
  1 to 2 tablespoon Sumac (I barely use 1 tablespoon)

Combine all dressing ingredients in a jar with a tight-fitting lid, cover, and shake to blend.

Directions

Split loaves of Pita bread by separating the top and bottom of the "pocket", and crisp in regular oven. (I place the pieces of bread in a plastic bag, sprinkle with drops of olive oil, and shake well before baking. This makes them extra crispy.)

Cut the vegetables into bite size pieces, and combine in large salad bowl
(De-seeding the tomato and cucumber helps prevent the pita from getting soggy)

Add crisped Pita

Add the dressing to Salad bowl and mix well

Serve

Jell-O, Pineapple and Cream Cheese Salad

Contributed by:	Liane Desmarais-Cavanagh
Source:	Doris Desmarais & Thelma Bolter-Swinford
Yield:	1 9 x 13" pan
Note:	Apparently Grandma D served this with cold ham and it goes very well in a buffet. I can honestly say I have never served this with meat. Coincidentally Ireceived a similar recipe from a Mormon friend (see dessert section), and she said it is always served at the reception after the funeral because it makes people smile.

Ingredients

1 pkg	Lemon Jell-O
1 pkg	Lime Jell-O
3 cup	boiling Water
1 can	Pineapple (crushed or bits, not rings)
4 oz. pkg	Cream Cheese (you can use the light variety)
1 cup	Whipped Cream
	sliced Almonds, toasted

Directions

Mix: Lemon Jell-O crystals with Lime Jell-O crystals.
Add 3 cups boiling water
Stir until all the crystals have dissolved

Measure out, and reserve 1 cup of the above mixture

Allow the 2 cups of Jell-O to cool and thicken slightly.
To the 2 cups of Jell-O add 1 can of drained crushed pineapple.
Stir well to combine
Place in pan (9" x 13") and chill in fridge at least 30 minutes or until quite firm.

Beat the 35% cream until soft peaks form

In a separate bowl soften the cream cheese
Fold in the whipped cream
Fold in the 1 cup of Jell-O that was reserved

Spread the Creamy Jell-O mixture on the top of the mostly set Jell-O/pineapple mixture.
The creamy mixture should rest on top of the Jell-O mixture.

Dust with toasted almonds and leave in the refrigerator to set "hard"

Cut in squares and serve on lettuce.

Orzo Salad

Contributed by:	Liane Desmarais-Cavanagh
Source:	Gina Chiarello
Yield:	Serves: 8
Note:	In my experience this tastes even better the day after you make it.

Ingredients

1½ cups	Orzo pasta, cooked to al dente
½ cup	Extra Virgin Olive Oil
½ cup	Red Wine Vinegar
2 teaspoons	kosher Salt
1	roasted Red Pepper, diced
1	roasted Yellow Pepper, diced (Gina also substituted fresh)
½ cup	Pine nuts
1½ cups	Basil (can be dried or fresh see below)
½ cup	finely diced Red Onion
1 cup	crumbled Feta cheese

Directions

Cook the orzo according to the directions on the box

While the pasta is cooking mix the Olive Oil, Vinegar and salt

When pasta is cooked, drain and while still hot toss with vinaigrette

Stir in the red and yellow peppers, pine nuts, onion and basil (if using dried).
(The heat will help the dried basil release its flavour. If you are using fresh basil; rip and add just before serving)

When cooled sprinkle with the feta cheese

Serve at room temperature

Potato Salad

Contributed by: Mireille Desmarais
Source: Totally original
Yield: 6 servings
Background: Mireille says this is John's favorite potato salad!

Ingredients

3 to 4	medium Potatoes cooked and chopped
1 raw	Carrot
1/3	Cucumber chopped
2 to 3	Radishes depending on the size
2	Scallions, cut
1 stalk	Celery chopped
2	Eggs hard boiled
	parsley to garnish

Directions

Combine in a large bowl.

Now make dressing (below)

Dressing:

¼ cup	Mayonnaise
¼ cup	Coleslaw dressing
	Salt & pepper

Mix well and pour over vegetables.
Combine well.

Store in the fridge until ready to serve.

Provençale Potato Salad

Contributed by:	Liane Desmarais-Cavanagh
Source:	Mireille Groseiller
Yield:	Serves: 8
Note:	This comes from our next door neighbour in France, so I had to guess at the quantities. These suit our taste, but feel free to play. The warm potatoes absorb a lot of the dressing so if you have a little left over, don't throw it out, you may need it!"

Ingredients

¼ cup	Chicken broth (I use canned low-salt)
¼ cup	dry White Wine
¼ cup	Olive Oil
4	Scallions, chopped
2 tablespoons	Dijon mustard
2 tablespoons	White Wine Vinegar
2 tablespoons	drained Capers
	Salt and Pepper
3¼ pounds	Red skinned potatoes (½"diameter)

Directions

Whisk first 7 ingredients in large bowl to blend
Season dressing to taste with salt and pepper
(Can be prepared 1 day ahead. If not using immediately cover and refrigerate.
 Bring to room temperature before continuing.)

Cook potatoes in large pot of boiling salted water until just tender (about 35 minutes).
Drain.
Return potatoes to pot.
Place pot over low heat until liquid from potatoes evaporates, about 2 minutes
Remove from heat

Cut warm potatoes into S   thick slices
Add to dressing
Toss gently to coat
Let stand at least 1 hour at room temperature
Toss again and serve

Savoury Carrot Salad

Contributed by: Heather Ross
Note: This makes an excellent winter salad, and is quick and easy to put together:

Ingredients
4	Carrots, shredded
2 tablespoons	Balsamic Vinegar
2 tablespoons	Extra Virgin Olive Oil
2 teaspoons	Dijon mustard
2	Garlic cloves, crushed
1 teaspoon	Basil, dried
	Salt & Pepper

Directions
Put shredded carrots in a bowl.
Mix the rest of the ingredients and pour over the carrots.
Gently toss.
Add salt and pepper to taste.

Serve right away, or chill first.
This salad is best eaten the day it is made.

Scandinavian Coleslaw

Contributed by:	Liane Desmarais-Cavanagh
Source:	Khrysta Kurt, Summer 2009
Yield:	10 people
Note:	Khrysta used to be our next-door neighbor. She said that when she was growing up (1920s Vienna) they only had mandarins at Christmas so this always reminds her of happy times. Coleslaw can be made 1 day ahead, chilled, and covered.

Ingredients

½ cup	Mayonnaise
¼ cup	Sour cream (low fat is fine)
2 tablespoons	Cider vinegar
¾ teaspoon	Sugar (I use Splenda)
½ teaspoon	Salt
½ teaspoon	Black pepper
2 pound	Cabbage, quartered, cored, & thinly sliced (8 cups) (can mix green and red)
3 medium	Carrots, shredded
2	Apples, cubed (I like Granny Smith)
	handful raisins**
	handful Pumpkin seeds**
	handful dried cherries or dried cranberries
2	Mandarins, sectioned

Directions

Whisk together: mayonnaise, sour cream, vinegar, sugar, salt, and pepper in a large bowl until well combined

Toss with cabbage and carrots

Let stand, uncovered, at room temperature, tossing occasionally, until a little wilted, about 30 minutes

Then add: apples, raisins, pumpkin seeds, dried cherries/cranberries

Just before serving gently fold in the Mandarin sections.

Serve at room temperature or chilled.

**I use a trail mix that includes; pumpkin seeds, raisins, sunflower seeds, currents, cashews, etc. it saves time and money."

Shrimp in Tomato Salad

Contributed by: Ellen Desmarais
Source: Genevieve Samson, a bookbinder at the National Archives, ca 1995
Yield: makes enough for 4
Note: This is a very good first course and so easy to prepare.

Ingredients

1 pound	frozen large Shrimp, thawed and cleaned (shrimp should be the size of a quarter)
1	Avocado (or tomato) per person, scooped
1	Plain yogurt
3 parts	Mayonnaise to 1 of yogurt
	Scallion, chopped

Directions

A few hours before serving, mix the mayonnaise, yogurt and green onions. Chill in the fridge a couple of hours.

Rinse and clean the shrimp, remove tails.

Scoop out the avocado or tomato; when ready to serve place on lettuce on a plate.

Fill the avocado or tomato with shrimp.

Pour the mayonnaise mixture over all and onto the plate.

Decorate with a slice or two of cucumber.

Strawberry Salad with Poppy Seed Dressing

Contributed by: Valerie Healy
Yield: 4 to 5 servings
Note: I make this once a year in strawberry season. Boys don't like it, but the girls do!

Ingredients:

6 cups	Baby Spinach and Romaine lettuce, mixed
¾ cup	Mayonnaise
3 tablespoons	granulated Sugar
¼ cup	Skim Milk
2 tablespoons	White Vinegar
2 tablespoons	Poppy Seeds
1 cup	Starwberries, sliced
½ cup	Orange Liquor
1	Red Onion, sliced

Directions

Wash and dry spinach & lettuce
Place in a salad bowl and chill until ready to serve

To make dressing, combine mayonnaise, sugar, milk vinegar and poppy seeds in a blender or whisk until smooth.
Chill 1 hour

Macerate strawberries in liquor 1 hour

Drain berries, mix with greens
Pour dressing over the salad to taste or serve separately
Top with onion to garnish

Vinaigrette

Contributed by: Heather Ross
Source: Ellen Desmarais
Yield: 1 cup
Note: This is my favourite basic salad dressing.

Ingredients & Directions

Into a small bowl put:

2 tablespoons	Dijon Mustard
¼ cup fresh	Lemon juice
¼ teaspoon	Sugar
¼ teaspoon	Salt
	masses of fresh ground pepper, to taste

Whisk all ingredients, taste and adjust accordingly.

Gradually add ¾ cup olive oil, whisking until the emulsion is creamy. Taste again. If too acidic, add a tiny bit more oil. If oil predominates, add another squirt of lemon.

Optional:
Freshly chopped parsley
Minced garlic

Nyons Vinaigrette

Contributed by: Liane Desmarais-Cavanagh

1/3 cup	Extra Virgin Olive Oil (preferably from Nyons)
1/3 cup	White Wine Vinegar
1 heaping teaspoon	Dijon Mustard
2 pinches	Herbs de Provence
1 pinch	Fleur de sel or Sel de mer
	Fresh ground 5 pepper corns

Pour oil into a jar that seals well
Add Dijon, Herbs, Fleur de sel and Pepper
Seal jar and shake well
Open jar and add Vinegar.
Seal jar and shake very well.
Open jar and taste (add extra oil or vinegar depending on taste preferences)

~Starch~

Colcannon

Contributed by:	Liane Desmarais-Cavanagh
Source:	Jenni Daly (now Cullen), Dublin, November 2004
Yield:	2 servings
Note:	A traditional Irish dish served to us in Dublin by an Irish friend whom we first met in Paris. Can be prepared in 45 minutes or less.

Ingredients

1¼ pounds	Russet (baking) Potatoes
3 cups	thinly sliced Cabbage
½ cup	Milk, scalded
2 tablespoons	unsalted Butter, cut into bits and softened

Directions

Peel the potatoes and cut them into 1" pieces.

In a saucepan cover the potatoes with salted water, and simmer them, covered, for 15 minutes, or until they are tender.

While the potatoes are simmering, in a steamer set over boiling water steam the cabbage for 5 minutes, or until it is tender.

Drain the potatoes in a colander, force them through a ricer or the medium disk of a food mill into a bowl.
Shake excess water off cabbage.

Stir into the potatoes the milk, the butter, the cabbage, and salt and pepper to taste.

(Traditionally served mounded with a divot of melted butter in the "crater" (volcano like).)

Couscous Salad with Shrimp and Mint

Contributed by: Liane Desmarais-Cavanagh
Source: From a friend's Moroccan mother who makes it all the time.
Yield: serves 6 or more
Note: This dish is very fresh and tasty. I serve this as a first course, as a side dish with grilled chicken, and (if there are any left-overs) it is wonderful stuffed inside pita bread as a sandwich!
Note from Ellen: My recipe contains raisins and mint, but it can be made with almost anything. My friends in France seem to prefer to make it with tomatoes and chopped onions.

Ingredients

½ cup   Olive Oil
¼ cup   Lemon juice, fresh is best
1 large   Garlic clove, minced
1 teaspoon   Celery seed

2 cups   Couscous (about 10 ounces)
2¾ cups   boiling water

1 pound   peeled cooked Shrimp (I add more!)
1½ cups   Tomatoes, chopped and seeded
1 cup   Celery, diced
½ cup   Scallions, chopped
S cup   fresh Mint, rinsed well and chopped
3 tablespoons   Capers, drained (I like to use more)

Directions

Whisk first 4 ingredients in small bowl.
Season dressing with salt and pepper.

Place couscous in large bowl.
Pour water over.
Cover and let stand until water is absorbed, about 10 minutes.
Fluff with fork.
Add shrimp, tomatoes, celery, green onions, mint and capers.
Mix in dressing.
Chill until cold, about 30 minutes or up to 2 hours.

Note: I have also added such things as:
- Cucumbers, peeled, seeded and chopped
- Pickles, patted dry and chopped
- Pickled pearl onions, patted dry and left whole
- tart Granny Smith apples, cored and chopped

Lemony Potato Salad

Contributed by: Liane Desmarais-Cavanagh
Source: Gourmet Magazine, Summer 2009
Yield: 8 servings

Preparation
Active time: 15 min
Total time: 45 min
What wine to serve: Artezin Mendocino, Zinfandel '07 or, Château de Chamirey

Ingredients

3 pounds	small boiling Potatoes
1 cup	chopped Celery (about 4 ribs)
½ cup	Mayonnaise
¼ cup	finely chopped Chives
1 teaspoon	Lemon zest
2 tablespoons	fresh Lemon juice
1 teaspoon	Sugar (I omit)

Directions

Cover potatoes with water in a large pot and season well with salt.
Bring to a boil, then simmer until tender, 12 to 20 minutes.

While potatoes cook, stir together in a large bowl:
    celery,
    mayonnaise,
    chives,
    lemon zest and juice,
    sugar,
    1 teaspoon salt, and
    ¾ teaspoon pepper.

Drain potatoes and cool completely, then halve or quarter.

Add to dressing and toss to coat.

Nana's Farting Beans

Contributed by: Valery Healy
Note: About the name…Whenever we have a family pot luck I ask Tristan, my 7 year old grandson, what he would like Nana to bring, his answer is always: "Nana's farting beans:. He loves the way they work on him!

Ingredients

Small Pot		*Large Pot*
1 pound	"Navy" Beans	2 pounds
1 teaspoon	Baking Soda	2 teaspoons
½ pound	Pork or Bacon	1 pound
1 teaspoon	Mustard	2 teaspoons
¼ cup	Sugar	½ cup
1 teaspoon	Salt	1 tablespoon
1 medium	Onion	2 medium
2 teaspoons	Vinegar	4 teaspoons
1 tablespoon	Brown Sugar	2 tablespoons.
½ cup	Ketchup	1 cup
dash	Pepper	bigger dash
½ cup	Molasses	1 cup

Directions

Cover beans with cold water and soak overnight.
In the morning drain and cover with water and 1 teaspoon soda.
Simmer 'til beans are soft (Blow on a few in a spoon and the skins should peel off).
Drain

In a bean pot put ½ beans, ½ pork and onion.
Mix other ingredients, pour some over beans.

Do this again with the rest of the beans etc.

Add enough hot water to come to bean level.

Bake at 275°F. For 8 hours, checking to be sure that the water is at bean level.

Note: I do this for a day, and reheat the next day for a while in the oven, they are even better the second day.

Polynesian Rice

Contributed by:	Ellen Desmarais
Source:	Judy Ross
Yield:	serves 8
Note:	This is a delightful rice to serve with cold meat or hot chicken. It has had a big success with our friends in France.

Ingredients

3 cups	cooked Rice (1 cup uncooked real rice)
1½ cups.	chopped Celery
1 10 oz. Pkg.	frozen Peas
¼ cup	chopped Onion

Toss rice, celery & onion together.

Dressing:

½ cup	Oil
2 teaspoons	Salt
1½ teaspoons	Sugar (or Splenda)
½ teaspoon	Celery salt
1 teaspoon	Soya sauce
2 teaspoons	Curry powder
1 tablespoon	Vinegar
1 can	Chinese noodles
½ teaspoon	Celery seed

Just before serving, mix dressing with rice etc. And toss together with 1 can (14 oz.) Chinese noodles.

Serve hot or cold.

Perogies (Rose Sawchuk's)

Contributed by: Liane Desmarais-Cavanagh
Source: Rose Sawchuk, October 1986
Yield: 48

Ingredients:
3 cups	pre-sifted all-purpose Flour
½ cup	Margarine
½ teaspoon	Salt
1	Egg
1½ tablespoons	Sour Cream
1¼ cups	Potato Water (room temperature)

Directions:
1. Pour flour and salt into a large bowl and stir with a spoon to combine thoroughly.
2. Cut cold margarine into flour with your hands until mixture resembles oatmeal.
3. Gently beat 1 egg in a separate small bowl.
4. Add the sour cream into the beaten egg mixture, then add the reserved room temperature potato water and whisk to combine thoroughly.
5. Make a well in the flour mixture and pour in the egg mixture.
6. With your hands, combine the wet and dry mixtures and form into dough.
7. Continue to combine until it pulls together to form dough. Knead in the bowl until it is soft and not sticky. It should easily come off of your hands as you knead it.
8. Cover dough with cling wrap or a damp cloth and let rest for 2 hours at room temperature.
9. When you are ready to fill perogies, divide dough into 3 pieces and cover 2 while you roll out one piece of dough.
10. Roll dough to a ¼" thickness - you want it to be thin, but not too thin (you don't want holes in the dough).
11. Cut 3" rounds with a cookie cutter or a glass with a sharp rim.
12. Press a round of dough in your hand and fill with 1 teaspoon of filling.
13. Fold round in half and neatly tuck filling inside with your index finger, away from the edges. If there is any filling on the seams it may unseal while boiling.
14. Starting from the bottom, pinch the edges closed to seal the perogy closed. Also ensure there are no air pockets inside the perogies - they may unseal as a result. Work your way along the edge pinching it closed and pulling the edges outward by gently sweeping the dough with your thumb to form a flat seam.
15. Fill a saucepan with water and salt and bring to a boil. Cook each different flavour of perogies in separate batches - do not cook all of them together at the same time.
16. Drop one type of perogies into boiling water. They will drop to the bottom of the pot while they cook. Do not crowd the pot by cooking too many at the same time.
17. Within a few minutes the perogies will rise to the top of the water and float. At this point, they will be finished.
18. Carefully remove the perogies from hot water with a slotted spoon and drain in a colander.
19. Options: Sauté finely chopped onions with butter and drizzle onto boiled perogies or pan fry the boiled perogies in the onions and butter until they are browned and crisp. If you are making fruit-filled perogies, simply toss with a dollop of butter so that they won't stick together.
20. Serve perogies with sour cream.

Potato and Cheese Perogy Filling

Ingredients:
4 white potatoes
1 cup of Cheddar cheese

Directions:
1. Bring 4 cut potatoes to a boil in a pot of water.
2. Grate 1 cup of Cheddar cheese.
3. Drain potatoes and reserve 1 ¼ cups of potato water for pierogy dough.
4. Cool potatoes slightly then begin to mash them.
5. Add grated cheese to the potatoes.
6. Mash potatoes and cheese thoroughly until they blend into a smooth paste.
7. Pour filling into a bowl and cool before filling pierogies.

Rose Sawchuk's Black Cherry Perogy Filling

Ingredients:
1 large can of black, pitted cherries
Sugar, to taste

Directions:
1. If you cannot find black cherries, red ones are fine, if you cannot find pitted cherries, then you may have to pit them yourself. Simply press down on each cherry with your thumb and remove the pit.
2. Drain the cherries and squeeze or pat dry in cheesecloth or paper towel.
3. Options: Use one whole cherry to fill each pierogy or chop the cherries and make a compote - simply place them into a bowl and add a bit of sugar, to taste.

Rose Sawchuk's Wine Sauerkraut Perogy Filling
Yield: 36

Ingredients:
1 onion
3 cups wine sauerkraut (in a can)
4 tablespoons of butter
Freshly ground pepper, to taste

Directions:
1. Squeeze the sauerkraut in cheesecloth or a tea towel and then chop finely.
2. Finely mince the onion.
3. Melt butter in a medium-sized fry pan and add minced onion. Sauté the onion over medium heat until it turns translucent.
4. Add sauerkraut and sauté for 10 minutes until soft. Season mixture with freshly ground pepper. Keep an eye on the heat so that you don't scorch the sauerkraut.
5. Pour filling into a bowl and cool to room temperature before filling pierogies.

Rice Pilaf with Pistachios and Golden Raisins

Contributed by:	Liane Desmarais-Cavanagh
Source:	Gourmet Magazine, Feb. 1990
Yield:	Serves 2.

Ingredients

¼ cup	finely chopped Onion
¼ teaspoon	Turmeric
[teaspoon	ground Cardamom
1½ teaspoons	unsalted Butter
S cup	long-grain Rice
T cup	Chicken Broth
2 tablespoons	Pistachios, toasted lightly, cooled, and chopped
2 tablespoons	Golden Raisins, soaked in boiling water to cover for 1 minute and drained
2 tablespoons	thinly sliced Scallion greens

Directions

In a small heavy saucepan cook the onion with the turmeric and the cardamom in 1 tablespoon of the butter over moderately low heat, stirring, until the onion is softened.

Add the rice and cook it, stirring, until it is coated with the butter.

Add the broth, bring the liquid to a boil, covered, and simmer the mixture for 17 minutes, or until the liquid is absorbed and the rice is tender.

Stir in the pistachios, the raisins, the scallion greens, the remaining ½ tablespoon butter, and salt and pepper to taste.

Roasted Sweet Potatoes and Fresh figs

Contributed by: Liane Desmarais-Cavanagh
Source: Jerusalem: A Cookbook (from Lil Levitin)
Yield: Serves 4.
Note: easy to make and satisfying crunch.

Ingredients

4 small (2¼ pounds)	Sweet Potatoes (2¼ pounds total)
5 tablespoon	Olive Oil
3 tablespoons	Balsamic vinegar (you can use a commercial rather than a premium aged grade)
1½ tablespoon	Superfine Sugar
12	Scallions, halved lengthwise and cut into 1½" segments
1 red	Chile, thinly sliced
6 (8½ oz)	ripe Figs, quartered
5 oz	soft Goat's Milk cheese (I use Loblaw's no-name)
	Sea Salt and freshly ground Pepper

Directions

Preheat the oven to 475°F

Wash the sweet potatoes, halve them lengthwise, and then cut each half again similarly into 3 long wedges.
Mix with 3 tablespoons of the olive oil, 2 teaspoons salt, and some black pepper.
Spread the wedges out, skin side down, on a baking sheet and cook for about 25 minutes, until soft but not mushy.
Remove from the oven and leave to cool down.

To make the balsamic reduction, place the balsamic vinegar and sugar in a small saucepan.
Bring to a boil, then decrease the heat and simmer for 2 to 4 minutes, until it thickens.
Be sure to remove the pan from the heat when the vinegar is still runnier than honey; it will continue to thicken as it cools.
Stir in a drop of water before serving if it does become too thick to drizzle.

Arrange the sweet potatoes on a serving platter.
Heat the remaining oil in a medium saucepan over medium heat and add the green onions and chile.
Fry for 4 to 5 minutes, stirring often to make sure not to burn the chile.
Spoon the oil, onions, and chile over the sweet potatoes.
Dot the figs among the wedges and then drizzle over the balsamic reduction.
Serve at room temperature.
Crumble the cheese over the top, if using.

Veg Rösti

Contributed by:	Liane Desmarais-Cavanagh
Source:	Jamie Oliver
Yield:	Serves 4.
Note:	easy to make and satisfying crunch.

Ingredients

600 g	Potatoes
3 large	Carrots
½ teaspoon	Dijon mustard
½	Lemon
	extra virgin Olive Oil
	Olive Oil (I know it's shown twice-it's the way Jamie Oliver has it in his recipe)
100 g	frozen Peas
100 g	baby Spinach
4 large	Eggs
50 g	Feta cheese

Directions

Preheat the oven to 180°C/350°F/gas 4.

Peel the potatoes and carrots, then coarsely grate them in a food processor or by hand on a box grater. Add a good pinch of salt, toss and scrunch it all together, then leave for 5 minutes.

Mix the mustard, a good squeeze of lemon juice, and a couple of lugs of extra virgin olive oil with a little pinch of salt and pepper in a medium bowl and put aside.

Drizzle a really good lug of olive oil into a large bowl and add a good pinch of pepper.
Handful by handful, squeeze the potato and carrot mixture to get rid of the excess salty liquid, then sprinkle into the bowl.
Toss in the oil and pepper until well mixed, then evenly scatter it over a large oiled baking tray (roughly 30cm x 40cm).
Roast for around 35 minutes, or until golden on top and super-crispy around the edges.

Meanwhile, blanch the peas for a minute in a large pan of boiling salted water, then scoop out, add to the bowl of dressing and pile the spinach on top.

Just before your r´sti is ready, with the water gently simmering, crack in the eggs, poach to your liking.

Remove rösti from oven.

Quickly toss the salad together to dress it and scatter in piles on the r´sti, then crumble over the feta, top with the poached eggs and serve.

Scalloped Potatoes with Goat Cheese and Herbs de Provence

Contributed by: Liane Desmarais-Cavangh
Source: Mary McQuaig
Yield: Serves 8.
Note: Interesting variation on an old favourite

Ingredients

1½ cups	Whipping Cream
1½ cups	Chicken Broth
1 cup	dry White Wine
½ cup	minced Shallots
1 tablespoon	minced Garlic
4 teaspoons	Herbes de Provence
¾ teaspoon	Salt
1 11 oz log	soft fresh Goat Cheese, crumbled
4 pounds	Russet Potatoes, peeled, thinly sliced

Directions

Preheat oven to 400°F.

Butter 13 x 9 x 2-inch glass baking dish.

Mix first 7 ingredients in large pot.
Bring to simmer over medium-high heat.
Add half of cheese; whisk until smooth.
Chill remaining cheese.
Add potatoes to pot; bring to simmer.

Transfer potato mixture to prepared dish, spreading evenly.
Cover with foil; bake 15 minutes.
Uncover and bake until potatoes are very tender and liquid bubbles thickly, about 50 minutes.

Dot potatoes with remaining cheese.
Bake until cheese softens, about 5 minutes.
Let cool 15 minutes before serving.

Tagliatelle with Saffron, Seafood, and Cream

Contributed by: Liane Desmarais-Cavanagh
Source: Chef in the Grand Titano Restaurant, San Marino
Yield: Serves: 4

Ingredients

A good pinch	Saffron
1 glass	white Wine
	Olive oil
1 large clove	Garlic, finely chopped
1 pound	dried Tagliatelle pasta
1½ pounds	mixed Seafood (red mullet, scallops, clams, de-bearded mussels, squid)
1 cup	Double Cream (heavy cream)
	Salt and freshly ground Pepper
	A bunch flat Parsley, chopped

Directions

Soak the saffron in the white wine.

Add a little oil and the garlic to a frying pan, and cook until softened.

Add the clams and mussels, shake the pan around, and add the white wine and saffron mixture.

Bring to a boil and cook until the shellfish opens, discard any shellfish that remain closed.

Then, lay the rest of the seafood, parsley, and the cream on top.
Simmer for 3 to 4 minutes and season to taste.

Cook the tagliatelle in salted, boiling water until al dente.

Drain and add to the fish, serve scattered with some of the leftover parsley and an extra drizzle of olive oil

Tartiflette

Contributed by:	Liane Desmarais-Cavanagh
Source:	The Chef at Les Trappeurs Tamie (Near Albertville, France)
	http://www.lestrappeurs-tamie.com/
Note:	A scary drive to get to the restaurant was well rewarded by this wonderful dish. Can be made 1 day ahead and re-warmed (but better if made fresh and kept warm until eaten).

Ingredients

1 kg	Potatoes
1 wheel of	Reblochon cheese
3 - 4 slices	good Ham
2	Onions
	Cream

Directions

Brown the onions and the ham
Add parboiled potatoes and cook until edges are browned.

Cut rind from cheese
Cut cheese into pieces

Put layer of potato mixture in Gratin dish sprinkle with ½ the cheese.
Top with remaining potatoes mixture
Dot with remaining cheese

Pour in Cream to just the top of the potatoes.
Bake in 325°F oven until liquid bubbles.

Two Potato Mash

Contributed by: Ellen Desmarais
Source: Patrick Savoie
Yield: According to the quantity of potatoes used.
Note: This is a delicious and unusual way to serve potatoes. The recipe is from Patrick Savoie, John's friend and colleague at the Senate.

Ingredients
Equal amounts of white potato and yams or sweet potatoes
Small container of sour cream
Chicken broth (optional)
Finely chopped onion or shallot
Salt & Pepper

Directions
Boil the white and sweet potatoes separately (the sweet potatoes cook much faster), mash each and then mix them together.

Add chopped onion if desired, about ½ the container of sour cream, salt, pepper, whip with a Mixmaster or portable blender.

The quantity of sour cream can be adjusted to your taste, or chicken broth may be used if you want the mixture to be lighter without adding more calories or fat.

Also, a slightly beaten egg may be added to the cooled potato mixture; in which case, bake in an oven at 350°F. about 45 minutes before you want to serve.

~Veggies~

Asparagus with Saffron Aïoli

Contributed by: Liane Desmarais-Cavanagh

Ingredients
Aioli:
¼ cup	Red Wine Vinegar (I use white wine/champagne vinegar)
1 tablespoon	Honey
Large pinch	Saffron threads
1 cup	Mayonnaise (If you don't have homemade use Hellman's)
2 cloves	Garlic, minced

Asparagus
2 pounds	Asparagus, trimmed
3 tablespoons	extra virgin Olive Oil
1 small	Red Bell Pepper, finely chopped (I omit)

Directions
For aioli:
Whisk vinegar, honey, and saffron threads in heavy small saucepan over medium-high heat. Bring to boil.
Remove from heat.
Cool completely.
Mix mayonnaise and garlic in medium bowl to blend.
Mix in cooled vinegar mixture.
Season aioli to taste with salt and pepper. (Can be made 1 day ahead. Cover and refrigerate.)

For asparagus:
Prepare barbecue (medium-high heat) (or ribbed fry pan).
Toss asparagus with oil on rimmed baking sheet.
Sprinkle with salt and pepper.
Grill asparagus until crisp-tender, turning occasionally, about 5 minutes.
Transfer to platter.
Drizzle aioli over asparagus.
Sprinkle with bell pepper.

Baby Carrots with Tarragon

Contributed by: Liane Desmarais-Cavanagh
Source: Ellen Desmarais
Yiled: Serves 6
Note: This is wonderful with roast lamb, and very good with baked chicken.

Ingredients

4 bunches	Baby Carrots (each about 8 ounces),
¼ cup	Water
3 tablespoons	minced fresh Tarragon (or 3 teaspoons dried tarragon)
2 tablespoons	Butter
1 tablespoon	White Wine Vinegar
1 tablespoon	Honey

Directions

Combine; carrots, ¼ cup water, 1½ tablespoons tarragon, butter, vinegar and honey in heavy large skillet.

Bring to a boil.

Reduce heat to medium; cover and simmer until carrots are almost tender, about 12 minutes.

Uncover; cook until carrots are tender and liquid is reduced to glaze, about 6 minutes longer.

Season with salt and pepper.
Transfer to platter.

Sprinkle with 1½ tablespoons tarragon.

Baby Onions with Orange Juice and Balsamic Vinegar

Contributed by: Liane Desmarais-Cavanagh
Yield: Makes 6 to 8 servings
Background: Great served with grilled chicken or pork. I love it 'cause I can make it the day ahead and serve it to guests with an antipasto first course.

Ingredients
2 pounds   fresh small Cipolline onions* or pearl onions
¼ cup   extra-virgin Olive Oil
¾ cup   fresh Orange Juice
¾ cup   Balsamic Vinegar

Directions
Blanch onions in large pot of boiling salted water 15 seconds.
Using slotted spoon, transfer to large bowl of ice water to cool.
Trim root end if necessary, leaving core intact.
Peel the outer paper layer off the onions.

Heat oil in large nonstick skillet over high heat.
Add onions and sauté until onions have deep golden brown spots, about 9 minutes.

Add orange juice and vinegar; bring to boil, scraping up browned bits.
Reduce heat to medium-low, cover, and simmer until onions are just tender when pierced with knife, about 8 minutes.

Using slotted spoon, transfer onions to medium bowl.
Boil juices in skillet until syrupy and reduced to T cup, about 3 minutes.
Pour over onions.

Serve warm or at room temperature.

(Can be made 1 day ahead. Cover and chill. Rewarm or bring to room temperature before serving.)

*here in Canada Cipolline onions are small, flat white Italian onions.

Brussel Sprouts with Panchetta

Contributed by: Liane Desmarais-Cavanagh
Source: Gordon Ramsay, Good Food Magazine, December 2005

Ingredients

1 kg	Brussels sprouts
100 g	Pancetta, thinly sliced, cut into 2cm strips
4 tablespoons	Goose fat,
a handful	Sage, shredded
12	Chestnuts, pre-cooked and peeled (optional)

Directions

Blanch the Brussels sprouts in a pan of boiling salted water for 3 minutes, then drain and tip into a bowl of iced water to cool quickly.

Drain well again and set aside until nearly ready to serve.

Sauté the pancetta in the hot goose fat until crisp.

Toss in the sprouts (and Chesnuts) and stir-fry for 2-3 mins,

Garnish with sage to serve.

Chou and Remoullade Salade

Contributed by:	Liane Desmarais-Cavanagh
Yield:	Serves 6

Ingredients

½ medium	green Cabbage, thinly sliced (about 8 cups)
½ small	Red Cabbage or Raddicio (about 4 cups)
2	Red Bell Peppers, cut into matchstick-size strips
3 cups	Celeriac, matchstick-size strips peeled and cleaned
T cup	Mayonnaise
2 tablespoons	Dijon Mustard
2 tablespoons	Cider/Sherry vinegar
4 teaspoons	Sugar (optional)
2 teaspoons	Celery/sesame seeds
1 tablespoon	slivered Almonds or chopped Pecans

Directions

Mix first 4 ingredients in large bowl.

Whisk mayonnaise and next 3 ingredients in small bowl to blend.

Pour dressing over vegetables.

Sprinkle with seeds

Season with salt and pepper.

(Can be made 6 hours ahead. Cover; chill.)

Eggplant Casserole

Contributed by: Liane Desmarais-Cavanagh
Source: Ellen Desmarais.
Yield: For 6 to 8 people
Note: I also add herbs de Provence and sometimes minced garlic to this casserole.

Ingredients

1 medium	Egg Plant
1 medium	Onion
	Bread Crumbs
	Milk
	Butter
	Salt & Pepper

Directions

Peel eggplant & cut into pieces

Peel and cut onion into pieces

Put in a pot and ½ fill with water

Bring to a boil & cook until eggplant is soft (about 7 min)

Grease casserole

Drain eggplant & onion

Put one layer of eggplant mixture into the casserole,
Next a layer of crumbs,
Sprinkle with salt & pepper

Repeat layering until casserole is full.

Pour milk into the corners until you can just see the milk
Dot with nutter

Bake in 375° oven for 45 minutes

Fried Eggplant (Melanzane fritte)

Contributed by: Ellen Desmarais
Source: My favourite Italian cookbook.
Yield: For 6 to 8 people
Note: Never add oil to the pan while the eggplant is frying. [I use canola oil, never olive oil for cooking.] The skin on North American eggplant is tough, so it is best to peel it for any recipe.

Ingredients

2 to 3 medium	Eggplants (3 to 4 ½ pounds)
	Salt
	Vegetable oil, enough to come 1 inch up the side of the pan.

Directions

Cut the eggplants lengthwise in slices about 3/8 Inch thick.

Set the slices upright in a pasta colander and sprinkle the first layer of slices liberally with salt before setting another layer next to it.

Put a soup dish under the colander to collect the drippings and let stand at least 30 min.

Add enough oil to a large skillet to come 1 inch up the side of the pan.
Turn on the heat to high.

Take as many slices of eggplant as you think will fit in one layer in the skillet and dry them well with paper towels.

When the oil is hot (test it with the end of one of the slices: it should sizzle), slide in the eggplant.

Fry to a nice golden brown on all sides, then transfer to a platter lined with paper towels to drain.

Dry some more slices and continue frying until they are all done. (If you see that the eggplant is browning too rapidly, lower the heat).

Eggplant, Parmesan Style (Melanzane alla parmigiana)

Contributed by: Liane Desmarais-Cavanagh
Yield: For 4 persons
Note: I like to prepare it the day ahead and bake it just before I serve it. I cut the eggplant to fit the baking pan, and lay in the eggplant with each layer going a different direction. (This adds more stability to the dish when cutting and serving)

Ingredients

2 medium	Eggplants (about 3 pounds), sliced, drained, and fried as in previous recipe.
2 cups	canned Italian tomatoes, drained of juice, seeds removed, and coarsely chopped
	Salt
1	whole-milk Mozzarella, coarsely grated on the largest holes of the grater.
4 to 5 tablespoons	freshly grated Parmesan cheese
1½ teaspoons	Oregano
2½ tablespoons	Butter

Directions

Preheat the oven to 400°F (if cooking the same day)

Line the bottom of a buttered bake-and-serve dish (10 inch square or its rectangular equivalent) with a single layer of fried eggplant slices.

Top this layer with chopped tomatoes.

Add a pinch of salt, a generous sprinkling of grated mozzarella, a tablespoon of grated Parmesan cheese, and a pinch of oregano and cover with another layer of sliced eggplant.

Continue building up layers of eggplant, tomatoes and cheese until you've used up all the eggplant.

The top layer should be eggplant. Sprinkle the remaining Parmesan cheese over it and dot with butter. (Can be made to this point 1 day ahead. Cover and refrigerate.)

Place in the upper third of the preheated oven.

After 20 minutes pull out the pan and, pressing with the back of a spoon, check to see if there is an excess amount of liquid. If there is, draw it off with the spoon. Return to the oven for another 15 min.

Allow it to settle and partly cool off before serving.

It should _not_ be piping hot.

(Festive) Green Bean Casserole

Contributed by: Liane Desmarais-Cavanagh
Source: Kay Cavanagh, June 1996
Yield: 12 – 15 people
Note: Kay made these green beans to serve at our wedding buffet. They were a huge hit!

Ingredients

5 cups	Green Beans, cut and hot tender-cooked
1 can (284 mL)	Campbell's Condensed Low Fat Cream of Mushroom Soup
¼ cup	softened Cream Cheese
1 tablespoon	Soy Sauce
[teaspoon	Pepper
¾ cup	dry hickory-smoked Potato Sticks
½ cup	sliced Almonds

Directions

Place green beans into shallow 1½ quart baking dish.

In small bowl, combine well: soup, cream cheese, soy sauce and black pepper.

Stir gently into beans.

Sprinkle with mixture of potato sticks and almonds.

Bake at 350°F for 30 minutes or until heated through.

Let stand for 5 minutes.

Not Your Mama's Green Bean Casserole

Contributed by: Liane Desmarais-Cavanagh
Source: Alton Brown
Yield: 4 – 6 servings

Ingredients:

For the topping:
2 medium	Onions, thinly sliced
¼ cup	all-purpose Flour
2 tablespoons	Panko bread crumbs
1 teaspoon	Kosher Salt
	Nonstick spray

For beans:
1 pound fresh	Green Beans, rinsed & trimmed
1 gallon	water
2 tablespoons	Kosher Salt

For sauce:
2 tablespoons	unsalted Butter
12 oz	Mushrooms, trimmed and cut into ½" pieces
1 teaspoon	Kosher salt
½ teaspoon	freshly ground black Pepper
2 cloves	Garlic, minced
¼ teaspoon	freshly ground Nutmeg
2 tablespoons	all-purpose Flour
1 cup	Chicken Broth
1 cup	Half-and-Half cream

Directions

Preheat the oven to 475°F.
Combine the onions, flour, panko and salt in a large mixing bowl and toss to combine.
Coat a sheet pan with non-stick spray and evenly spread the onions on the pan.
Bake in the oven until golden brown, tossing every 10 minutes, for approximately 30 minutes.
Once done, remove from the oven and set aside until ready to use.
Turn the oven down to 400°F.
While the onions are cooking, prepare the beans.
Bring a gallon of water and 2 tablespoons of salt to a boil in an 8-quart saucepan. Blanch for 5 minutes.
Drain in a colander and immediately plunge the beans into a large bowl of ice water to stop the cooking. Drain and set aside.
Melt the butter in a 12" cast iron skillet set over medium-high heat.
Add the mushrooms, salt and pepper and cook, stirring occasionally, until the mushrooms begin to give up some of their liquid, approximately 4 to 5 minutes.
Add the garlic and nutmeg and continue to cook for another 1 to 2 minutes.
Sprinkle the flour over the mixture and stir to combine. Cook for 1 minute.
Add the broth and simmer for 1 minute.
Add the half-and-half and cook until the mixture thickens, approximately 6 to 8 minutes.
Remove from the heat and stir in ¼ of the onions and all of the green beans.
Top with the remaining onions.
Place into the oven and bake until bubbly, approximately 15 minutes.
Remove and serve immediately.

Parmesan Roasted Green Beans

Contributed by: Liane Desmarais-Cavanagh
Source: Tyler Florence
Note: Wonderful with grilled meat

Ingredients

1 pound	thin Green Beans (haricots verts)
	Extra-virgin olive oil
	Kosher salt and freshly ground black pepper
1 cup	grated Parmigiano-Reggiano
½ cup	caramelized Onions (optional)

Directions

Preheat the oven to 400 degrees F.

Trim off the tough end of the beans and arrange the beans on a non-stick cookie sheet.

Sprinkle caramelized onions evenly over green beans (optional)

Drizzle with olive oil season with salt and pepper, to taste.

Sprinkle the cheese evenly over the top and bake until the cheese melts and forms a crisp shell over the beans, about 10 minutes.

Let the beans sit a few minutes for the cheese to cool slightly.

Lift the beans out onto a platter and serve.

Roast Vegetables

Contributed by: Ellen Desmarais
Source: Taken from the newspaper long ago.
Yield: Serves 6
Note: A very good make-ahead recipe. You will need a Pyrex dish or casserole.

Ingredients
Suggested vegetables:
1	Yellow Pepper
1	Green Pepper
1	Onion
1 small	Eggplant
1 or 2	Zucchini
1	Tomato
	Salt & Pepper
	Oil (about 4 tablespoons)

Directions
Preheat the oven to 325°F.

Deseed the peppers and cut into thin strips. Keep the colours separate

Peel the onion and cut into thin rings.

Wash and cut the eggplant and zucchini into thin strips.

Cut the tomatoes in half, remove the seeds, then cut into segments.

Fill the oven-proof dish using the strips of vegetables, alternating the colours. For example: onion, then green pepper, then zucchini, then one tomato, then the eggplant and finally the yellow pepper. This is only to make it look pretty.

Sprinkle with salt & pepper,
Pour the oil over the vegetables,
Cover with foil
Cook for 1 hour until vegetables are fairly dry.

Serve hot or cold

When baked, let it cool then divide into plastic dishes or small bags and freeze or keep in the fridge (for 3 or 4 days, not longer).

Serve with any kind of meat or with eggs or make it your meal.

Shitakes with Ginger and Scallions

Contributed by: Liane Desmarais-Cavanagh
Yield: Makes 4 side-dish servings.
Note: If your mushrooms are dirty, allow time for wiping them clean with slightly dampened paper towels before lighting the charcoal.

Ingredients

1½ tablespoons	dry Sherry
1 tablespoon	Soy Sauce
1 tablespoon	Ginger minced peeled fresh
1½ teaspoons	Rice Vinegar (not seasoned)
½ teaspoon	Sugar
2½ tablespoons	Vegetable Oil (I use Grape Seed)
1½ pound large	fresh Shiitake Mushrooms (3 inches wide), stems cut off and discarded
½ teaspoon	Salt
½ teaspoon	Pepper
2	Scallions, cut into very thin strips (2 inches long)

Directions

Prepare grill for cooking over medium-hot charcoal (moderate heat for gas).

Stir together sherry, soy sauce, ginger, vinegar, sugar, and ½ tablespoon oil in a large bowl until sugar is dissolved.

Toss mushrooms with salt, pepper, and remaining 2 tablespoons oil, then grill on lightly oiled grill rack, covered only if using a gas grill, turning over occasionally, until lightly browned and tender, 4 to 6 minutes total.
Transfer mushrooms with tongs to bowl with sauce, then add scallions and toss until combined.

Cooks' notes:

• If you aren't able to grill outdoors, mushrooms can be grilled in a hot lightly oiled well-seasoned large (2-burner) ridged grill pan over moderately high heat.
• If you aren't able to find large shiitakes, you can use smaller ones but will need to grill them on a lightly oiled perforated grill sheet to prevent them from falling through the grill rack.

Spiced Sesame Snap Peas

Contributed by: Ellen Desmarais
Source: A magazine, a long time ago.
Yield: Serves 4
Note: This is my favorite pick-me-up vegetable course for an otherwise dull meal. This is a little spicy; reduce the garlic if you prefer softer flavours.

Ingredients

2	Shallots, minced
2 cloves	Garlic, minced
1 tablespoon	Vegetable (or peanut) Oil
1 tablespoon	Sesame Oil
1½ pounds.	Sugar Snap Peas, cleaned
1 large	Carrot, julienned and blanched
1 teaspoon	Soy Sauce
1 teaspoon	Lemon juice
	pinch of chili pepper
½ teaspoon	Sesame seeds
	salt & pepper to taste

Directions

In a large skillet, over medium heat, sauté shallots and garlic in vegetable oil about 3 minutes.

Increase heat to medium-high and add sesame oil.
Add peas and carrot, tossing frequently about 3 minutes.
Add soy sauce and lemon juice.
Sprinkle with chili pepper, sesame seeds, salt and pepper.

Toss and serve.

Tsimis

Contributed by: Liane Desmarais-Cavanagh
Source: Lil Levitin.
Yield: Serves 6
Note: This is one of many versions of this dish.

Ingredients
2 pounds	Carrots (about 6 large carrots), peeled and cut into 1/4-inch coins
2 tablespoons	Canola Oil
1 teaspoon	Kosher Salt, plus more to taste
¼ teaspoon	freshly ground black Pepper, plus more to taste
1 cup	Honey
	Juice of 2 lemons
3 sprigs	Thyme
1 cup	quartered pitted Prunes
½ cup	golden Raisins
½ teaspoon	ground Ginger
¼ teaspoon	ground Cinnamon
	Chopped fresh flat-leaf parsley, for garnish

Directions
Preheat the oven to 350°F.

In a roasting pan, toss the carrots with the oil, salt, and pepper.
Cook in the oven, stirring occasionally, until the carrots are lightly browned and somewhat tender, 40 to 50 minutes.
Meanwhile, combine the honey, juice from 1½ lemons (reserve the remaining lemon half), thyme, and 1/3 cup water in a large pan or skillet.
Bring to a simmer and cook the mixture over medium-high heat for 5 minutes, then remove and discard the thyme.
Remove the pan from the heat.

When the carrots are done cooking, pour the carrots, prunes, and raisins into the pan with the honey mixture and stir to coat completely.

Add the ginger and cinnamon, and simmer the carrot-honey mixture over medium-high heat, stirring frequently, until the liquid has reduced to a thick glaze, 10 to 15 minutes.
Then add the juice from the remaining ½ lemon and remove the pan from the heat.

Season with salt and pepper to taste.

Garnish with the chopped parsley.

~ Main Course (meat) ~

7 Layer Dinner

Contributed by: Valerie Healy
Source: Judy Ross
Note: This recipe originally came from a Newfie in Schefferville. Judy's family doesn't care for it, but my family does, especially Trevor.

Ingredients

Thinly sliced	raw Potatoes
Thinly sliced	raw Carrots
Thinly sliced	raw Onions
¼ cup	uncooked Rice
1 can	Peas
1 pound.	Sausage
1 can	Tomato soup
	Salt & Pepper

Directions

This is another recipe that can be made as big or small as you need.

Layer in order, and add a soup can of water over everything.
Cover.

Bake at 350°F for 2 hours.

Take cover off, turn sausage and bake another hour.

Beef in Guiness

Contributed by:	Liane Desmarais-Cavanagh
Source:	From: Joan (Siobhan) Daly, Dublin, May 2006
Yield:	Serves 4

Ingredients:

2½ pounds	Shin of Beef or other stewing/braising Steak
2 Large	Onions, sliced
6	Carrots, sliced
2 tablespoons	Seasoned Flour
	A little beef dripping or oil
8 fl.oz.	Guinness
8 fl.oz.	Beef Stock
2	Bay Leaves
2 sprigs	Fresh Thyme
1 tablespoons	freshly chopped Parsley

Instructions

Cut the beef into chunks and toss in the flour to coat on all sides.
Melt the dripping or oil in a large saucepan until very hot, add the beef and seal quickly on all sides.
Remove from the pan with a slotted spoon and set aside.

Heat the fat again until hot then add the onions and fry gently until soft and transparent.
Return the beef to the pan together with the carrots, bay leaves, thyme, stock and Guinness.
Mix well, bring to the boil then reduce the heat, cover and simmer for 1½ hours, stirring from time to time.

To serve - transfer to a warmed serving dish, sprinkle with chopped parsley and serve hot.

Blanquette de Veau

Contributed by: Liane Desmarais-Cavanagh
Source: Chef Boulud, Café Boulud
Yield: 8 people
Note: Great winter meal Serve with: white Burgundy), or Pinot Gris (from Alsace)

Ingredients

10 ounces	Pearl Onions
4½ pounds	Veal shoulder, boned, trimmed, cut into 1-inch pieces
9 cups+	Chicken Stock (or veal stock if you have it)
3	fresh Thyme sprigs
2	Bay leaves
5 tablespoons	Butter
1½ pounds	Celeriac, peeled, cut into 1½" pieces
4 large	Carrots, peeled, cut into 1½" lengths
3 medium	Turnips, peeled, each cut into 6 pieces
8 ounces	Button Mushrooms
6 ounces	Green Beans, ends trimmed
3 tablespoons	all-purpose Flour
½ cup	Whipping Cream
½ tablespoon	fresh Lemon juice
½ bunch	fresh Chives, cut into 2-inch pieces

Directions

In large pot of salted water blanch pearl onions for 1 minute.
Using slotted spoon, remove onions from pot, trim ends and peel.
Add veal to pot and cook 4 minutes.
Drain veal; rinse with cold water.
Rinse pot and return veal to pot.
Add 8 cups chicken stock and bring to boil.
Reduce heat and simmer 30 minutes.
Add thyme and bay leaves and simmer until veal is tender, stirring occasionally, about 30 minutes longer.
In another large heavy pot, melt 2 tablespoons butter over medium heat.
Add pearl onions, celery root, carrots, turnips, mushrooms and 1 cup chicken stock.
Cover and cook until vegetables are tender and almost all liquid has evaporated, about 15 minutes.
Add green beans and cook until just tender, about 2 minutes.
Drain veal, reserving 2 cups liquid (less than 2 cups liquid remains? add stock to measure 2 cups).
Mix veal into vegetables.
Melt remaining 3 tablespoons butter in heavy medium saucepan over medium heat.
Mix in 3 tablespoons flour.
Cook until butter mixture turns golden brown, stirring constantly, about 2 minutes.
Whisk in 2 cups reserved cooking liquid.
Cook until thickened, stirring frequently, about 5 minutes.
Stir in whipping cream.
Season sauce to taste with fresh lemon juice, salt and pepper.
Pour cream sauce over cooked veal and vegetables.
Garnish with fresh chives, if desired, and serve immediately.

Brisket with Dried Apricots, Prunes and Spices

Contributed by: Liane Desmarais-Cavanagh
Source: Lil Levitin, August 2005
Yield: 8 servings
Note: This recipe takes 2 days to make, and it can be kept 2 days before serving, so it's a great (and tasty) make-ahead dish for pot-luck.

Ingredients

T cup	quartered dried Apricots (about 4 ounces)
9 large cloves	Garlic
3½ teaspoons	ground Cumin
1 teaspoon	Salt
¼ teaspoon	ground Cinnamon
¼ teaspoon	ground black Pepper
1 4½- 5-pound	flat-cut beef Brisket
3 tablespoons	Olive Oil
4 cups	chopped Onions
2 medium	Carrots, coarsely chopped
1 tablespoon	minced peeled fresh Ginger
1 teaspoon	ground Coriander
[teaspoon	Cayenne pepper
1 cup	dry Red Wine
3 cups	homemade Beef Stock (or canned low-salt beef broth)
T cup	pitted Prunes, quartered
	chopped fresh Cilantro

Directions Day 1:

Combine S cup apricots, 3 garlic cloves, 1 teaspoon cumin, salt, cinnamon, and ¼ teaspoon pepper in processor.
Using on/off turns, chop to coarse puree.

Using small sharp knife, make ½-inch-deep slits all over brisket.
Set aside 1 tablespoon apricot mixture.
Press remaining apricot mixture into slits.

Position rack in bottom third of oven and preheat to 300°F.

Heat oil in heavy large ovenproof pot over medium-high heat.
Sprinkle brisket all over with salt and pepper.
Add brisket to pot and sauté until brown, about 5 minutes per side.
Transfer to plate, fat side up; spread with reserved 1 tablespoon apricot mixture.

Add onions to same pot. Sauté over medium-high heat 5 minutes.
Add carrots, ginger, coriander, cayenne pepper, remaining 6 garlic cloves and 2½ teaspoons cumin; sauté 3 minutes.
Add wine and boil until reduced almost to glaze, stirring up any browned bits, about 5 minutes.
Return brisket to pot.

Brisket with Dried Apricots, Prunes and Spices con't

Add stock and bring to simmer.
Spoon some of vegetable mixture over brisket.
Cover pot and place in oven.
Roast brisket 2½ hours, basting every 30 minutes with pan juices.

After 2½ hours, add prunes and remaining S cup apricots.
Cover; roast until brisket is tender, about 30 minutes longer.

Cool brisket uncovered 1 hour.
Chill uncovered until cold, then cover and keep chilled overnight.

Directions Day 2:
Spoon off any solid fat from top of gravy; discard fat.

Scrape gravy off brisket into pot.

Place brisket on work surface.

Slice brisket thinly across grain.

Bring gravy in pot to boil over medium-high heat.
Boil to thicken slightly, if desired.
Season gravy with salt and pepper.

Arrange sliced brisket in large ovenproof dish.
Spoon gravy over.
Cover with foil. (It can be put in the fridge at this point until you are ready to heat and serve)

Rewarm covered brisket in 350°F oven about 30 minutes (or 40 minutes if chilled).

Sprinkle with cilantro and serve.

Broccoli and Chicken Casserole

Contributed by: Ellen Desmarais
Source: Sandy West, 1965
Yield: Serves 8
Note: Use the quantity of broccoli that seems in proportion. I thaw frozen broccoli and cut the pieces into smaller sizes, or use fresh broccoli not cooked. Instead of the soup and mayonnaise, I make a light white sauce. I omit the cheese, the potato chips and the onion rings. Mix everything, including the noodles or pasta in the casserole! I look at it as a diabetic's version!

Ingredients
2 bags	frozen Broccoli (1 large bag, or use fresh broccoli lightly cooked)
2 cups	diced cooked Chicken (or turkey)
2 cans	Cream of Chicken soup
1 cup	real Mayonnaise
1 tablespoon	Lemon juice
1 can	dry Onion Rings (if available)
4 oz.	grated Sharp Cheese
½ cup	soft Bread Crumbs
1 cup	crushed Potato Chips (optional)
1 tablespoon	melted Butter

Directions
Arrange broccoli in a greased casserole or 9 X 13 inch pan.
Place chicken on broccoli.

Combine soup with mayonnaise, lemon juice and onion rings.
Sprinkle with cheese.

Mix bread crumbs with chips and butter, spread on casserole.

Bake uncovered at 350°F for about 25 to 30 minutes.

Serve with noodles or pasta or rice.

Charlotte's Chili

Contributed by: Valerie Healy
Source: Charlotte
Note: Whenever I'm having everyone in, but not sure of when, this is a favourite. So it doesn't matter when they arrive, it is ready in the slow cooker. Great after a day of sliding or skating.

Ingredients

1 pound	Hamburger
2 large	Onions
2 cans	Tomato Soup
1 can	Kidney Beans
1½ tablespoons	Vinegar
3 tablespoons	Sugar
2 cans	Mushrooms
3 teaspoons	Chili Powder
3 teaspoons	Garlic powder
1 tablespoon	Salt
Two 19 oz tins	Tomatoes
1S cups	Water
1 large	Green Pepper

Chicken Breast Diane

Contributed by: Ellen Desmarais
Source: Recipe cards distributed by Steinbergs in the '60s.
Yield: 4 servings
Note: This has been a favourite recipe for a long time, so I felt confident when I served it to Chef Serge Caffarel in France. And I was surprised when he told me it was a traditional French recipe and has the same name in French: Poulet à la Diane and that I had done it very well!

Ingredients

For 4 servings you will need:

4 large	boneless Chicken breast halves or 8 small
½ teaspoon	Salt
¼ to ½ teaspoon	Black Pepper
2 tablespoons	Olive or Salad oil (I prefer Peanut oil)
2 tablespoons	Butter or margarine
3 tablespoons	chopped fresh Chives or Scallions
	Juice of ½ lime or lemon
2 tablespoons	Brandy or Cognac (optional)
3 tablespoons	Dijon-style mustard
¼ cup	Chicken Broth

Directions:

Place chicken breast halves between sheets of waxed paper or plastic wrap.
Pound slightly with mallet to make them an even thickness.
Sprinkle with salt and black pepper.

Heat 1 tablespoon each of oil and butter (or margarine) in large skillet.
Cook chicken over high heat for 4 minutes on each side.
Do not cook longer or they will be overcooked and dry.
Transfer to warm serving platter.

Add chives or green onion, lime juice and brandy, parsley and mustard to pan.
Cook 15 seconds, whisking constantly.
Whisk in broth.
Stir until sauce is smooth.

Whisk in remaining butter and oil.
Pour sauce over chicken.

Serve immediately.
Good served with noodles with tomato sauce, steamed broccoli and a fresh salad.

Chicken with Cinnamon and Apples from Metz

Contributed by: Liane Desmarais-Cavangh
Source: *Quiches, Kugels and Couscous* by Joan Nathan.
Yield: 4 to 6 servings
Note: Never fails to taste great

Ingredients

One 3½ to-4-pound	Roasting Chicken
	Salt and freshly ground pepper to taste
1 teaspoon	ground Cinnamon
1	Onion, peeled and cut into chunks
1 cup	Chicken broth
1 1/3 cups	White Wine
3	Apples, cored and cut horizontally into 4 pieces (the French would use Reine-des-Reinettes apples or Pippins)
2 tablespoons	Sugar

Directions

Preheat the oven to 375°F.

Season the chicken with salt and freshly ground pepper to taste and ½ teaspoon of the cinnamon. Put in a roasting pan with the onion.
Pour the chicken broth and wine over the chicken, and roast in the oven for 45 minutes.

After the chicken has been cooking for 45 minutes, surround it with the apples sprinkled with the remaining cinnamon and the sugar.

Baste with the wine, and roast for about 45 more minutes, or until the apples are very soft and the chicken is cooked.

Chicken Christian Bérard

Contributed by:	Liane Desmarais-Cavanagh
Source:	Michèle Filippi, October 2002
Yield:	Serves: 4
Wine:	Paternel Blanc or Vouvray
Note:	Michèle, my God-Mother, was friends with Christian Bérard, a successful fashion and theatre designer in Paris in the 1940's. He invented this dish and taught her how to make it. All measurements are approximate as the original recipe had no quantities.
	PRO: Guaranteed to impress even the most difficult of guests!
	CON: Must be made at the last minute

Ingredients

4	Chicken Breasts, boneless and skinless
2 tablespoons	Butter
2 tablespoons	Oil
	Salt
	Pepper
4 tablespoons	Paprika
1 cup	White wine (or ½ cup Cognac)
2 – 3 tablespoons	Dijon Mustard
½ cup	35% Cream
½ to ¾ cup	Conté Cheese, grated (I have used Emmental when I couldn't get Conté)

Directions

In pie plate mix together Salt, Pepper and paprika.
Dredge chicken in Paprika mixture (coat well)

In a large skillet (over medium heat), heat oil and butter (until butter has melted).
Brown chicken (both sides) in skillet.
Add white wine, reduce temperature to Medium, and set the timer for 15 to 20 minutes (ish)

While the chicken is cooking, mix in a bowl: Cream, Mustard and _half_ the Conté cheese.

When the timer goes off remove the chicken from the skillet and place in an oven proof dish.

Add the Cream/Mustard/Cheese mixture to the skillet and reduce by half.
(The reduction may take several minutes so I usually tent the chicken with foil to keep it warm)
When sauce is reduced pour over the chicken.

Turn on broiler

Sprinkle remaining Conté over chicken and place under the broiler (not too close) until cheese is golden brown.

Serve on rice with side greens (asparagus is best)

Chicken Piccata

Contributed by: Liane Desmarais-Cavanagh
Source: Chef Pat – Valetta, Malta, 2011
Yield: 4 servings

Ingredients

2	Chicken breasts, skinless and boneless, butterflied and then cut in half
	Sea salt and freshly ground black pepper
	All-purpose flour, for dredging
6 tablespoons	unsalted Butter
5 tablespoons	extra-virgin Olive Oil
⅓ cup	fresh Lemon juice
½ cup	Chicken stock
¼ cup	brined Capers, rinsed
⅓ cup	fresh Parsley, chopped

Directions

Season chicken with salt and pepper.
Dredge chicken in flour and shake off excess.

In a large skillet over medium high heat, melt 2 tablespoons of butter with 3 tablespoons olive oil.
When butter and oil start to sizzle, add 2 pieces of chicken and cook for 3 minutes.

When chicken is browned, flip and cook other side for 3 minutes.
Remove and transfer to plate.

Melt 2 more tablespoons butter and add another 2 tablespoons olive oil.
When butter and oil start to sizzle, add the other 2 pieces of chicken and brown both sides in same manner.
Remove pan from heat and add chicken to the plate.

Into the pan add the lemon juice, stock and capers.
Return to stove and bring to boil, scraping up brown bits from the pan for extra flavour. Check for seasoning.

Return all the chicken to the pan and simmer for 5 minutes.
Remove chicken to platter.

Add remaining 2 tablespoons butter to sauce and whisk vigorously.
Pour sauce over chicken and garnish with parsley.

Chicken Sauté Provence Style

Contributed by: Liane Desmarais-Cavanagh
Source: Chef at a Roman Cooking Class I took at Pont du Gard
Yield: Serves 4-6
Note: In the Vaucluse area of Provence (where Ste Cécile les Vignes is located), tomatoes are nicknamed *pommes d'amour* – love apples – and this dish of pan-cooked chicken includes lots of them. It might once have been made outdoors, over a wood dire. If possible, try to use a youngish chicken, ideally one raised in the open, its diet enriched by corn, for the most characterful results.

Ingredients
3½ pounds	Frying chicken cut into 10 or 12 pieces
¼ cup	extra virgin Olive Oil
1	Onion, sliced
½ cup	medium-dry White or Rosé Wine
1 fresh	Bouquet Garni (oregano, marjoram, bay and basil)
12 oz	ripe, flavorful Tomatoes, peeled and chopped
2 tablespoons	Tomato paste
12 pitted	salt-cured Black olives, lightly crushed
4 cloves	Garlic, finely chopped
	a small handful of fresh parsley, finely chopped
	Salt and freshly ground black pepper

Directions
Pat dry the chicken pieces and rub all over with salt and pepper.
Heat the oil in a very large, heavy-based skillet or a flameproof casserole dish.
Fry half the chicken over high heat for 10 minutes, pressing the pieces down hard for maximum contact with the skillet, and turning them often until golden brown.
Transfer the chicken to a plate, and cook the second batch in the same way.
Set aside with the first lot.

Put the onion in the skillet and sauté for 1 minute, stirring.
Pour in the wine and add the bouquet garni, scrapping up the sediment as the wine reduces by half.
Add the tomatoes, tomato paste, and olives, and cook for 3-5 minutes over high heat while stirring.
Return the chicken to the skillet, cover with foil or a lid and cook for 8 – 10 minutes or until very tender.

Mix the garlic and parsley together, then scatter this topping over the chicken and serve hot.

Curried Lamb (Chicken or Turkey)

Contributed by:	Valerie, Judy and Ellen
Source:	Can't remember
Yield:	4 servings
Note:	Ellen can't remember where she found this recipe, but since everybody enjoys it so much, it is obviously a success.

This recipe if a favourite of Judy's, and she especially likes it for left-over barren land caribou roast!.

Valerie said: …when Mum, Judy and I went to Vancouver on the train one of the meals we were served was curried lamb. I loved it. How lucky for me that Ellen had the recipe. My family does not care for lamb – only me – so that is why I use chicken or turkey. This is one of Jeremy's favorites.

Ellen always uses it when there is left-over lamb. Ingredients are readily available both in Canada and in France.

Ingredients

3 cups	diced Lamb
3 tablespoons	cooking Oil
½ cup	chopped Onion
½ cup	chopped peeled Apple

Mix the following together:

2 tablespoons	Flour
1 tablespoon	Curry powder
1 teaspoon	Sugar
½ teaspoon	Salt
1/8 teaspoon	Pepper
2 cups	Chicken broth
1 tablespoon	Lemon juice
½ cup	Raisins

Directions

Heat oil; add onion and apple. Cook gently until onion is tender.
Blend in flour, curry powder, sugar, salt & pepper.
Stir in chicken broth and juice.
Add raisins and simmer, stirring constantly, until sauce is smooth and thickened.
Just before serving, add the meat and simmer gently until the flavour blends.
Serve with rice.

Drunken Chicken

Contributed by:	Liane Desmarais-Cavanagh
Source:	Anne Willan, April 2004
Yield:	4 servings
Note:	This is amazing. The chicken roasts in less than an hour, turning to an even, golden brown, my only caution is to avoid letting it colour too much. The chicken is best freshly roasted just before it is served. I don't rotate the bird while roasting! It's too hard to handle a hot slippery bird. Wine for the marinade; any dry white will do. Wine for the sauce; a luscious sweet white is needed and a Muscat from Northern Italy or Provence works nicely. Wine to drink; Sauvignon Blanc.

Ingredients

One 4- 5 pound	Roasting Chicken
	Salt and Pepper
4 tablespoons	Butter
1 cup	sweet White Wine
1 tablespoon	Flour
1 cup	Chicken Stock

For the marinade

2 cups	dry White Wine
¼ cup	Brandy
1	Carrot, grated
1	Onion, grated
2	Bay leaves
2 to 3	sprigs Thyme
2 to 3	sprigs Marjoram or Parsley

Directions

Wipe the chicken inside and out with paper towels.
Combine all the marinade ingredients in a large heavy-duty plastic bag set over a bowl.
Add the chicken and seal the bag with as little air as possible, leaving it in the bowl.
Marinate the chicken in the refrigerator for a day, turning it from time to time; the bag ensures that all of the chicken is kept moist with marinade.

To roast the chicken,
Heat the oven to 425°F
Take the chicken from the marinade, pat it dry with paper towels, and sprinkle it inside and out with salt and pepper.
Discard the marinade.
Truss the chicken, set it on its back in a roasting pan; cut the butter in slices and set them on the breast.
Roast the chicken, basting often, until it sizzles and starts to brown, about 15 minutes.
Turn the chicken onto one leg and continue roasting for another 15 minutes, basting often.
Turn the bird onto the other leg and roast for 15 more minutes.

And finally, turn it onto its back to finish cooking, allowing 50 minutes to 1 hour total cooking time. To test, lift the bird with a two-pronged fork and pour juice from the cavity; it should run clear, not pink.

When the chicken is done, transfer it to a platter and cover it with foil to keep warm.
Discard fat from the pan, leaving behind the cooking juices.
Stir in the flour and cook, stirring, for 1 minute.
Add the sweet white wine and simmer for 1 to 2 minutes, stirring to dissolve the juices.
Add the stock and simmer again until the gravy is slightly thickened and reduced by half.
Strain it into a saucepan, reheat it, taste, and adjust the seasoning.

Discard trussing strings from the chicken

Quick fix:
Cut the chicken into 6 to 8 pieces, or use ready-prepared breasts or thighs (my recommendation).
Marinate them for 1 to 2 hours.
Drain and pat the pieces dry on paper towels, then coat them in seasoned flour.
Melt the butter in a sauté pan or skillet and fry the chicken pieces until well browned on all sides.
Cover the pan and roast in a 350°F oven until the chicken pieces are very tender when pierced with a two-pronged fork, 20 to 30 minutes.
Transfer them to a platter and keep warm.
Discard excess fat from the pan and make the gravy as directed.

Endives and Ham

Contributed by:	Ellen Desmarais
Source:	Ann Lienardy, in Rome in 1987.
Yield:	According to the number of endives.
Note:	A lovely light meal, but rich. The recipe was given to me by my seatmate in Rome (who was from Belgium) in 1987. If the endives are large, cut them in half. Get ham slices from the butcher so they are cut from a large ham.

Ingredients

Endives –	2 per person for a meal; 1 per person if it is for the first course.
Ham slices:	one for each endive.
2 cups	Bechamel Sauce
½ cup	Emmenthal Cheese
	Garlic,
	Salt & Pepper,
	Nutmeg

Directions

Cook endives* in skillet, over medium heat, with butter, garlic, salt & pepper until tender.

Prepare béchamel sauce (butter, 3 tbsp. Flour, 2 c. milk) like "white sauce".

Wrap endives in a slice of ham and arrange in a baking dish.

Pour the béchamel sauce over, sprinkle with nutmeg and cover with the grated cheese.

Bake at 350°F for 20 minutes; then broil until the cheese browns a little.

*To prepare the endives – wash the endives and trim off the base a little, then cut the base into quarters. Squeeze out any excess water, then place in the skillet to cook. I cook them with a cover on the pan.

Fish Marseillaise

Contributed by: Ellen Desmarais
Source: I don't know where this recipe originated, it is dated 1972 in my cookbook and it is still a good recipe.

Ingredients
1 pkg	frozen Fish fillets
½ cup	Chicken broth
2 tablespoons	melted Butter
1 teaspoon	dry Mustard
½ teaspoon	Tarragon (or chopped fresh)
	Salt & pepper

Directions
Place fillets in a single layer on greased dish (or on parchment paper).
Mix other ingredients and pour over fish.
Bake 20 to 25 minutes at 350°F.

Ginger Flank Steak

Contributed by:	Liane Desmarais-Cavanagh
Source:	WH Smith Books cooking contest 1995
Yield:	Makes 6 servings
Note:	A soy-sake marinade is the base for a delicious reduction sauce. For convenience, begin this one day ahead and refrigerate the steak in its marinade overnight. Very good served fresh and hot off the grill...but even better the next day. Larry's favourite!
Wine:	A fruity Zinfandel.

Ingredients

½ cup	Soy Sauce
½ cup	Sake
¼ cup (packed)	dark Brown Sugar
3 tablespoons	fresh Ginger, peeled and minced
1 tablespoon	Balsamic Vinegar
4 cloves	Garlic, crushed
2 pound	Flank Steak

Directions

Combine first 6 ingredients in 13 x 9 x 2-inch glass baking dish.
Add meat.
Cover and refrigerate at least 2 hours and up to 1 day.
Let stand at room temperature 1 hour before continuing.

Remove steak from marinade; reserve marinade.
Add steak to skillet (I usually BBQ) and cook to desired doneness, about 4 minutes per side for medium-rare.
Transfer to cutting board.
Tent with foil and let stand 5 minutes.

Meanwhile, place reserved marinade in small saucepan.
Whisk in cornstarch.
Whisk over high heat until sauce thickens and boils, about 3 minutes.
Remove sauce from heat.
Season sauce to taste with salt and pepper.

Cut steak across grain on diagonal into ½-inch-thick slices.
Arrange steak slices (atop vegetables) on a platter.
Spoon some of sauce over meat and vegetables.

Serve, passing remaining sauce separately.

Hamburger, Corn & Cheese Casserole

Contributed by: Liane Desmarais-Cavanagh
Source: Connie Spicer
Yield: Serving: 8
Note: My mother-in-law shared this family favourite recipe with me. And I make it any chance I get! Tastes like childhood.

Time to Prepare: 30-40 minutes
Time to Cook: 45 minutes

Ingredients

2 pounds	Hamburger
2 cups	Noodles; cooked (elbow macaroni)
1	Onion, chopped and caramelized
2 cups	Cheddar cheese, grated
¼ cup	Oil; vegetable
1½ cups	Corn kernels
2 cups	Tomato soup
1 teaspoon	Salt
½ teaspoon	Pepper
1 tablespoon	Ketchup

Directions

Put beef, onion & oil in fry pan.
Stir to break up meat till it browns.
Drain off fat.
Put meat mixture in bowl.
Put corn, soup, salt and pepper, mustard, ketchup, and 1.5 cups cheese in bowl.
Stir and mix with meat.
Cook noodles, drain and combine with all ingredients.
Pour into greased casserole.
Sprinkle grated cheese on top.
Cover & bake at 350°F for 45 min.
Remove cover & bake till cheese is bubbly.

Hamburger Casserole (Grama H's)

Contributed by: Liane Desmarais-Cavanagh
Source: Christina Henderson via Ellen Desmarais
Yield :   8 people
Note :   Comfort food. Can be made ahead and re-warmed

Ingredients

2 pounds	Ground Beef (not lean)
2 cups	Macaroni (any kind)
1 cup	Onions, diced and browned
2	Zucchini, cut into chunks
1	Eggplant (narrow), cut into chunks (I added this)
1 jar	stewed tomatoes (bite size)
1 small can	pure Tomato paste (I use double intense Italian tomato paste in a tube)
1 cup	grated Cheese (I toss with panko crumbs to absorb excess casserole moisture)
	Salt and Pepper
	Herb de Provence (I added this)
	Sliced toasted Garlic (I added this)

Directions

Early in the day, slice, salt and let your eggplant drain of water
Blanch your onions (makes them easier to peel)
Grease your casserole

Boil water and cook pasta
Drain pasta and fold in the tomato paste (the heat and moisture of the pasta makes the tomato sauce spread more evenly)

Turn on your Oven to 350°F

Add 1 tablespoon of oil to a large skillet, heat oil
Add Hamburger to skillet, and stir to break up the meat as it browns
When browned remove meat from skillet and put in large bowl
Keep fat in skillet
Add onions to skillet and sauté - When golden remove and add to meat mixture
Add Zucchini and Eggplant to skillet
Sauté unit most of the juice has been mostly removed and they are nicely browned.
Remove and add to meat mixture
Brown slices of garlic in what is left of the fat - When golden add to meat mixture
Add jar of stewed tomatoes to meat mixture
Stir meat mixture so all ingredients are well combined
Gently fold in Noodles
Pour into greased casserole.
Sprinkle grated cheese on top.
Cover & bake at 350°F for 45 min. (or until cheese is bubbly).

Lasagna (Slow Cooker)

Contributed by: Liane Desmarais-Cavanagh
Source: allrecipes.com
Yield: Serves 10
Note: You start this recipe in the skillet and finish it in the slow cooker.

Ingredients

1 pound	lean Ground Beef
1	Onion, chopped
2 teaspoons	Garlic, minced
1 (29 oz) can	Tomato sauce
1 (6 oz) can	Tomato paste
1½ teaspoons	Salt
1 teaspoon	Oregano, dried
1 (12 oz) pkg	Lasagna noodles
12 oz	cottage cheese
16 oz	Mozzarella, shredded

Directions

In a large skillet over medium heat cook the ground beef, onion, and garlic until brown.
Add the tomato sauce, tomato paste, salt, and oregano and stir until well incorporated.
Cook until heated through.

In a large bowl mix together the cottage cheese, grated Parmesan cheese, and shredded mozzarella cheese.

Spoon a layer of the meat mixture onto the bottom of the slow cooker.
Add a double layer of the uncooked lasagna noodles.
Break to fit noodles into slow cooker.
Top noodles with a portion of the cheese mixture.
Repeat the layering of sauce, noodles, and cheese until all the ingredients are used.

Cover, and cook on LOW setting for 4 to 6 hours.

Lemon Chicken (Crock Pot)

Contributed by: Valerie Healy
Source: Judy Ross, from Marc Dougherty, 1986
Yield: Serves 4 to 6
Note: This came originally from Judy and I modified it to suit myself. It is one of my favourite meals. Original recipe had smaller quantities but this is a rough guide of what I usually use; brown sugar, ketchup and lemon juice could be increased another tablespoon each to supplement the sauce. Water and Cornstarch may also need to be increased for thickening.

Ingredients

Original quantities		Valerie's quantities
5-6	boneless, skinless chicken pieces	3-4 pounds
¼ cup	Flour	
	pinch of salt	
2 tablespoons	Cooking Oil	
1	frozen Lemonade	6 oz.
6 tablespoons	Ketchup	3 tablespoons
2 tablespoons	Lemon concentrate	1 tablespoons
6 tablespoons	Brown Sugar	3 tablesppons
4 tablespoons	cold Water	2 tablespoons
4 tablespoons	Cornstarch	2 tablespoons

Directions

Mix flour and a pinch of salt in a zip-lock bag.
Coat chicken and brown in oil.
Pat dry (to absorb the oil).
Put in slow cooker.

While the chicken is browning dissolve cornstarch in water and add remaining ingredients.
Thicken over medium to high heat, stir it or it will stick and/or burn.
Pour over chicken in crock pot.
Cook on high for 4 hours.
Check it once in a while.
You may want to turn down to low and turn the pieces.
Serve over rice.

Lime Broiled Chicken

Contributed by: Liane Desmarais-Cavanagh
Source: Connie (Cavanagh) Spicer, June 1, 1996
Yield: Makes enough to marinate 4 chicken breasts (can be doubled)
Note: This was my wedding day gift from my mother-in-law, one of the best gifts we received! Now this recipe is a family favourite! Serve with: Chardonnay

Ingredients
½ cup   Lime juice (preferably fresh)
¼ cup   Soya Sauce
1 tablespoon fresh* Ginger, grated (I have been known to add more!)
1 tablespoon fresh* Garlic, minced

*While we think the recipe is best with fresh spices, it's okay to use dried

Directions
Pour lime juice and soya sauce into a bowl
Add ginger and garlic
Stir to mix

Pour into large zip lock bag

Add skinless boneless chicken
Suck out the air and marinate in the fridge for at least 4 hours (I leave overnight)

When ready to cook,
Remove chicken from bag and broil/BBQ 5 min* each side
(Chicken cooks very fast because it has been "precooked" by the lime juice)

Note: this is also a wonderful marinade for Turkey breast and Pork tenderloin

Meatballs

Contributed by: Valerie Healy

Ingredients

3	beaten Eggs
¾ cup	Milk
3 cups	soft Bread Crumbs (about 4 ½ slices)
½ cup	finely chopped Onions
2 teaspoons	Salt
3 pounds	Ground Beef

Directions

In large bowl combine all ingredients and mix well. (I find my hand works best.)

Make 1 inch ball and bake at 350ºF. for 30 to 35 minutes.

I divide these in three lots and freeze them in Ziploc bags.

Variations:

Bar-B-Que Meatballs

Contributed by: Valerie Healy
Source: Laurel Gunter
Note: Can also be made in slow cooker for pot luck.

Ingredients

¾ cup	White Sugar,
2 tablespoons	Flour
¼ cup	White Vinegar
¾ cup	Ketchup
2 cups	hot Water

Directions

Mix the above together in double boiler.

Cook until thick.

Add meat balls (recipe above) and let them heat through.

Sweet and Sour Meatballs

Contributed by: Valerie Healy

Ingredients

One 13½ oz.	can Pineapple tidbits
½ cup	Brown Sugar
3 tablespoons	Cornstarch
1 cup	Water
1/3 cup	Vinegar
1 cube	Beef boullion
1 tablespoon	Soy sauce
1/3 recipe	Meatballs (see meatball recipe on previous page)
1	Green Pepper
One 5 oz. can	Water chestnuts (optional)

Directions

Drain pineapple, reserve syrup.

In double boiler mix brown sugar and corn starch.

Blend in reserved syrup, water, vinegar, boullion and soy sauce.
Cook until it is thick.

Stir in meatballs, pineapple & green pepper.

Simmer covered.

Serve over rice.

Meat Loaf

Contributed by: Valerie Healy
Yield: 1 large meatloaf
Note: I recommend using "Epicure" brand onion soup mix because it reduces the level of salt, and extra lean Hamburger (of course). Ellen uses "Knorr" brand.

Ingredients

1 pouch	Onion soup mix
1½ - 2 pounds	extra lean Hamburger
2	beaten Eggs
¼ cup	Ketchup
½ cup	fine Bread Crumbs
¾ cup	warm Water

Directions

Mix thoroughly and put in loaf pan.

Bake at 350°F. for 1½ to 2 hours.

Meat Pies (Ellen's)

Contributed by: Liane Desmarais-Cavanagh
Source: Ellen Desmarais
Yield: Make 5 pies

Ingredients

4 pounds	Pork, ground
2 pounds	Veal, ground
6 teaspoons	Salt
1½ cups	fine Bread Crumbs
1½ cups	Onion, chopped
4 teaspoons	Sage
4 teaspoons	Savory
	Salt & Pepper to taste.

Directions

Put meat in a large pot, and cover meat with water
Sprinkle in 6 teaspoons salt
Cover and cook 2 hours (skim of scum, if there is any, as cooking)
Remove from heat, and once cooled to room temperature place in fridge

Next day, remove fat from jelly.
Re-heat the mixture and drain off liquid
To the drained meat add: onions, spices and bread crumbs (add just enough bread crumbs to make it sticky)
Mixture should be moist not wet

Make pie crust,
Fill with meat mixture
Bake approx 1 hour at 375°F.

When cooked remove from oven and let rest 'till room temperature.

Wrap tightly and freeze.

Meat Pies (Liane's)

Contributed by: Liane Desmarais-Cavanagh
Source: Inspired by Ellen Desmarais
Yield: Make Six 9" pies

Ingredients

4 pounds	Pork, ground (1.8 kg)
3 pounds	Veal, ground (1.3 kg)
6 teaspoons	Sea Salt
1½ cups	fine Bread crumbs
2 cups	Onion, chopped & caramelized with Balsamic vinegar
4 teaspoons	Herb de Provence
3 teaspoons	Celery Seeds
½ cup	Leeks, chopped white part only
	Salt & Pepper to taste.

Directions

Mix meat together
Put raw meat in a large pot, and just cover meat with water
Sprinkle in 6 teaspoons sea salt
Cover and simmer 2 hours (skim of scum, if there is any, as cooking)
Remove from heat, cool to room temperature and then place in fridge (or in garage if cold enough)

Next day, remove fat from jelly.

Re-heat the mixture and drain off liquid (save liquid for stock)

Caramelize onions

To the drained meat add: onions, HdeP, celery seeds, leeks and bread crumbs (add just enough bread crumbs to make it sticky)

Make pie crust (*5 Roses* recipe currently the best)

Fill with meat mixture and put on top layer of pastry.

Cut slits into upper pastry to allow steam to escape

Bake approx 1 hour at 375°F.

When cooked remove from oven and let rest till room temperature.

Put in zip-lock bags and suck the air out
Freeze.

Re heat in 350°F oven for one hour

Moroccan Chicken Stew

Contributed by: Ellen Desmarais
Source: Taken from the International Olive Oil Council booklet. It looks complicated, but it is not, although it takes some attention the first time you make it.
Yield: Makes 6 to 8 servings.

Ingredients

1/3 cup	Olive Oil divided
1 tablespoon	Honey
3 pounds	Chicken thighs
	Salt & Pepper
1 cup	hot Chicken Broth
½ cup	Raisins
1 teaspoon	crushed Saffron threads (or turmeric)
2 cloves	Garlic, minced
2 tablespoons	minced fresh Ginger (or 2 teaspoons dried, ground)
2	Spanish Onions, coarsely chopped
1 teaspoon	Cumin
½ teaspoon	Cinnamon
½ teaspoon	Hot Pepper flakes
1 can	Chick Peas, drained
	Chopped fresh coriander or flat-leaf parsley

Directions

Preheat oven to 450°F.

Brush 13 X 9 inch baking pan with a little of the olive oil.

Spread honey under the skin of chicken thighs, dividing evenly.
Brush skin with a little of the remaining oil, and season lightly with salt and pepper.
Place chicken pieces skin-side up in prepared pan.
Bake in center of oven for 30 minutes.

Without moving oven rack, broil for a few minutes, repositioning the pan as needed to crisp and brown chicken skin evenly.

Lift chicken pieces out and set aside.

Drain accumulated juices from plan and discard.
Set pan aside.

Meanwhile, combine broth, raisins and saffron.
Set aside.

See next page…….

Moroccan Chicken Stew con't

In large skillet, heat remaining oil over medium heat.
Add onions and cook, stirring frequently, for 5 minutes.

Stir in garlic, ginger, cumin, cinnamon and hot pepper flakes.
Cook for 5 minutes, stirring occasionally.

Add broth mixture and cook uncovered over medium-low heat, stirring occasionally, for 20 minutes or until onions are soft and liquid has evaporated.
(Note: Cook only 10 or 15 minutes otherwise it is too dry). Remove from heat; season to taste with salt and pepper.

Stir chick peas into onion mixture; spread in baking pan.

Nestle chicken pieces into onion mixture, leaving some of skin exposed.

Bake at 375°F for 30 minutes or until chicken is fork-tender and top lightly crusted.

Garnish with chopped coriander or parsley.

Serve with green beans and couscous.

Prepare couscous during the last step.
Boil water or chicken broth and pour over couscous in a pot; let sit for 1 or 2 minutes, stirring with a fork to prevent lumps.
Add a lump of butter and cook over low heat 4 or 5 minutes.
Use slightly more liquid than dry couscous: 2 cups liquid to 1½ cup couscous for this recipe.

Moussaka

Contributed by:	Ellen Desmarais
Source:	A British newspaper
Yield:	Makes 6 servings.
Background:	We liked the Moussaka when we were in Greece but I didn't have a good recipe until last year when I found this one in "The Telegraph".

Ingredients

1 large or 2 small	Eggplants
1 pound	Ground Beef
1	Onion, chopped
1 clove	Garlic, minced
¼ teaspoon	Cinnamon
¼ teaspoon.	Nutmeg
½ teaspoon.	fines herbs
2 tablespoons	chopped Parsley
1 can	Tomato sauce
½ cup	Red Wine (optional)
	olive oil
	Butter or margarine (if needed for frying eggplant)
	salt & pepper
2 cups	Béchamel sauce (recipe below)
	grated cheese

Directions

Peel and cut the eggplant into ½ inch slices; sprinkle with salt, and set aside on paper towel to absorb the moisture. Leave an hour, or more, wipe the slices of eggplant; put oil in a frying pan and fry the eggplant over high heat.
When cooked, lay the eggplant on a paper towel to drain. (I use peanut or canola oil.)

Sauté the meat in margarine & oil with salt and pepper, onions and garlic, crumbling the meat with a fork.
When the meat is evenly browned, add the cinnamon, nutmeg, fines herbs, parsley and tomato sauce. Mix well, add wine, and simmer for 20 minutes.
In a greased 8 X 8 pan for the oven place a layer of eggplant, top with the meat mixture, sprinkle with grated cheese, cover with the remaining eggplant and meat until it is all used.
Top the moussaka with béchamel sauce. (You can add ¼ teaspoon nutmeg to the béchamel sauce and a good quantity of grated cheese.)
Bake in a 350ºF oven for 1 hour. Allow to cool before serving.

Béchamel sauce   - makes 2 cups
2 cups hot Milk   3 tablespoons Flour
¼ cup Butter   Salt and Pepper
¼ teaspoon Nutmeg
Melt the butter in a saucepan, add flour and stir until smooth.
Lower heat, and gradually add the hot milk, stirring constantly until it thickens.
Season with salt & pepper & nutmeg.

No Peek Casserole (Crock Pot)

Contributed by: Valerie Healy
Source: Christina Henderson
Note: Valerie recommends using "Epicure" brand onion soup mix because it contains less salt than other brands.

Ingredients

2 pounds.	Stew cubes
1 envelope	Onion soup
One 10 ½ oz.	can of Mushroom Soup
One 4 oz.	can of Mushrooms

Directions

Combine all ingredients in crock pot.
Cover and cook on low for 8 hours.
Serve over noodles or rice.

Sherried Beef (oven version of above recipe)

Contributed by: Judy Ross
Source: Joan Gibbs, 1984
Yield: 8 servings

Ingredients

3 pounds	cubed Beef Chunks
2 cans	Golden Mushroom Soup
¾ cup	cooking Sherry
1 can	Mushrooms
1 envelope	Onion Soup mix

Directions

Place beef in casserole. Mix other ingredients and pour over meat.
Cover and bake for 3 hours at 325°F.

Orange and Soy-glazed Duck

Contributed by: Liane Desmarais-Cavanagh
Yield: Serves 4
Note: This is a great dish when you are short of time – it is quick to cook and tastes delicious. Serve the duck breasts with your choice of vegetables such as steamed broccoli or bok choy, or sautéed spinach.

Ingredients

4	Duck breast fillets, about 8 ounces each
	freshly squeezed juice of 1 orange
3 tablespoons	Soy sauce
2 tablespoons	Maple syrup (Eastern Townships is best!)
½ teaspoon	Chinese five-spice powder
2	Garlic cloves, crushed
	freshly ground Szechuan Peppercorns or black pepper
	steamed broccoli or bok choy, or spinach, to serve.
1	Orange, cut into wedges, to serve

Directions

Using a sharp knife, score the fat on each duck breast crosswise several times.
Put the breasts into a shallow dish.

Put the orange juice, soy sauce, maple syrup,
Chinese give-spice powder, garlic and pepper into a small pitcher or bowl, mix well, then pour the mixture over the fillets.
Cover with plastic wrap and marinate in the refrigerator for as long as possible.
You can leave them overnight, but return them to room temperature for 1 hour before cooking.

Preheat the oven to 400°F.

Heat a ridged stovetop grill pan until hot, add the duck breasts, skin side down, and sear for 1-2 minutes. Transfer to a roasting pan, adding the marinade juices.
Cook the duck in the preheated oven for about 10 minutes or until medium rare.
Remove the duck from the oven, wrap it in foil and keep it warm for 5 minutes.

Pour the juices from the roasting pan into a small saucepan, and, using a large spoon, very carefully skim the fat off the surface.
Transfer the pan to the top of the stove and bring the juices to a boil for 2 minutes, until thickened slightly.

Serve the duck breasts sprinkled with the juices and accompanied by vegetables and wedges of orange.

Osso Bucco

Contributed by: Liane Desmarais-Cavanagh
Source: Ellen Desmarais, October 2002 (in France)
Yield: Serves 6

Ingredients

4 pounds	shanks of Veal, cut in 2" pieces
½ cup	Flour
1 tablespoon	Salt
3 tablespoons	Olive Oil
2 tablespoons	Butter
1 cup	Water
½ cup	White Wine
1 or 2 cloves	Garlic, crushed
½ teaspoon	Basil, crushed
Pinch	Thyme
1 tablespoon	minced Parsley
2 tablespoons	Tomato paste
2	Onions, chopped
1 teaspoon	Lemon zest
4	Carrots, scraped and diced
1 stalk	Celery, chopped
1 tablespoon	minced Celery leaves

Directions

Dust the veal shanks with the flour blended with the salt.
Brown over high heat in the oil and butter.
Lower heat, add the water and wine slowly, stirring to blend and let simmer gently.

Crush the garlic and mash to a paste with the herbs.
Blend in the tomato paste and add this mixture to the broth with the chopped onions and the lemon zest (only the yellow part of the rind, none of the white).

Cook covered at least 2 hours, until meat is nearly falling from bones.

During last half hour, add carrots and celery stalk and leaves.
Cook until carrots are tender.

Transfer meat to a platter.
Strain the sauce and thicken if desired with 2 tablespoons butter worked into a ball with 2 tablespoons flour and an additional teaspoon minced parsley.

Add to sauce, simmer until smooth.

Serve with noodles.

Pappardelle with Boar Ragu

Contributed by: Liane Desmarais-Cavanagh
Source: Renato Janelle's grandmother's cook book
Yield: makes 4 Servings

Ingredients

1 pound	fresh Boar, Pork or Venison sausage, cut into chunks
1 medium	Spanish onion, cut into ¼ inch dice
1 medium	Carrot, peeled and finely chopped
2 cloves	Garlic, thinly sliced
1 stalk	Celery, cut into ¼ inch dice
4	whole fresh sage leaves
2 cups	Dry White Wine
One 16-oz. can	peeled whole Plum Tomatoes, crushed by hand with juices
1 cup	brown Chicken Stock

Directions

In a heavy-bottomed casserole or Dutch oven, heat the olive oil over medium high heat until almost smoking.
Cook the sausage in the olive oil until it is browed, 10 -12 minutes.

Remove the meat to a plate and add the onions, carrot, garlic celery and sage to the casserole.
Cook over low heat until softened 7 – 9 minutes.

Add the wine, crushed tomatoes and their juices and chicken stock and bring to a boil.

Return the meat to the pan, then lower the heat, partially cover and simmer for 1 hour.

Keep warm.

Pork Tenderloin (Gloria Marshall's)

Contributed by: Ellen Desmarais
Source: Gloria Marshall, former neighbour on Belvedere Crescent
Yield: Serves 4 (or more, depending on size of tenderloin)
Background: Gloria served this and I thought I had never eaten anything so good!

Ingredients:
2	Pork Tenderloins, medium size
½ cup	Soy sauce
½ cup	Rye Whiskey (or chicken broth)
4 tablespoons	Brown Sugar
1 pkg	Club House 4 Peppercorn sauce
½ cup	whole Cranberry Sauce (not the jelly)

Directions
Marinate tenderloins in soy sauce, whiskey and sugar for 2 to 3 hours.

Drain and reserve marinade.

Place in a greased baking dish (lined with aluminum foil to save cleaning up)
Bake at 375°F for 25 to 30 minutes or until tender (this will depend on the size) basting with reserved marinade a few times.

To serve, slice on the diagonal and serve with Peppercorn-Cranberry Sauce (below):

To make the sauce:
1 pkg of Club House 4 Peppercorn Sauce.

Use recipe on package and when it is finished cooking,
Add ½ cup of whole cranberry sauce.
You may use more cranberry sauce if you wish.
Be sure it is the whole cranberry, not the jelly.

Rabbit in Mustard Sauce

Contributed by: Liane Desmarais-Cavanagh
Source: Michèle Filippi
Yield: 4 servings
Note: A French classic that makes your mouth sing. Serve with crusty bread and a white Bordeaux, or a white Cotes du Rhone blend.

Ingredients

1	Rabbit, cut into serving sized pieces
	Salt
4 tablespoons	Butter
2 large	Shallots, chopped
½ cup	White Wine
½ cup	Water
½ cup	Mustard (preferably grainy country Dijon – not the bright yellow mustard)
1 teaspoon	Thyme, leaves only
½ cup	heavy Cream (35%) (I like using Crème Fraiche)
4 tablespoons	Parsley, finely chopped

Directions

Salt your rabbit pieces and set aside at room temperature for 30 to 60 minutes

Heat the butter in large sauce pan on medium heat
Pat the rabbit pieces dry and brown them in the butter (remember to leave space between the pieces and cook them slowly so they don't scorch)
As the rabbit pieces are browned, remove them to a bowl
Add the shallot to the pan and brown them as well, this will take 3-4 minutes.

Deglaze the pan with the white wine (you may have to raise the heat)
Loosen any browned bits on the bottom of the pan with a wooden spoon.
Add the mustard, thyme and water and bring to a rolling boil.
Taste the sauce for salt and add some if needed.

Add the rabbit pieces, coating them with the sauce, then turn the heat down to low.
Cover and simmer gently for 45 minutes. (You want the meat to be nearly falling off the bone. It might need more time, but should not need more than an hour total.)

When the meat is ready, gently remove it to a platter.
Turn up the heat and reduce the sauce by half.

Add the cream and parsley.
Stir to combine and return the rabbit to the pan.
Coat with the sauce and serve at once.

Three-Ingredient Prime Rib Roast

Contributed by: Liane Desmarais-Cavanagh
Source: Internet
Note: Coffee and prime rib seem like unlikely partners, but this recipe reveals they both have an earthy quality that makes them a natural match. Just be sure to scrape off any excess coffee rub from the meat before serving. Roasting: 15 min/per pound

Ingredients
S cup	finely ground coffee
2 tablespoons	kosher salt
1 tablespoon	freshly ground black pepper
¼	vanilla bean, split and seeds scraped
One 12-pound	bone-in prime rib roast (5 bones)

Directions
In a bowl, thoroughly blend the coffee with the salt, pepper and vanilla bean seeds.
Set the rib roast in a roasting pan and rub it all over with the coffee mixture, concentrating most of the rub on the fatty part of the meat.
Turn the roast bone side down and let stand at room temperature for 30 minutes.

Preheat the oven to 450°. F
Roast the meat for 15 minutes.

Reduce the oven temperature to 325° and roast meat for 15/min/per pound (rare) or until an instant-read thermometer inserted in the thickest part of the meat registers 125° for medium-rare.

Transfer the roast to a carving board and let rest for 20 minutes.
Scrape off any excess coffee rub.
Carve the meat in ½"-thick slices and serve.

Make Ahead
The coffee-rubbed roast can be refrigerated overnight.
Bring to room temperature before roasting.

Tipsy Chicken

Contributed by: Liane Desmarais-Cavanagh
Source: Ellen Desmarais, October 2002
Yield: Makes 4 servings.

Ingredients

4	Chicken breasts, skinless & boneless,
4	Shallots, thinly sliced
½ cup	dry White Wine
½ cup	Cream
2 tablespoons	Dijon Mustard
1 teaspoon	Butter
1 teaspoon	Oil

Directions

Melt butter and oil in a large skillet over med/high heat
Brown Chicken breasts on all sides.
Add shallots and brown
Add white wine
Cook for 20 minutes
Remove chicken from skillet and place in warm oven

While chicken is cooking mix Cream, Mustard and chopped parsley in a bowl
Stir cream mixture into wine in skillet

Bring to a simmer and cook till slightly thickened (about 2 minutes)
Add the chicken back into the skillet and cook for a further 10 minutes

Should be served soon after cooking, it does not sit well.

Serve with rice

Savoury Sirloin Steak

Contributed by: Judy Ross and Valerie Healy
Source: Joyce MacKenzie, Shigawake, Sept. 1977
Note: Also submitted by Valerie Healy under the heading "Savory Sirloin Steak".
from Valerie: I only made this recipe once. Here's why: when Allan and I were married I could make Kraft Dinner and pour corn flakes, maybe a little more but you get the idea – not much experience in cooking. Once I got going, Mum was a great help but to start I was on my own. Anyway, I thought this recipe sounded like a good Sunday dinner. I followed the recipe to a Tee. The only thing was I thought 1 clove of garlic was a bulb. Well – stink. We lived in a one bedroom apartment; we opened the patio door and the window to try to air it out – in January! In Quebec! It was so strong we went to Mum's for the afternoon. When we were walking home we could smell dinner about a block away. I'm sure over the years I have had other cooking disasters but non more memorable than that one!

Ingredients

1½ pounds.	Steak (cut in 1 inch cubes)
2 tablespoons	Shortening
1 pkg. (9 oz.)	frozen Green Beans
1 can	Cream of Mushroom Soup
¾ cup	Water
2 tablespoons	Sherry
1 clove	Garlic
1 medium	Bay leaf
	Salt & pepper

Directions

Brown meat.

Add beans.

Mix other ingredients together and pour over meat.

Bake in a slow oven until tender. (The longer this is baked the better it is.)

Scallops Au Gratin

Contributed by: Ellen Desmarais
Source: Jacqueline Buchanan, 1964
Yield: serves 4
Note: This is the best ever recipe to cook scallops. The note in my original copy is "Serves 2, or 2 + Liane".

Ingredients
1 pound	Scallops (of a good size, not the minis)
¼ cup	Butter melted
½ cup	Bread cubes (fresh)
¾ cup	Swiss cheese grated
2 tablespoons	chopped Onion
½ teaspoon	Salt
	Pepper & paprika

Directions
Thaw the scallops in the fridge.
Put in shallow pan; brush with about 1 Tbsp.
Melted butter.
Bake 20 minutes at 350ºF. Mix rest of butter and other ingredients.
Spread this over fish and bake until cheese is melted.
Serve immediately.
Serves 2 generously.

Can be served with rice and a vegetable or salad.

Serve with a dry white wine.

Spare Ribs

Contributed by: Ellen Desmarais
Source: Doris Desmarais ("Mrs. D")
Yield: serves 4 to 6
Note: This is the recipe Mrs. Desmarais gave me in the '60s and it is still a family favorite. The sugar content is quite high. Mrs. Desmarais served this with fried rice, but we usually serve it with plain rice and a vegetable or salad.

Ingredients

3 pounds	Pork Spareribs (broken through the center)
2 cloves	Garlic
2 teaspoons	Cinnamon
3 tablespoons	Molasses
¼ cup	Vinegar
¾ cup	Brown Sugar (can be reduced)
1 cup	Pineapple juice (or water, to reduce sugar)
4 or 5	Pineapple slices
1 teaspoon	Salt

Directions

Boil the ribs to remove the fat, then drain. (about ½ hour in bubbling water).

Make sauce of above ingredients, except the pineapple slices.

Place slices of spare rib in roast pan lined with aluminum foil.
Brush each piece with sauce and place pineapple rings on top.

Bake 1 hour at 350°F (turning the ribs once) with cover

Then remove cover and finish baking about ½ more.

Sunday Dinner Chicken

Contributed by: Ellen Desmarais
Source: Minute Rice package, 1963
Yield: Serves 4
Note: This recipe dates from about 1963 when we lived at 4542 Beaconsfield Avenue. A family favorite ever since, it's easy, forgiving and very good.

Ingredients
1	Chicken (fryer), cut up
4 tablespoons	Butter
2 cups	Water or chicken broth
1 large	Onion, chopped
1½ teaspoons	Salt
	Dash pepper
1 can	Carrot slices, drained (or fresh cooked)
1 can	whole Green Beans, drained (or prepared fresh, or frozen peas)
1 1/3 cups	Minute Rice (1 cup for 2 persons)
1 tablespoon	Flour
½ cup	Heavy Cream (35%)
1	Egg yolk, slightly beaten

Directions
To cook chicken:
Brown in 3 tablespoons butter in deep skillet.
Add water (or chicken broth), onion, salt & pepper. Cover and simmer 30-40 minutes or until chicken is tender. Remove chicken & keep warm.
Measure broth & add water to make 2 1/3 cup. (2 cups per person).

To fix rice:
Combine 1 1/3 cup broth, the vegetables and rice in the saucepan.
Bring to a boil. Cover, remove from heat. Let stand 5 minutes.

To make sauce:
Melt remaining tablespoon of butter in skillet.
Blend in flour.
Gradually add remaining cup of broth and the heavy cream, stirring until thickened.
Blend a little hot sauce into egg yolk.
Gradually stir into sauce in skillet.
Cook until bubbly.
Arrange rice around chicken.
Top with sauce.

ALTERNATE (serves 4):
Brown chicken and onions, add 2 cups of hot chicken broth and 1 cup of regular long-grain rice and simmer for 20 minutes, or until rice is cooked.
Add the cooked vegetables, a little broth if it seems very sticky and then the cream.
Cook until it bubbles and remove from heat.

Trout In Paper

Contributed by: Ellen Desmarais
Source: Toni Forsythe, 2013
Yield: As many as you wish.
Background: Toni served this delicious recipe the first time we had eaten parchment wrapped fish. Now I have my own cookbook for wrapped cooking!

Ingredients per person:

1 piece	Trout
	chopped green Onion or Shallots
	very thin slice of Lemon
	small piece of Broccoli or other vegetable
1 teaspoon	browned Butter

Directions

Cut pieces of parchment paper large enough to wrap around a piece of fish and twist the ends to close.

Arrange the ingredients on the piece of paper, pour the browned butter over.
Fold paper in a drugstore fold and twist ends.

Cook in a medium oven 375° to 400° for 10 minutes.
Remove, leave in paper and let sit for 5 minutes.

Might try adding 1 teaspoon white wine or lemon juice.

Tuna Burgers

Contributed by: Valerie Healy
Source: Peggy Healy

Ingredients

1 can	Tuna
2 tablespoons	Mayonnaise
1 tablespoon	Mustard
1 tablespoon	Relish
1 tablespoon	finely chopped Onion
	Cheese slices
	Hamburger buns

Directions

Mix ingredients

Place cheese slices on bottom of buns,
Add tuna and top of bun.

Wrap in foil and bake a little while so cheese melts and burgers heat through.

V-8 Stew

Contributed by: Valerie Healy
Note: I received this recipe from a bank customer when I worked at Scotiabank. This is a very flexible recipe. Make it as large or small as you want. I also add turnip. I use a bottle of V-8 juice too. So it can make a big stew for a gang. Cook it on low all day in the slow cooker. Smells great to come home to.

Ingredients
1 pound	Stew Beef
1 cup	Carrots
1 cup	Potatoes
1 cup	Celery
1 cup	chopped Onions
1 tablespoon	Minute Tapioca
1 teaspoon	Salt
1 teaspoon	Vinegar
1 cup	V-8 juice

Wine Braised Short Ribs

Contributed by: Liane Desmarais-Cavanagh
Yield: 6 servings
Note: To test if ribs are done pull on a bone, it should come out of the meat clean. Serve with: Merlot

Ingredients

5 pound	bone-in Beef Short Ribs, cut crosswise into 2" pieces
	Kosher Salt and freshly ground Pepper
3 tablespoons	Vegetable Oil
3 medium	Onions, chopped
3 medium	Carrots, peeled, chopped
2 stalks	Celery, chopped
3 tablespoons	all-purpose Flour
1 tablespoon	Tomato paste
1 750-ml bottle	dry Red Wine
10 sprigs	flat-leaf Parsley
8 sprigs	Thyme
4 sprigs	Oregano
2 sprigs	Rosemary
2 fresh or dried	Bay leaves
1 head	Garlic, halved crosswise
4 cups	low-salt Beef Stock

Directions

Preheat oven to 350°F.
Season short ribs with salt and pepper.
Heat oil in a large Dutch oven over medium-high heat.
Working in 2 batches, brown short ribs on all sides, about 8 minutes per batch.
Transfer short ribs to a plate.
Pour off all but 3 tablespoons drippings from pot.
Add onions, carrots, and celery to pot and cook over medium-high heat, stirring often, until onions are browned, about 5 minutes.
Add flour and tomato paste; cook, stirring constantly, until well combined and deep red, 2-3 min.
Stir in wine, then add short ribs with any accumulated juices.
Bring to a boil; lower heat to medium and simmer until wine is reduced by half, about 25 minutes.
Add all herbs to pot along with garlic.
Stir in stock.
Bring to a boil, cover, and transfer to oven.
Cook until short ribs are tender, 2-2½ hours.
Transfer short ribs to a platter.
Strain sauce from pot into a measuring cup.
Spoon fat from surface of sauce and discard; season sauce to taste with salt and pepper.

Serve in shallow bowls over mashed potatoes with sauce spooned over.

~ Desserts & Sweets ~

Apple and Pear Crumble with Crème Anglaise

Contributed by:	Liane Desmarais-Cavanagh
Source:	Doris Desmarais (Granma D)
Yield:	Makes 10 to 12 servings.
Note:	While this is a tasty recipe the topping does not always come out crunchy (depends on the juiciness of your fruit).

Ingredients

2½ cups	Rolled Oats
1½ cups	Golden brown sugar, packed
1 cup	All-purpose flour
1 cup	Unsalted butter, chilled, cut into ½-inch cubes (+ Butter for greasing dish)
3 pounds	Granny Smith apples, peeled, halved, cored, each half cut into 6 slices
1 pound	Bartlett Pears, should be firm, cored and sliced
½ cup	Pecans (I also like to use pine nuts)
3 tablespoons	Lemon juice, fresh
½ tablespoon	Cinnamon, ground
½ tablespoon	Nutmeg, ground
½ tablespoon	Ginger, ground

Serve with: Vanilla ice cream or Crème Anglaise (see recipe)

Directions

Mix oats, 1 cup sugar, and flour in bowl.
Add butter; rub in with fingertips until topping comes together in moist clumps.
(Can be made 1 day ahead. Cover; chill.)

Preheat oven to 37 °F.
Rub 13 x 9 x 2-inch glass baking dish with butter to coat bottom and sides (or use non-stick spray)
Mix apples, pears, lemon juice, cinnamon, nutmeg, ginger, and ½ cup brown sugar in bowl.
Transfer to baking dish.
Sprinkle with Pecans (or pine nuts).
Sprinkle topping over and press lightly into the apples.
Bake crumble until apples are tender and topping is brown and crisp, about 55 minutes.
Cool slightly.
Spoon warm crumble into bowls and serve with ice cream or Crème Anglaise.

Apple Crisp

Contributed by: Ellen Desmarais
Source: Thelma Bolter-Swinford
Yield: 6 servings
Note: This favourite dessert has many versions, but this remains our classic favorite.

Ingredients

6 medium	Apples
¼ cup	Sugar, granulated
½ teaspoon	Cinnamon
¼ cup	Butter
½ cup	Flour
¾ cup	Brown sugar
½ teaspoon	Nutmeg
1 or 2 tablespoons	Sherry or fruit juice

Directions

Peel apples and slice into a buttered baking dish.

Sprinkle the apples with the granulated sugar and cinnamon.

Combine butter, flour and brown sugar and nutmeg, and spread on top of the apples.

Bake about 30 minutes in a moderate oven – 350° F- until apples are soft and top is a golden brown. Serve with cream, ice cream or crème Anglaise (see recipe).

Note: Raisins or cranberries can be added to the apples.

Baked Pears with Honey and Ginger

Contributed by: Liane Desmarais-Cavanagh
Source: Ellen Desmarais, Fall 1995
Yield: 8 Servings
Note: An easy make-ahead dessert that can look and taste very sophisticated

Ingredients

	Non-stick vegetable oil spray
8 firm but ripe	Bartlett pears, peeled, halved, cored
1 cup packed	Golden brown sugar
3 teaspoons	Ginger, ground
6 tablespoons	Honey
3 tablespoons	Lemon juice, fresh is best
2 teaspoons	Lemon zest
10 tablespoons	Unsalted Butter
1 quart	Vanilla frozen yogurt (I like ice cream)

Fresh mint sprigs (optional)
Lemon peel strips (optional)

Directions

Preheat oven to 375°F
Spray 2 large ovenproof skillets with oil spray.
Arrange half of pears cut side down in each skillet.
Sprinkle ½ cup sugar and 1½ teaspoons ginger over pears in each skillet.
Mix honey, lemon juice and peel in small bowl.
Drizzle over pears.
Dot pears in each skillet with 3 tablespoons butter.

Place skillets with pears in oven.
Bake until juices bubble thickly and pears are tender when pierced with small sharp knife, basting occasionally, about 15 minutes.
Turn pears over.
Bake 5 minutes longer.
Remove pears from oven.
(Can be made 1 day ahead. Cool. Transfer pears and cooking syrup to large glass baking dish; cover and chill. Rewarm uncovered in 375°F. oven 15 minutes before continuing.)

Arrange 2 pear halves on each of 8 plates.
Transfer cooking syrup to 1 large skillet.
Bring syrup to simmer, whisk in 4 tablespoons butter.
Spoon over pears.
Place 1 scoop yogurt alongside.
Garnish with mint and lemon peel, if desired.

Beer Cake

Contributed by: Liane Desmarais-Cavanagh
Source: Mrs. Primeau (Iroquois Falls, Ont)
Yield: 12 Servings
Note: Marc's mother used to make this cake for him for his Birthday every year and ship it down to Ottawa on the bus! One year she couldn't do it and asked me to make it for him, and that's how I got the recipe. Trust me, you don't taste the beer.

Ingredients

1 cup	Butter (shortening)
2 cups	Brown Sugar
2	Eggs
3 cups	Flour
1 teaspoon	Cinnamon, ground (I prefer Nutmeg)
½ teaspoon	Allspice, ground
½ teaspoon	Cloves, ground
2 teaspoons	Baking Powder
½ teaspoon	Salt
½ teaspoon	Baking Soda
1 cup	Nuts, chopped
1 cup	Raisins (or currents)
1 bottle	Beer (dark is best)
½ cup	Water

Directions

Preheat oven to 350°F

Mix together first three ingredients in large bowl.

Mix together dry ingredients together in Med Bowl

Add dry ingredients to wet slowly

Add chopped nuts, raisins, beer and water

Mix well

Bake;
- in a Springform pan, at 350° for 1 hour + 15 minutes (or until toothpick comes out clean).
Or
- in two 8" cake pans for 45 minutes

Dust with icing sugar.

Bird's Nest Cookies

Contributed by: Liane Desmarais-Cavanagh
Source: Christina Henderson, Fall 1976 (?)
Yield: 16 cookies
Note: One autumn (in the late '70s) Grama H came to stay with my while my parents went to France. One Saturday afternoon she taught me how to make cookies. This was one of the recipes.

Ingredients

¼ cup	White Sugar
1	Egg yolk
1 cup	Flour
Pinch	Salt
½ cup	Butter (or Shortening)
1	Egg white, lightly beaten (for dipping cookies)
1 cup	Nuts, chopped fine

Directions

Mix first 5 ingredients as for Shortbread

Roll into small balls

Then dip each small ball into white of egg and roll into chopped nuts

Place on a greased cookie sheet and make a hole in the centre with a thimble.

Bake about 10 minutes in a 325°F oven

You will find that in most cases the hole will be filled up so just press the thimble into the hole again, and bake until golden brown (about 5 more minutes).

When cool fill with apple jelly.

Brandied Peaches or Pears

Contributed by: Judy Ross
Source: Manon Reford – 1984
Note: This recipe can also be used with Pears: peel pears but leave stems on. Be careful as they discolour quickly.

Ingredients

	Fresh peaches
	Lemon Juice
2 cups	Water
1 cup	Sugar
4 oz	Brandy

Directions

Peel peaches and leave whole (i.e. leave stone inside).

Add lemon juice to cold water (to maintain colour during preparation)

Prepare medium syrup: Bring to a boil 2 cups water & 1 cup sugar

Place peaches in sterilized jars.

Pour 4 oz brandy over fruit (cheap brandy works just fine) then fill jar with hot syrup.

Boil for 20 minutes in a water bath.
Remove from water; firm lids and let cool.

Store in a cool dark place.
Keep until Christmas.

Brownies (Sandy West's)

Contributed by:	Ellen Desmarais
Source:	Sandy West, also in Mabel Holmes handwritten cook book
Note:	These are chewy brownies, as opposed to cake-like in Mum's famous recipe.

Ingredients

½ cup	Butter or margarine
2 squares	Chocolate (or 6 tablespoons cocoa & 2 tablespoons butter)
1 cup	Sugar
2	Eggs
½ cup	Flour
½ cup	Walnuts, chopped
1 teaspoon	Vanilla

Directions

Melt butter and chocolate in top of double boiler (or in the Microwave).

Remove from heat, stir in sugar and eggs (mix well), flour and chopped nuts.

Bake in 8 x 8 inch pan at 325°F for ½ hour.

(if you double the recipe use a 9 x 13 inch pan)

Brownies with Marshmallows & Icing

Contributed by: Ellen Desmarais
Source: Christina Henderson
Yield: 9 x 13 pen
Note: This is Mum's famous brownie recipe. Nobody ever made better.

Ingredients (for Brownies)
½ cup	Butter
2	Eggs
½ teaspoon	Vanilla
½ teaspoon	Baking Soda
½ cup	Nuts
1 cup	White Sugar
¼ cup	Milk
pinch	Salt
¾ cup	Flour
2 squares	Chocolate
some	Marshmallows, cut up* (enough to cover the top of cooked brownies)

(for Icing)
1½ squares	Chocolate
1 tablespoon	Butter.
¼ cup	Milk
Pinch	Salt.
Some	Icing sugar so it will run out of bowl.
	Vanilla (to taste)

Directions
Preheat oven to 350°F
Melt butter and chocolate together.
Beat eggs, sugar, salt, milk, flour and soda.
Add melted chocolate.
Add nuts.
Spread on shallow pan 9 x 13 inch (greased).
Bake 15 or 20 minutes at 350°F.
(while brownies are cooking make icing:
    Melt 1½ squares chocolate & 1 tablespoon butter.
    Add ¼ cup milk, and salt.
    Add enough icing sugar so it will run out of bowl.
    Vanilla to taste.

Remove brownies from oven.
Let cool 5 minutes.
Spread cut marshmallows on top, then pour the melted chocolate over them.
* To cut marshmallows: dip scissors in water periodically.

Butterscotch Ice Box Cookies

Contributed by: Ellen Desmarais
Source: Doris Desmarais
Yield: 4 doz or more
Note: This is the cookie the Mrs. Desmarais made for Christmas. They are quite plain but very good. It is convenient to be able to store rolls or the cookies in the freezer until you want to cook them. Do <u>not</u> double the batch.

Ingredients

1 cup	Butter
2 cups	Light Brown Sugar
2	Eggs, unbeaten
3½ cups	Flour
½ teaspoon	Salt
1 teaspoon	Baking Soda
½ teaspoon	Baking Powder
1 teaspoon	Vanilla
½ cup	glazed Cherries, chopped
½ cup	Walnuts, chopped
½ cup	candied Ginger, chopped

Directions

Sift together flour, baking powder, baking soda, and salt.

Cream butter and sugar gradually, beating between additions
Add eggs and mix well

Add dry ingredients and mix well

Fold in nuts and fruits
(The dough may be divided so that you can add chopped nuts or cherries or candied ginger to each section as desired.)

Form dough into logs (about the diameter of the finished cookie), then wrap dough in cling-wrap.

Chill for several hours (overnight if possible)

Cut into 1/8 inch slices (or as thin as possible)
Arrange on <u>greased</u> cookie sheet

Bake at 375°F to 400°F for 6 to 8 minutes

Cool on cookie rack and store in an airtight container.

Butterscotch Sauce for Plum Pudding

Contributed by: Ellen Desmarais
Source: Thelma Bolter-Swinford
Yield: ¾ cup
Note: Thelma's recipe for plum pudding sauce, adapted for the microwave. It is delicious on Judy's plum pudding

Ingredients
2 tablespoons	Margarine
4 tablespoons	Brown sugar
2 teaspoons	Rum flavouring
1 tablespoon	Water

Directions
Mix all ingredients in a (microwave safe) 1 cup Mason jar (or 2 cup measuring cup),
Microwave on High for 1 minute.
Let it cool,
Serve on warm plum pudding.
Keeps well in the fridge in a closed jar.

Alternate Butterscotch Sauce
(Source: Good Housekeeping Cook Book, 1955)
Makes 4 servings

Ingredients
1 cup	Brown sugar, packed
¼ cup	Light cream
2 tablespoons	white Corn Syrup
2 tablespoons	Butter or margarine

Directions
Combine all the ingredients in a saucepan.
Bring to boil; cook, stirring, 3 to 4 minutes or until thickened.
Serve on butter-pecan or other ice cream, warm cake squares, etc..

Carrot Cake (Fern Radmore's)

Contributed by: Liane Desmarais-Cavanagh
Source: Fern Radmore
Yield: 10 Servings
Note: My friend, who *loves* Carrot Cake, maintains it is the best recipe

Ingredients

2/3 cup	Flour
½ cup	Sugar, granulated
1 teaspoon	Baking Soda
¾ teaspoon	Baking Powder
1 teaspoon	Cinnamon, ground (I omit)
¼ teaspoon	Cloves, ground
1 teaspoon	Nutmeg, freshly grated
¼ teaspoon	Allspice, ground
¼ teaspoon	Salt
1/3 cup	Vegetable Oil (not olive, something with very little taste)
2	Eggs
1 cup	Walnuts, chopped (I use chopped Pecans)
½ cup	Pineapple, crushed
1 cup	Carrot, finely grated
½ cup	Raisins (or currants)

Cream Cheese Frosting:

One 8 oz pkg	Cream cheese
6 tablespoons	Butter
1 teaspoon	Vanilla extract
1¾ cups	Confectioners' Sugar
¼ teaspoon	Ginger, ground (I also add minced candied ginger)

Directions

Preheat the oven to 350°F.
Butter a 9" x 5" (or 4½" x 8 ½" loaf pan.)
Coat the pan with flour, tapping out the excess.
In a bowl, whisk together the: flour, granulated sugar, baking soda, baking powder, spices, and salt
Then sift them into a second bowl to make sure the spices are well combined.
In a small bowl, whisk together the oil and eggs until blended,
Stir the egg mixture into the flour with a rubber spatula.
Fold in the walnuts (pecans), pineapple, and grated carrot.
Transfer the batter to the prepared pan and smooth the top with an offset spatula.
Bake for 50 minutes, or until a toothpick inserted in the center comes out clean.
Let cool until easy to handle, and turn out onto a cake rack.
While the cake is cooling, make the frosting.
In a bowl, combine the cream cheese, butter, vanilla, and confectioners' sugar.
Beat on medium speed until well combined and fluffy, about 10 minutes or until smooth.
Fold in ginger
When cake is completely cool spread frosting on loaf.

Carrot Cake (Kathleen Sullivan's)

Contributed by: Liane Desmarais-Cavanagh
Source: Kathleen Sullivan, colleague at CFIA
Note: This version is popular with many of my friends. **Note from Ellen**: This is the recipe I use in France since all the ingredients are available there.

Ingredients

1 pound	Carrots (6 or 7 large carrots), peeled
2½ cups	Flour
1¼ teaspoons	Baking Powder
1 teaspoon	Baking Soda
1¼ teaspoons	Cinnamon, ground
1 teaspoon	Nutmeg, ground
1/8 teaspoon	Cloves, ground
¼ teaspoon	Allspice, ground
½ teaspoon	Salt
1½ cups	Confectioners' sugar
½ cup	Dark Brown Sugar, packed
1¼ cups	Vegetable Oil
4	Eggs, lightly beaten
1 cup	Pecans, chopped
½ cup	Golden raisins

Directions

Preheat the oven to 350°F.

Butter & flour two 9" round pans (or one 9" x 13" cake pan)
(In addition, you can also place a cut-out parchment circle on the bottom of the pan)

Grate the carrots with a grater or a food processor. (I like them as fine as possible so they "hide")

In a large bowl, mix together the dry ingredients: flour, baking powder, baking soda, cinnamon, nutmeg, cloves, allspice, salt, confectioner's sugar, and brown sugar).
Add the Raisins/currents and toss to coat well with flour

Stir in the oil and eggs, then the carrots.

Pour the batter into the prepared pan

Bake for 30 to 40 minutes, or until a toothpick comes out clean.

Cool completely, then frost with cream cheese frosting.

Carrot Cake (Wanda Doyle)

Contributed by: Valerie Healy
Source: Wanda Doyle
Note: "Because of the oil this cake stays moist a long time…if it lasts!"

Ingredients

1½ cups	Oil
2 cups	Sugar
4	Eggs, beaten
2 cups	Flour
½ teaspoon	Baking Powder
1 teaspoon	Vanilla
2 teaspoons	Cinnamon
2 teaspoons	Baking Soda
½ teaspoon	Salt
1 cup	Walnuts, chopped
14 oz.	Crushed Pineapple, drained
2 cups	Carrots, grated

Directions

Preheat the oven to 350°F.

Mix oil and sugar
Add eggs & blend thoroughly
Add flour, Baking Powder, Baking Soda & salt
Add nuts, pineapple & carrots

Pour the batter into the prepared 12" x 18" baking dish* at 350ºF for 1 hour.
(*I use a 9" x 13" lasagna pan, it's a little deeper)

While cake cooks, make icing:

8 oz pkg	Cream Cheese
2 teaspoons	Vanilla
½ cup	Butter
2 cups	Icing Sugar

Beat all ingredients well

Remove cake from oven and cool completely

Spread icing on cooled cake.

Cherry Cheese Coffee Cake

Contributed by: Liane Desmarais-Cavanagh
Source: Jackie Sampson
Yield: 12 Servings
Note: I first had this at a "Hen Party" in 2001. It was very pretty and yummy. Takes a little maneuvering to get it to look as good as the picture, but it's worth the effort.

Ingredients

One 8 oz. pkg	Philly Cream Cheese, softened
S cup	Icing Sugar
1	Egg, separated
½ teaspoon	Vanilla or ½ teaspoon almond extract
2 pkgs (8 oz.)	Pillsbury crescent rolls
1 cup	Cherry Pie filling (canned)

Glaze = ½ cup Powdered (Icing) Sugar + 1 to 2 teaspoon Mil

Directions

Preheat oven to 350°F

In large bowl, combine cream cheese, S cup powdered sugar, egg yolk, and vanilla; mix until smooth.
Unroll crescent rolls and reserve four triangles for decoration.
Separate remaining dough into 12 triangles and arrange on a 15" round baking sheet with points toward the center.
Roll dough into a 14" circle to seal the seams.
Cut an oculus in the center of the dough with a glass and discard.
Spread cream cheese mixture over dough to within ½" of the edges; top with pie filling.
Roll remaining dough into a rectangle; 6" wide and 7" long.
Cut lengthwise into 12 strips.
Twist strips and place in a spoke-like fashion over filling.
Press ends to seal at center and outer edges.
Brush strips with lightly beaten egg white.

Bake 25-30 minutes or until golden brown; cool slightly.

Make glaze and drizzle over coffee cake. (best if not served hot!)

Cherry Surprise

Contributed by: Valerie Healy
Source: Maisy Day via Christina Henderson (1967)
Note: from Grama H "This is from Judy's cook book"

Ingredients:
1½ cups	Icing Sugar
1½ cups	Coconut
½ cup	Butter, soft
1 teaspoon	Almond flavouring
1 small bottle	Marachino Cherries

Directions
Drain Cherries well
Mix all other ingredients.

Roll mixture around each cherry and then roll them in Graham cracker crumbs
Store in fridge

If mixture becomes too dry to roll around cherry add a dash of cream or condensed milk but not more than 1 tablespoon.
If mixture is to moist to handle chill in fridge for a few minutes

Chocolate Chip Cookies with Walnut

Contributed by: Mireille Desmarais
Source: Clara Robinson contributed the recipe to the:
90th Anniversary edition, Olive Branch Rebekah Richmond, Quebec, Cook book 1895 to 1985
Yield: Makes about 5 dozen cookies

Ingredients

2½ cups	Flour
¼ teaspoon	Salt
¾ cup	Sugar
1	Egg
2/3 cup	Chocolate Chips (mini) (dusted with flour)
1 teaspoon	Baking soda
¾ cup	Margarine – (either Becel or Fleishmann's will do)
1 cup	Brown Sugar (packed)
1½ teaspoons	Vanilla
½ cup	Walnuts, chopped (& dusted with flour)

Directions

Preheat oven to 350ºF

Combine: flour, baking soda, and salt in a bowl and set aside.

In a large bowl combine the margarine and sugar
Beat with an electric mixer, until smooth.

To the Margarine add the egg and vanilla and beat until combined
Gradually add the flour mixture to the butter mixture and beat until smooth

Fold in the chocolate chips and walnuts until all of the ingredients are mixed well.

Measure out cookie dough, 1 teaspoonful per cookie, onto an un-greased baking sheet

Bake at 350ºF for 10 to 15 minutes or until the cookies are just browned.

Remove from the cookie sheet to cool on rack.

Chocolate Fudge

Contributed by: Valerie Healy
Source: Marlene McCourt

Ingredients

2 cups	Brown Sugar
1 cup	White Sugar
1 cup	Evaporated Milk
½ cup	Butter
22	large Marshmallows
One 6 oz pkg	Butterscotch chips
One 6 oz pkg	Chocolate chips
1 teaspoon	Vanilla

Directions

Bring Brown & White Sugar, evaporated milk, and butter to a boil over medium heat, stirring often

Boil 15 minutes

Remove from heat and add:
    22 large marshmallows
    One 6 oz pkg Butterscotch chips
    One 6 oz pkg Chocolate chips

Stir until morsels are melted and mixture is smooth
Add 1 teaspoon vanilla
Add nuts (if desired)

Pour into 8" x 8" greased pan

Chocolate & Ice Cream Dessert (Polly Johnson's)

Contributed by: Liane Desmarais-Cavanagh & Ellen Desmarais
Source: Polly Johnson, Philadelphia, 1961
Yield: 6 to 8 Servings (or just Liane!)
Note: Better on the second day, and may be doubled for a 9" x 13" pan
Take from the freezer at least 10 minutes before cutting and serving

Ingredients

2 squares	Baker's chocolate
2 cups	Vanilla wafers*, crushed
3 Eggs	Egg yolks
½ cup	Confectioners' sugar
3 Eggs	Egg whites beaten
1 pint	Ice cream (I like vanilla)

Directions

Put 1 cup of crumbs in buttered tray (8" x 8").

Beat the egg whites until stiff.

Mix sugar, egg yolks and melted chocolate; fold gently in to beaten egg whites.

Place mixture over crumbs; place slices (or scoops) of ice cream on top.

Cover with remaining crumbs on top.

Keep in the freezer.

* Use as much as you need, this is a very generous amount.

Chocolate Trifle

Contributed by:	Valerie (Henderson) Healy

Ingredients

	Mrs Ross' One bowl Chocolate cake (see recipe page 246)
1 can	Cherry Pie filling
1 pkg	Chocolate Instant pudding (made as instructed)
	Whipped Cream (whipped)

Directions
Make the above listed ingredients and assemble as instructed below:
Line the bottom of the bowl with one layer of cake – cut however to cover the bottom
Top with ½ can cherry pie filling
Top that with ½ of the Chocolate pudding

Now another layer of Chocolate cake
The remaining ½ can of cherry pie filling
The remaining ½ of the Chocolate pudding

Top with Whipped cream

Chocolate Zucchini Cake

Contributed by: Judy Ross
Source: Aleda Van Horn – Valley Weaver's Guild – 1980
Yield: 1 large or 2 small cakes
Background: Peel and seed zucchini if skin is tough and zucchini are really large. Cupcakes were popular in school lunches – easy to pack and no messy icing. Freezes well

Ingredients

2 cups	Zucchini, finely diced
½ cup	soft Margarine
½ cup	Cooking oil
1½ cups	White Sugar
2	Eggs
½ cup	Sour Milk
1 teaspoon	Vanilla
2½ cups	Flour,
¼ cup	Cocoa
½ teaspoon	Baking Powder
1 teaspoon	Baking Soda
½ teaspoon	Cinnamon
½ teaspoon	Ground Cloves

Directions

Preheat oven to 325°F

Cream margarine, oil and sugar together.

Add eggs, vanilla and milk; beat with a mixer.

Add sifted dry ingredients; mix well.

Stir in diced zucchini.

Place in greased and floured 9" x 12" pan (or 2 layer cake pans).

Sprinkle the top with ¼ cup chocolate chips.

Bake at 325°F for 40 – 45 minutes.

Chocolate, Apricot, Brandy & Almond Cake

Contributed by: Liane Desmarais-Cavanagh
Source: maybe Ellen Desmarais (from the Daily Telegraph)
Yield: Serves 10
Note: This is lovely if serves a little warm with either cold Crème Anglais or ice cream.

Ingredients

180 g	Apricots, chopped (about 1.2 cups)
60 ml	Brandy (¼ cup)
360 g	Chocolate (about 2 cups)
300 g	Butter (about 1 1/3 cups)
225 g	Almonds, blanched (about 2½ cups)
9	Eggs, separated
150 g	Sugar (about 12½ tablespoons)

Directions

Preheat the oven to 300° F.
Grease and line a 10" Springform pan.

Soak the apricots in the brandy.

Melt the chocolate and butter in a steel or glass bowl over a pan of boiling water.

Grind the almonds to medium corse

Whisk the egg yolks with 100 g sugar until light and pale.
Add the soaked apricots and the almonds to the egg yolk mixture, followed by the melted chocolate, and stir gently.
Whisk the egg whites and the remaining sugar
Then fold the egg white mixture into the chocolate mixture.

Bake at 300°F for 30 minutes - make sure it's still a little wobbly in the centre, and cool before you turn it out.

Clafoutis aux Cerises (Cherry Custard Dessert)

Contributed by: Ellen Desmarais
Source:
Yield: Serves 4-6
Note: In France, Dominique's mother gave us a huge basket of cherries; when I confessed that I didn't have any recipe except cherry pie, she gave me this one which I understand is traditional. It is best with really good cherries.

Ingredients

	Butter for greasing
1½ pounds	Bing cherries*, pitted (1 cup will cover bottom of small oblong Pyrex)
4	Eggs
	Salt
½ cup	Sugar
½ cup	Flour
5 tablespoons	Butter
1 cup	Milk
	Sugar for sprinkling

Directions

Preheat oven to 325°F

Generously butter a wide, shallow baking dish and arrange the cherries evenly over the bottom.

Beat the eggs lightly in a large bowl; beat in a pinch of salt and the sugar.
Sift in the flour gradually, still beating.
Melt two-thirds of the butter and beat it in.
Stir in the milk.

Pour this batter over the cherries and dot with the remaining butter.

Bake in a preheated 400° F oven for 35-40 minutes, until the batter is set.
If you don't want to serve immediately, it may help to prevent the batter sinking if you turn the oven down to 325°F. and bake for a few minutes longer.

Sprinkle with sugar and serve hot or lukewarm, with cream.

* You can substitute, peaches (peeled and pitted)

[I mix by hand, because an electric beater puts too much air in the eggs. I always cook it at 325° F (or even less) for about 40 minutes. Test for doneness with a knife blade as for other custards. Do not over cook ...]

Cockeyed Cake

Contributed by: Judy Ross, Ellen
Source: From Judy's first cookbook *I Hate to Cook!* By Peg Braken, 1965
Note: This has been everyone's favorite chocolate cake for over 50 years!

Ingredients

9 x 13 pan	**Ingredients**	*9 x 9 or 9" round*
3 cups	Flour	1½ cups
½ cup	Cocoa	3 tablespoons
2 teaspoons	Baking soda	1 teaspoons
2 cups	Sugar	1 cup
½ teaspoon	Salt	½ teaspoon
2 teaspoons	Vanilla extract	1 teaspoon
2 tablespoons	Vinegar	1 tablespoon
½ cup	Cooking oil	¼ cup
2 cups	cold Water	1 cup

Directions

9 x 13:
Sift dry ingredients together in a large bowl.
Make three holes and into first pour the vanilla, the second the vinegar, and the third the cooking oil. Pour the cold water over all of it and mix until the batter is smooth and you can't see the flour. Pour into greased pan and bake at 350°F for 40-45 minutes.

9 x 9 or round pan:
Sift dry ingredients directly into greased pan, then continue as above.
Bake for 30 minutes.

Remove cake from oven and let it cool just a bit.
Stir and blend the topping* and then pour and spread it over the cake.
Set the cake back in the oven for 5 minutes, or until the frosting bubbles - or set it under the broiler for about 2 minutes.

*Topping:

While the cake is baking, mix the following ingredients together in a saucepan and set it on the exhaust element of the stove.

9 x 13 pan	**Ingredients**	*9 x 9 or 9" round*
¼ cup	softened Margarine	2 tablespoons
2/3 cup	Brown Sugar	½ cup
2 tablespoons	Milk	1 tablespoon
to taste	Nuts and Coconut	to taste

Coffee Shortbread Fingers

Contributed by: Liane Desmarais-Cavanagh
Source: Connie Cavanagh-Spicer (Liane's Mother-in-law)
Yield: 4 dozen cookies
Note: Great twist on an old favourite

Ingredients:

1 cup	Butter, soft (not melted)
¾ cup	Brown Sugar (lightly packed)
1 teaspoon	Instant Coffee powder
2 cups	Flour (sifted)

If dipping in nuts:
1	Egg white, lightly beaten
½ cup	finely chopped nuts

Directions

Preheat oven to 300°F

Cream together
    1 cup Butter, soft (not melted)
    ¾ cup Brown Sugar (lightly packed)

Blend in
    1 teaspoon Instant Coffee powder

Gradually add
    2 cups Flour (sifted)

Mix until well blended

Chill the dough

On a lightly floured surface roll the chilled dough to a ½" thickness.
Cut into 2 x 1/2" 'fingers'

(Optional: Dip shortbread in 1 egg white (slightly beaten and Roll in chopped nuts)

Place on ungreased baking sheet.

Bake in preheated 300° F oven for 20 – 25 minutes

Remove from oven, cool on rack and store in airtight container.

Cream Pie Fillings

Contributed by: Ellen Desmarais
Source: Thelma Bolter-Swinford
Yield: 1 pie
Note: These recipes are from the days before pie mixes.

Ingredients

½ cup	Sugar, granulated
¼ teaspoon	Salt
5 tablespoons	Flour
1 tablespoon	Butter
1 teaspoon	Vanilla
2 cups	Milk
2	Egg yolks

Directions:

Combine in double boiler: sugar, salt, flour, milk and egg yolks.
Cook over boiling water until as thick as thick custard sauce.

Remove from heat, add butter and vanilla.

Cool and add to cooked pie shell.

Chocolate Cream Pie:

Make cream pie, adding 2 or 2 ½ squares unsweetened chocolate.
Melt chocolate with the butter and add to mixture just before removing from heat.

Crème Anglaise

Contributed by:	Liane Desmarais-Cavanagh
Source:	Ellen Desmarais, Fall 1998
Yield:	Makes 1T cups
Note:	I have friends who call this custard, but I don't think it's as thick. I love it on Cockeyed Cake, Apple Crumble, fruit pie, or just licked off a spoon!

Ingredients

1 cup	Half-and-half Cream (10%)
½ cup	Heavy Cream (35%)
2 large	Egg yolks
3 tablespoons	Sugar
1 teaspoon	Cornstarch

Directions

In a 1½ quart heavy saucepan bring half-and-half and heavy cream just to a boil.

While cream mixture is heating, in a bowl whisk together yolks, sugar, and cornstarch until slightly thickened and pale, about 2 minutes.

Temper the egg mixture with some of the hot cream (by whisking in a slow, thin stream of hot cream into the yolk mixture)
Now, using a wooden spoon, stir the cream as you pour the tempered yolk mixture into the cream.

Cook custard over moderately low heat, stirring constantly with a wooden spoon, until a thermometer registers 180°F, about 2 minutes (do not let custard boil).

Transfer custard to a clean bowl and cool to warm, stirring occasionally to prevent a skin from forming.

When the Crème Anglaise is at room temperature, pour into a clean glass jar that can be sealed.

Crème Anglaise may be made 2 days ahead and chilled, covered.

Reheat sauce (gently) if desired.

Date Filled Cookies (Aunt Emma's)

Contributed by: Heather Ross
Source: Aunt Emma via Christina Henderson – Christmas 1969
Note: Judy's note: Emma, sister of Christina, was married to Amos Ward and lived most of her life if Melbourne. Mum made these for us every year, at Christmas; it took me until Christmas 2009 to be brave enough to try making them myself!
Heather's note: One day I hope to practice this recipe until I get a result that is similar to Grammie H's. These were favourite cookies when I was growing up, and I'm sure my kids would love them.

Ingredients

1 cup	Brown sugar
¾ cup	Sour milk
1½ cups	Oatmeal
1 teaspoon	Baking Soda
Pinch	Salt
3 cups	Flour
1 pkg (500g)	Dates, chopped (at least 2 cups when chopped)
1/3 cup	Brown sugar
½ cup	Water
1	Orange, grated rind from

Directions

Cookie Dough:
Pour 1 cup melted shortening (Substitute: ¾ cup Canola oil) over:

1 cup	Brown sugar
¾ cup	Sour milk
1½ cups	Oatmeal
1 teaspoon	Baking Soda
Pinch	Salt

Blend ingredients and then add approximately 3 cups flour.
Chill the dough before rolling out.

Date Filling:
Cook over medium-low heat until smooth:

1 pkg	Dates, chopped (500g; at least 2 cups when chopped)
1/3 cup	Brown sugar
½ cup	Water
	Grated rind of 1 orange

Note: filling should be fluid enough to drop from a spoon

Roll chilled cookie dough as thin as possible.
If using a *small cutter*; place filling on one cookie and cover with a second cookie.
If using a *large cutter*; place filling on one half of the cookie and fold the other half over the top.
Bake at 350°F for 10 minutes.

Date Squares

Contributed by: Ellen Desmarais
Source: Christina Henderson
Yield: 8 X 8" pan
Note: At the top of the recipe Mum (Teeny) wrote " '86 " so I assume that was the year she wrote it out for me. Again, I have never found a better recipe.
Note from Judy: Mum said this was the only thing she could cook when she got married.

Ingredients
2 cups	Dates, chopped
1 tablespoons	Flour
1 cup	Water, hot
1 tablespoons	Orange rind, grated
½ cup	Sugar
1 cup	Flour
1 teaspoon	Baking soda
½ teaspoon	Salt
2 cups	Rolled Oats
½ cup	Brown sugar
¾ cup	Butter

Directions
Toss dates in the flour.
Add hot water to dates with ½ cup sugar.
Simmer till thick.
Stir in rind and cool.

Sift together 1 cup Flour, Baking Soda, Salt and Oats and work in butter.

Press ½ of mixture in an 8 x 8 inch pan,
Spread with the dates mixture
Cover with the rest of the oat mixture.

Bake in moderate oven until brown (i.e., 350ºF, 45 minutes).

Decadent Chocolate Squares

Contributed by:	Ellen Desmarais
Source:	St. George ?
Note:	The heading on my copy of this recipe is "Recipes from the St. George". Who or what that is, I don't remember, but they have a sweet tooth. These squares are really decadent.

Ingredients
½ cup	Butter
Two 8 oz. pkgs	Chocolate chips
1 cup	Peanut Butter
3 cups	Mini Marshmallows, coloured

Directions
Over low heat melt Butter, Chocolate chips, and Peanut Butter

Melt and stir until smooth.

Cool until you can hold your hand on the bottom of the pot.

Stir in mini marshmallows;

Press into a small pan (round or square 8 or 9 inch).

Chill until firm.

Cut and serve.
(Store any leftovers in the fridge.)

Delicate Lemon Pudding

Contributed by:	Ellen Desmarais
Source:	Ivy Fuller ("my Grade 4 teacher") from the *1954 Personal Recipes of the Ladies Auxiliary to the Canadian Legion, Richmond, Quebec*
Yield:	4 servings
Note:	I have found this recipe in various cookbooks, all with different names, but since this was the first one I used, I stick with it. The recipe makes a lovely light flavoured dessert.

Ingredients

2 tablespoons	Butter
2/3 cup	Sugar
2	Eggs, separated
2 tablespoons	Lemon juice
1 teaspoon	Lemon rind, grated
2 tablespoons	Flour
1 cup	Milk

Directions

Preheat oven to 375°F

Butter baking dish (8"x8")

Put water in (roasting) pan (big enough to accommodate the water and the baking dish)

Cream the butter; add sugar and cream well.

Beat the egg yolks until thick and lemon coloured; add to creamed mixture with lemon juice and rind.

Fold in flour and stir in milk.

Beat the egg whites until stiff; fold into first mixture.

Pour into greased baking dish (1 to 1½ quarts), set in a pan of hot water.

Bake in moderate oven (375°F) 35 to 40 minutes.

Chill and serve

"Drumstick" Cake

Contributed by:	Liane Desmarais-Cavanagh
Source:	Zac De Vouge's Mum, July 2011
Yield:	6 to 8 servings
Note:	Tastes like a summer day in Richmond

Ingredients

½ cup	Margarine, melted
1½ cup	Graham Wafers
2 tablespoons	Crunchy Peanut Butter
One 8 oz pkg	Cream Cheese (softened)
¼ cup	Granulated Sugar
2	Eggs
1 teaspoon	Vanilla
1 large container	Cool Whip (not frozen)
½ cup	Peanuts, unsalted (I prefer dry roasted)
½ cup	Chocolate Syrup
½ cup	Caramel syrup

Directions

Bottom Layer
In a bowl mix together Margarine, Graham Wafers, and Peanut Butter
Scoop out ¼ cup and reserve
Press remaining mixture into a 9" x 13" pan

Middle Layer
With an electric mixer bled together: Cream Cheese, granulated sugar, Eggs, and Vanilla
Add container of Cool Whip and mix until well incorporated
Spread over Crumb mixture

Top layer
Sprinkle the reserved ¼ cup of crumb mixture over middle layer
Sprinkle chopped unsalted peanuts
Squirt chocolate syrup over cake
Squirt caramel syrup over cake

Put in freezer for a few hours before serving

Easy Christmas Fruitcake.

Contributed by: Mireille Desmarais
Source: The United Church of Canada "Let's Bake Bread together" © 1988
Note: The Best Recipe ever! You will find pieces of candied fruit and a mixture of fruit at the Bulk Barn (A store that sells food in bulk) with 3 different size containers. When I make this fruitcake each year I use my electric mixer to help mix the wet ingredients well.

Ingredients

2½ cups	all-purpose Flour
1 teaspoon	Baking soda
2	Eggs, lightly beaten
1 can	Eagle Brand condensed milk (I use light condensed milk)
1 jar	Robertson's or Cross & Blackwell mincemeat pie filling
1 pound jar	Candied fruit and
1 small container	Candied Cherries, cut up

Directions

Preheat oven to 300°F

In a large bowl I mix the 2 lightly beaten eggs, 1 can of condensed milk, mincemeat pie filling and a small container of cut up cherries.

Mix your dry ingredients well

Add your dried ingredients to your wet.

Then you mix the entire mixture using your best mixing utensil you use for baking.

Butter the entire area of an Angel food cake pan or a loaf pan and line it with parchment paper. or waxed paper if the parchment paper is too stiff.

Bake for 2 hours at 300°F oven.

Cool 5 minutes before turning out.

English Gingerbread Cake

Contributed by:	Liane Desmarais-Cavanagh
Source:	Sar'Ann Allen, December 1982
Yield:	12 – 14 servings
Note:	The cake tastes better the day after baking and will keep (in an air tight container) for up to 4 days.

Ingredients

10 tablespoons	Butter, unsalted, at room temperature, (+ more to grease the pan)
1 cup + 2 tablespoons	Cake Flour, sifted, (plus more to dust the pan)
1S cups	Lyle's golden syrup, or dark corn syrup
¼ cup	Dark Brown Sugar, packed
1½ tbsp.	Marmalade (Robertson's thick cut is best)
T cup	Milk
2	Eggs
1 cup	Whole Wheat Flour
1½ teaspoons	Baking Powder
1 teaspoon	Cinnamon, ground
1 teaspoon	Ginger, ground
½ teaspoon	Baking Soda
¼ teaspoon	Salt
3 tablespoons	Sugar
2 tablespoons	Lemon juice, fresh
	Confectioners' sugar, for garnish

Directions

Preheat oven to 32 °F.
Grease bottom and sides of an 8" x 8" metal baking pan with butter and line bottom of pan with parchment paper.
Grease parchment paper with butter and dust paper and sides of pan with a little cake flour.
Heat: 8 tablespoons butter, golden syrup, brown sugar, and marmalade in a 2 qt. saucepan over medium-high heat.
Cook, stirring often, until syrup thins and sugar dissolves, about 5 minutes; let cool for 10 minutes.
Whisk in the milk and eggs; set syrup mixture aside.
In a large bowl, sift together: cake flour, whole wheat flour, baking powder, cinnamon, ginger, baking soda, and salt.
Add reserved syrup mixture and whisk until just combined.
Pour batter into reserved baking pan.
Bake at 325°F until a toothpick inserted into center of cake comes out clean, about 50 minutes.
Transfer cake to a rack and let cool for 10 minutes.
Meanwhile, heat remaining butter along with sugar and lemon juice in a 1 qt. saucepan over medium heat and cook, stirring often, until sugar dissolves, about 3 minutes.
Using a pastry brush, brush half the lemon syrup over top of cake.
Invert cake onto cooling rack, discard parchment, and brush the remaining lemon syrup on bottom and sides of cake.
Invert the cake onto a serving stand and wrap in plastic wrap; let cool completely.
To serve, cut cake into squares and sprinkle with confectioners' sugar.

Eton Mess

Contributed by: Liane Desmarais-Cavanagh
Source: Gussie Long's Cookbook (dated June 21, 1923)
Yield: 4 Servings
Note: Serve shortly after you make it, meringue gets mushy if it's left too long. Good with Late Harvest Semillion, Gewürztraminer Late Harvest

Ingredients
4 large   Egg whites
1 cup + 1 tablespoon Sugar
¾ pound   Strawberries
2 tablespoons   Harvey's Bristol Cream (Sherry)
½ cup   Whipping Cream (35%), well chilled

Directions
Make Meringue
Preheat oven to 225°F. & Line a baking sheet with parchment paper
Crack egg whites into clean copper bowl, and add a pinch of salt
Beat whites until they just hold soft peaks.
Gradually add (in measured amounts) 1 cup sugar, beating all the while.
Now beat until meringue holds stiff, glossy peaks.
Spoon meringue into 4 mounds (on parchment paper) onto baking sheet.
Spread each into a egg sized rounds.
Smooth the tops.
Place on the middle rack of the oven for about an hour (or an hour and a half) until crisp and firm but not golden! (If you are doing this in the summer and the weather is humid, cooking time may take longer.)
When baking complete turn off oven, but leave meringues inside to come to room temperature.
Cool meringues completely (only then can you gently remove them from the parchment paper).
Slice strawberries and, in a small bowl, stir together with Sherry and 1 soup spoon of sugar.
Let stand 20 minutes.
Drain strawberries in a sieve set over a bowl.
Reserve syrup.
Beat cream in a chilled bowl until it just holds stiff peaks.
Add reserved syrup.
Assemble parfaits (bottom to top):
    Meringue on bottom
    Strawberries next
    finally layer of cream.
    Repeat until glass is full.
    Top with single perfect strawberry and sprig of mint
NB:
Meringues can be made 1 week ahead, wrapped well individually, and kept at cool room temperature
- I have made this in parfait glasses using bakery fresh meringues, and layering meringue, strawberries, cream, meringue, strawberries, cream. (note the meringues can't be dry and crumbly)

Fruit Squares

Contributed by:	Ellen Desmarais,
Source:	Christina Henderson, Fall 1995
Yield:	One 8 X 8" pan
Note:	This is Mum's recipe and I have never found one better. It's like butter tarts but better.

Ingredients

½ cup	Butter or shortening
1 cup	Flour
¼ cup	Brown sugar
½ teaspoon	Salt
2	Eggs, well beaten
½ cup	Corn syrup
3½ tablespoons	Flour
½ teaspoon	Vanilla
1 cup	Brown Sugar
¼ cup	Raisins,
¼ cup	Walnuts
¼ cup	Cherries
½ teaspoon	Salt

Directions

Mix butter, flour, brown sugar, and salt together and spread in a 7" x 11" pan
Bake about 15 minutes

Top with the following mixture:

2	Eggs well beaten
½ cup	Corn syrup
3½ tablespoons	Flour
½ teaspoons	Vanilla
1 cup	Brown Sugar
¼ cup each	Raisins, Walnuts, Cherries
½ teaspoons	Salt

Bake at 350°F until golden brown – about 30 to 40 minutes.

Gingerbread Cookies

Contributed by: Mireille Desmarais
Source: Derek (1983)
Note: Derek, came in with a batch of Gingerbread cookies in December 1983. He was a student at Rideau High School, Printing class.

Ingredients

½ cup	Butter (If you use ½ butter and ½ margarine the dough will spread and will give you a crackled look, after it comes out of the oven.
½ cup	Sugar
½ cup	Molasses
1	Egg Yolk (Yellow part)
2 cups	Flour
1 teaspoon	Salt
½ teaspoon	Baking Soda
1½ teaspoons	Cinnamon (or you can use Allspice)
1 teaspoon	Ground Cloves
1 teaspoon	Ginger and
½ teaspoon	Nutmeg

Directions

Preheat oven to 350°F

Cream together the butter, sugar and the molasses and then the yellow yolk.
Mix well.

Mix together: Flour, Salt, Baking Soda, Cinnamon, Ground Cloves, Ginger and Nutmeg
Sift all dried ingredients together.

Combine the wet and the dry ingredients and mix well.

Roll out a portion of ½ the dough and keep the rest covered with a damp dish cloth and put it in the refrigerator, until you are ready to do the 2nd ½ of the batch.

Meanwhile work the dough with your hands, roll out use cookie cutters.
Small cookie cutters can be used as well.

Bake at 350°F for 8 to 10 minutes.

Gingersnaps

Contributed by: Liane Desmarais-Cavanagh
Source: Lisa Czajkowski's Great Grandmother (from East Farnham, Quebec)
Yield: Makes 5 dozen
Note: These are the dark and grown-up version of ginger cookies.

Ingredients

1 cup	Butter
1 cup	Sugar
1	Egg
1 cup	Molasses
2 tablespoons	Vinegar
5 cups	all-purpose Flour, sifted
1½ teaspoons	Baking Soda
½ teaspoon	Salt
2 to 3 teaspoons	Ginger, ground
1 teaspoon	Cinnamon
1 teaspoon	Cloves, ground

Directions

Cream together butter and sugar
Beat in egg, molasses, and vinegar

Sift together dry ingredients

Blend dry ingredients into cream mixture

Chill 3 hours

Preheat oven to 375°F

Roll out dough on lightly floured surface to 1/8 inch thick
Cut into shapes

Place 1 inch apart on cookie sheet

Bake at 375°F for 5 to 6 minutes

Grand Marnier Crepe Cake

Contributed by:	Liane Desmarais-Cavanagh
Source:	Michèle Filippi, Fall 1999
Yield:	12 servings
Note:	My god-mother told me how to make this, and it is the simplest dessert ever! It needs to be made 1 day ahead so that the cream will have time to be absorbed. Don't hesitate to use store bought crêpes if you can get really good thin ones.

Ingredients

6 large	Eggs
1 cup	Milk, 3.25%
3 cups	Heavy Cream (35%), chilled
1 teaspoon	Vanilla, real
1 cup	All-purpose flour
[teaspoon	Salt
1 cup	Confectioners' sugar
2 teaspoons	Orange zest
2 tablespoons	Unsalted Butter, melted
1 tablespoon	Grand Marnier (or Cointreau)

Directions

For crèpes:

In a medium bowl combine: flour, salt, ¼ cup confectioners' sugar, and 1 teaspoon zest
In a small bowl mix: eggs, milk, ½ cup cream, and ½ teaspoon vanilla
Now add the wet ingredients to the dry and blend until just smooth.

Brush a 10-inch non-stick skillet lightly with some of melted butter, then heat over medium-high heat until hot.
Pour in a scant ¼ cup batter, immediately tilting and rotating skillet to coat bottom. (If batter sets before skillet is coated, reduce heat slightly for next crêpe.)
Cook until underside is golden and top is just set, 15 to 45 seconds.
Loosen edge of crêpe with a heat-proof rubber spatula, then flip crêpe over with your fingertips and cook 15 seconds more.
Transfer to a plate and top with parchment paper to keep them from sticking together.
Continue making crêpes, brushing skillet with butter each time and stacking on plate.

for filling:

Beat remaining 2½ cups cream, ½ teaspoon vanilla, ¾ cup confectioner's sugar, 1 teaspoon zest, and Grand Marnier in a large deep bowl with an electric mixer until cream holds stiff peaks.

Assembly:

Centre a crêpe on a serving plate and spread with ¼ cup Grand Marnier whipped cream.
Continue stacking crêpes and spreading with cream, ending with a crêpe.

Chill, covered, 24 hours (this stage is critical as it allows the cake to 'set'
Serve.

Gumdrop Cookies

Contributed by:	Mireille Desmarais
Source:	Eleanor and Arthur Bieber's recipe from: *Personal Recipes of the Ladies Auxiliary to the Canadian Legion, Richmond, Quebec (1954 ed.)*
Yield:	Makes about 3 dozen.
Note:	To cut gumdrops, use a pair of scissors dipped in water occasionally.

Ingredients:

½ cup	Shortening
½ cup	Brown Sugar
½ cup	White Sugar
1 teaspoon	Vanilla
1	Egg, beaten
1 cup	Flour (regular white)
½ teaspoon	Baking Soda
½ cup	Baking Powder
¼ teaspoon	Salt
½ cup	Shredded Coconut
½ cup	Walnuts, chopped
½ cup	Gumdrops, small & cut into pieces
1 cup	Oatmeal, quick-cook variety

Directions

Beat the shortening until soft.
Gradually beat in the brown sugar, white sugar and vanilla until light and creamy.

In a separate bowl sift the flour before measuring;
Add the Baking Soda, Baking Powder and salt
Resift the dry ingredients to ensure everything is well incorporated.

In a separate bowl combine the Coconut, Walnuts, gumdrops, and Oatmeal.
Sprinkle a ¼ of the flour mixture over the coconut, walnuts, gumdrops and oatmeal.
Toss to coat.

Beat the sifted flour mixture into the butter mixture in two parts alternating with the beaten egg.
Now add the Coconut mixture to the butter mixture.

Pinch off pieces of dough and roll them into 1 inch balls.

Flatten balls with a spatula dipped in milk.

Bake the cookies in a moderate oven about 350° – 375°F for about 10 minutes.

Hot Cross Bun Pudding

Contributed by: Ellen Desmarais
Source: A hot cross bun package!
Yield: 6 servings
Note: This is the best bread pudding recipe I`ve ever used; fast, easy and delicious. It's also a great use for stale buns.

Ingredients

4	Hot Cross Buns, cubed (or raisin bread cubed)
2	Eggs
2 cups	Milk
1 teaspoons	Vanilla
½ cup	Equal or Splenda
	Cinnamon, to taste
	Nutmeg, to taste
	Raisins, to taste

Directions

Preheat oven to 350°F

Spread hot cross bun cubes in lightly greased baking dish.

Whisk together eggs, milk, vanilla and sugar-substitute.

Pour over bun cubes and stir to coat.

Bake in 350°F oven for 35 to 40 minutes or until a knife inserted in centre comes out clean.

Serve warm, at room temperature, or chilled.

Hot Milk Cake

Contributed by: Judy Ross
Source: Connie Morrison, Schefferville, March 1972
Note: Aunt Bertie Stevens made this cake often.

Ingredients

	9 x 9		*9 x 13*
Melt	2½ to 3 tablespoons	Shortening	1/3 cup
in	½⁺ cup	Milk	1⁺ cup
Beat:	2	Eggs	3
Add:	1 cup	White Sugar	2 cups
Sift:	1 cup	Flour	2 cups
	1½ teaspoons	Baking Powder	1 tablespoon
	Dash	Salt	Dash

Alternately add flour mixture and liquid mixture to eggs and sugar.

| **Add**: | 1 teaspoon | Vanilla | 1 teaspoon |

Grease and paper bottom of pan (**NOT** sides).
Bake 30 minutes at 350°F.
Let stand 5 minutes after baking before removing from pan.

Layered Lemon Squares

Contributed by: Valerie Healy
Source: Charlotte Griffith
Yield: This makes an 8 x 8 and a 9 x 13 pan!
Note: Light and refreshing and can be taken to pot-luck and still have enough to leave some at home.

First Layer
2 cups   all-purpose Flour
1 cup   Butter or Margarine
1 cup   finely chopped Pecans

Mix and pat into pan and bake at 350º for 15 min.
Cool

Second layer:
Two 8 oz pkgs   Cream Cheese
1 cup   Icing Sugar
1 cup   Whipping Cream

Spread over cooled crust

Third layer:
2 pkg   Lemmon pudding/pie filling

Fourth layer:
2 cups   Whipping Cream
2 tablespoons   Sugar (granulated)
1 teaspoon   Vanilla

Top with slivered Almonds

Lemon Cheesecake Dessert

Contributed by: Ellen (Henderson) Desmarais
Source: Marie-Claire Fournier
Yield: One 9" X 13" pan
Note: This is a rather old fashioned dessert, but it makes a large one, is refreshing and is usually a great success. It was given to me by Marie-Claire Fournier in 1983 when I worked at the National Archives.

Ingredients

1 cup + 2 tablespoons	Graham cracker crumbs
¼ cup	Butter, melted
1 can (385 ml)	Carnation milk (whole, not 2%) well chilled
1 cup	White sugar
1 tablespoon	Vanilla
1½ pkg.	Lemon Jell-O
1 cup	Water
1 pkg (250g)	Cream cheese, soft

Directions

Melt butter & mix with graham crackers, spread all but 2 tablespoons on the bottom of 9" x 13" pan.

Whip carnation milk then add sugar and vanilla.

Dissolve Jell-O in water; add soft cream cheese and beat well.

Add Jell-O mix to milk and beat well.

Pour over crumbs then put remaining crumbs on top.

Refrigerate at least half a day then cut like a cake.

Makes 1 large pan or 2 small cake pans.

Lemon Crème Brulée Tarte

Contributed by: Liane Desmarais-Cavanagh
Source: Bon Appétit Magazine (2004)
Background: The filling is wonderful, pastry just okay, better if using the 5 Roses pie crust. (must try Val's recipe for pie crust!)

Ingredients
Crust
1 cup	all-purpose Flour
¼ cup	powdered Sugar
	Pinch of salt
6 tablespoons	Butter - unsalted, chilled and cut in ½" cubes
4 teaspoons	Whipping Cream (35%), chilled
1	Egg white, beaten to blend

Filling
¾ cup + 2 tablespoons	Sugar
¾ cup	Whipping Cream (35%)
4 large	Egg yolks
2 large	Eggs
½ cup	Lemon juice, fresh
1 tablespoon	Lemon zest
	Lemon slices (optional)

Directions
For crust:
Combine flour, sugar, and salt & blend, cut in the butter until coarse meal forms.
Add 4 teaspoons cream.
Blend until moist clumps form, adding more cream by the teaspoon if dough is dry.
Gather dough into ball; flatten into disk. Wrap and chill at least 2 hours.
Preheat oven to 350°F.
Roll out dough on floured surface to 12" round, and transfer to 9" diameter pan with removable bottom.
Fold overhang in, pressing to form double-thick sides.
Bake until golden, pressing with back of fork if crust bubbles, about 18 minutes (small cracks may appear).
Brush inside of hot crust twice with egg white.
Maintain oven temperature.

For filling:
Whisk ¾ cup sugar, cream, yolks, and eggs in bowl to blend well.
Mix in lemon juice and lemon peel.
Pour filling into warm crust.
Bake until filling is slightly puffed at edges and set in centre, about 30 minutes.
Cool completely, about 1 hour.
Preheat broiler. Place tart on baking sheet. Cover edge of crust with foil to prevent burning.
Sprinkle tart evenly with 2 tablespoons sugar.
Broil tart until sugar melts and caramelizes, turning sheet for even browning, about 2 minutes.
Transfer tart to rack. Cool until topping is crisp, about 1 hour.
Push tart pan bottom up, releasing tart.
Place on platter, garnish with lemon slices, if desired, and serve.

Lemon Custard

Contributed by: Ellen Desmarais
Yield: 4 to 6 people
Note: This is a well-tested recipe from Thelma's kitchen.

Ingredients

1/3 cup	Sugar
3	Egg yolks, beaten
3 tablespoons	Cornstarch
2 cup	Milk, scalded
¼ teaspoon	Salt
1 tablespoon	Lemon juice
1 teaspoon	Lemon zest

Directions

Combine sugar, cornstarch, salt, in top of double boiler.

Stir in egg yolks to blend.

Add hot milk gradually, stirring constantly.

Set over boiling water to cook, stirring constantly, until thick.

Add lemon juice and rind and cool.

Serve chilled.

Lemon Pie

Contributed by: Ellen Desmarais
Source: Thelma Bolter-Swinford
Note: If you don't have a lemon pie mix, this is Thelma's recipe to make it from scratch.

Ingredients
1 cup	Sugar
3 tablespoons	Corn starch
2	Lemons
	Grated rind of 1 lemon

Directions
Put juice in cup and fill with water to make 1 cup; add another cup of water.
Cook until clear.
Add 2 egg yolks.
Remove from heat.
Pour into a prepared, precooked pie crust.

Top with meringue:
2	Egg whites
4 tablespoons	Sugar

Whip, add sugar.

Brown at 300°F to prevent further cooking of pie.

Mixed Nut Bars

Contributed by: Valerie Healy
Source: Christine Gawlick
Yield: one 9 x 13 pan
Note: Another quilting friend from London. Bet you can't eat just one!

Ingredients & Directions

1½ cups	all purpose Flour
¾ cup	Brown Sugar
¼ teaspoon	Salt
½ cup	Butter, cold!

Pre heat oven to 350°F
Grease 9 x 13 pan

Mix together flour, sugar and salt, and sprinkle into pan
Cut butter into greased pan

Bake 10 min at 350°F

Sprinkle 11 ½ oz mixed nuts on top of base

Melt together:
1 cup	Butterscotch chips
½ cup	Corn Syrup
2 tablespoons	Butter

Pour over nuts

10 more minutes at 350°F

Mum's Doughnuts

Contributed by: Valerie Healy
Source: Christina Henderson (via Judy (Henderson) Ross)
Yield: Makes about 3 doz large doughnuts
Note: Notes (written by Judy to Val): Milk – we used to think that "foam milk" made the best doughnuts. If Mum didn't have milk from Aunt Emma's she would use whole milk. – Well in Schefferville we used what I had and that was powdered skim milk. Surprise, surprise I got lighter doughnuts that didn't "choke" and I've been using skim milk ever since. This recipe was given to Mum by Aunt Bertie – I suppose some 40 – 50 years ago. Mum and I both usually double this recipe to make the mess worthwhile! Best results when lard is used for frying. I usually have 3 pounds on hand – start with 2 and add to it if necessary.

Ingredients
- 1½ cups Sugar
- 3 Eggs
- ½ teaspoon Vanilla
- 3½ cups Flour
- ½ teaspoon Baking Powder
- 1 teaspoon Baking Soda
- 1 teaspoon Nutmeg
- 1 pinch Ginger
- Dash Salt
- 1 cup Milk

Directions
Beat together: 1½ cups Sugar, 3 Eggs, ½ teaspoon Vanilla
Place in Sifter: 3 ½ cup Flour, ½ teaspoon Baking Powder, 1 teaspoon Baking Soda, 1 teaspoon Nutmeg, 1 pinch Ginger, Dash Salt
Sow: 1 cup milk (see note) (generous cup)
Melt: Shortening to measure 3 tablespoons
Add dry ingredients alternately with milk to egg mixture
Add melted shortening about half way through, before batter is too stiff
Refrigerate a minimum of a few hours or up to a few days (or at this point, place in the freezer to proceed later)

Place approx 1/3 of batter on floured board and knead in flour until easy to handle*
(* leave remainder in the fridge)

Pat out; cut; fry @ 400° - 425° F.

Noodle Kugel

Contributed by:	Liane Desmarais-Cavanagh
Source:	Lil Levitin, 1997
Yield:	8 servings
Note:	I know it seems strange to have noodles for dessert, but this is really good. Not to sweet

Ingredients

½ pound	wide Egg Noodles
1 pound	creamed or whipped Cottage Cheese
1 cup	Sour Cream
¼ pound	unsalted Butter, melted
½ cup	Sugar
2	Eggs, beaten
¾ cup	golden Raisins
2 medium	Granny Smith apples, peeled and sliced thin
pinch	Salt
pinch	Cinnamon
1 teaspoon	Vanilla extract
	Butter for greasing baking pan
	Sour Cream and fresh berries as an accompaniment (if desired)

Directions

Preheat the oven to 350°F.

Boil the noodles until al dente, and drain.

In a large mixing bowl, combine drained noodles and remaining ingredients (through and including vanilla extract) and toss well.

Transfer the mixture to a buttered 13 x 9 x 2-inch baking dish, and bake 40 minutes, uncovered.

Cover with foil and bake an additional 20 minutes, or until cooked through.

Remove from oven and let cool before cutting into squares.

Serve warm or at room temperature with sour cream and/or fresh berries on the side, if desired.

One Bowl Chocolate Cake

Contributed by: Judy Ross via Valerie Healy
Source: Mrs. Alice Ross – Sept. 1971
Note: Necessary when making Chocolate Trifle (page 215)

Ingredients

½ cup	Shortening
1½ cups	Sugar
2	Eggs
1 teaspoon	Vanilla
1¼ cups	Milk (*)
½ cup	Cocoa
1¾ cups	Flour
1 teaspoon	Baking Soda
½ teaspoon	Baking Powder
¾ teaspoon	Salt

Directions

Preheat oven to 350°F

Cream shortening and sugar; add eggs, and vanilla; blend well.

Alternately add dry ingredients and milk.
Beat two minutes on medium speed.

Spread in greased and floured 9 x 13 pan, or two 9" layer pans.

Bake at 350°F for 25-35 minutes.

(*)Substitution for milk: 1½ cups water + ½ cup skim milk powder.

Note: To save time, the dry ingredients, (including skim milk powder) can be premeasured and placed in airtight jars.

Orange Delight

Contributed by: Valerie Healy
Source: Mrs. Wheelock, Richmond, via Christina Henderson
Note: Mr. Wheelock was the Principal at St. Francis School in Richmond. Mrs. Wheelock made this recipe for a year-end party.

Ingredients

2 packages	Gelatin
1 cup	Cold Water
2 cups	boiling Water
2 cups	White Sugar
Two 6 ounce	Frozen Orange (juice)
1 pint	Whipping Cream (35%)
1 large	Angel Cake

Directions

Soak the gelatin in cold water 5 minutes, add boiling water and dissolve.
Add sugar and stir until all is dissolved.
Add frozen orange juice.
Put in fridge till it starts to thicken (Mum's expression was "until it is like liver").

Fold the whipped cream into orange mixture.

Butter bottom of 9 x 13 inch pan.
Layer:
  ½ crumbled cake
  ½ mixture
  ½ crumbled cake
  ½ mixture

Decorate with oranges and cherries.

Note: This dessert was served at Valerie & Allan's wedding September 24, 1977.

Oven Style Caramel Corn

Contributed by: Valerie Healy
Source: Heather Davidson

Ingredients
2 cups	Brown Sugar
½ cup	Butter
½ cup	Corn Syrup
1 teaspoon	Salt
1 teaspoon	Vanilla
½ teaspoon	Soda
One 8 qt.	Pop corn

Directions
Place first 4 ingredients in 2 quart saucepan.
Bring to a boil.
Boil for 5 minutes stirring constantly.
Do not over boil.

Add vanilla and soda, stirring after each addition, drizzle over popped corn.

Place on 2 cookie sheets.
Bake at 250º F for 1 hour, stirring 3 – 4 times.

Peanut Butter Cookies - Connie's

Contributed by:	Liane Desmarais-Cavanagh
Source:	Connie (Cavanagh) Spicer
Yield:	3 dozen
Note:	Great no-fail recipe

Ingredients

½ cup	Butter
½ cup	Peanut Butter
½ cup	White Sugar
½ cup	Brown Sugar, lightly packed
1	Egg, lightly beaten
1½ teaspoons	Molasses
1¼ cups	Flour,
1 teaspoon	Baking Soda
½ teaspoon	Salt

Directions

Preheat oven to 375°F

In large mixing bowl cream together
    ½ cup Butter
    ½ cup Peanut Butter
Gradually beat in
    ½ cup Sugar (white)
    ½ cup Brown Sugar, lightly packed
Add: 1 Egg, lightly beaten & ½ teaspoon Vanilla
Beat Well

In a separate bowl sift together
    1¼ cups Flour,
    1 teaspoon Baking Soda
    ½ teaspoon Salt

Blend dry ingredients into Peanut butter mixture, adding 1/3 at a time
Shape into dough balls which are about 1" in diameter.

Place on greased cookie sheet and press
Dip fork in warm water and press into cookie balls to make a cross-tine pattern

Bake in a preheated 375°F oven for 10 to 12 minutes
Remove and place on a rack to cool

Store in air tight container

Peanut Butter Cookies – Mireille's

Contributed by:	Mireille Desmarais
Source:	Doris Desmarais
Yield:	4 dozen cookies
Note:	This is recipe has been in the family for many years and has been appreciated by my father.

Ingredients

1½ cups	Flour
½ teaspoon	Baking Soda
¾ cup	Peanut butter, creamy type
1/3 cup	Margarine (Becel or Fleishmann's original)
½ cup	White Sugar
½ cup	Brown Sugar
1	Egg

Directions

Preheat the oven to 350° F.

In a medium bowl sift together the flour, baking powder, baking soda and the salt.

In a large bowl, combine the peanut butter and margarine
Beat with an electric mixer, until smooth
Add the brown and white sugar
Add the egg
Add the flour mixture and continue beating, until all of the flour is well incorporated.

Shape into 3/4 inch balls and place them on an ungreased cookie sheet.

Press the balls flat with the tines of a fork, making a criss-cross pattern on the top of each of the balls of the cookie dough.

Baking for 10 to 15 minutes, until the edges are barely browned.

Remove from the cookie sheet to cool.

Peanut Butter Cookies – Grama H's

Contributed by: Liane Desmarais-Cavanagh
Source: Christina Henderson
Yield: 4 dozen cookies
Note:

Ingredients

1 cup	Butter
1 cup	Peanut Butter
1 cup	White Sugar
1 cup	Brown Sugar
1½ teaspoons	Baking Soda
1 teaspoon	Vanilla
¼ teaspoon	Salt
2	Eggs
2 cups	Flour

Directions

Cream white sugar & butter
Add peanut butter and brown sugar
Mix
Beat eggs separately and add vanilla
Sift flour, baking soda, & salt
Combine
Mixing well

Do not grease pan

(NB: there was no notation for temperature or baking time, but I suspect 350°F for 8 to 10 minutes)

Pear Crumble

Contributed by:	Ellen Desmarais
Source	Home Makers Magazine
Yield:	6 people
Note:	This recipe was taken from the "Home Maker's" magazine which used to be distributed door-to-door. The date on it is 1993. It is always a surprise because it is unusual and very tasty.

Prep time: 15 minutes / Cooking time: 40 to 45 minutes

Ingredients

6 large	Pears (about 1.25 kilo)
¼ cup	Lemon juice
¼ cup	Currants (or raisins)
½ cup	Brown Sugar, packed
½ cup	all-purpose Flour
½ cup	Rolled Oats
½ cup	Chopped Walnuts, toasted
1 teaspoon	Lemon zest
¼ teaspoon	Salt
¼ teaspoon	Cinnamon
¼ teaspoon	Nutmeg
¼ cup	Butter

Directions

Peel core and thinly slice pears. I
In large bowl, combine pears, lemon juice, currants, half of the sugar and 2 tablespoons of flour; set aside.

In separate bowl, stir together remaining sugar and flour, the oats, walnuts, lemon rind, salt, cinnamon and nutmeg.
Cut in butter until mixture is crumbly.

Spread pear mixture in greased, shallow 8 cup (2 litre) baking or gratin dish.
Sprinkle evenly with oat mixture.

Bake in 375ºF oven 40 to 45 minutes or until crumble topping is beginning to brown and pears are tender.

Serve the crumble warm with softly whipped cream, ice cream or cheddar cheese.

Pie Crust

Contributed by: Valerie Healy
Source: Louise Mader
Note: This is the best pie crust recipe ever, hands-down. It came from a dear friend Louise Mader. We were Beaver Leaders together – She had four boys too. We looked like Jack Sprat and his wife. She was tall and thin, me shout and wide – then put us in those ridiculous hats!! I came away every week with a headache the size of Innerkip – not Louise. She was ready to take on another round. The Mader's raised pigs, she did all the work with the babies, kept house, did Beavers, was very active in the church, all this and she was the <u>best</u> cook. When her children were old enough to go to high school she took on a job outside the home to help with expenses. On December 11, 1997, she flipped the pick-up she was driving on black ice, she died instantly. She was 42. You know the saying "the good die young" very true in this case.

Ingredients

2 cups	Flour
1 cup	Shortening
½ teaspoon	Salt
2 teaspoons	Sugar

Blend with Pastry Blender

1 teaspoon	Vinegar
½ cup	Water

Pineapple Lemon Mousse (aka Mormon Funeral Dessert)

Contributed by: Liane Desmarais-Cavanagh
Source: Sheila Schultzke
Yield: 10 – 12 people
Note: This makes my brother-in-laws smile every time I serve it! Best part is it can be made a day in advance.

Ingredients

Two 3 oz pkgs	Lemon (or Lime)-flavored Jell-O
One 20 oz. can	crushed Pineapple (in its own juice)
¾ cup (about)	Pineapple juice
½ cup	Water
3 tablespoons	fresh Lemon juice
2 tablespoons	grated Lemon peel
2 cups	chilled Whipping Cream (35%)
4 teaspoons	Vanilla extract

Directions

Place gelatin in large bowl.

Drain pineapple thoroughly in sieve set over large measuring cup.
Add enough additional pineapple juice to juice in cup to measure 1½ cups.

Transfer juice to small saucepan and bring to boil.
Pour boiling juice over gelatin.
Stir until gelatin dissolves.

Mix in drained pineapple, water, lemon juice and lemon peel.
Refrigerate until mixture thickens and <u>just begins</u> to set, stirring occasionally, about 1 hour.

Beat cream and vanilla in another large bowl until stiff peaks form.
Fold into gelatin mixture in 2 additions.

Transfer mousse to serving bowl or spoon into goblets.
Cover and refrigerate until well chilled, at least 4 hours.

Pink Marshmallow Squares

Contributed by: Valerie Healy
Source: Gladys Galbraith via Christina Henderson
Note: Gladys Galbraith was a friend of Mum's from Rebekahs. Whenever Mum was asked for a pan of squares this is what she would often make. Her theory was that they wouldn't turn out right unless you used a stand mixer, not a hand one. I never tested the theory. She also felt they looked very pretty on a plate of squares and she seemed to be the only one who made them.

Ingredients and Directions

3 cups	Butter
1/3 cup	Brown Sugar
1½ cups	Flour

Work like pie crust, stir with a spoon 'till forms a ball
Pat down in pan and prick with a fork
Bake at 325°F for 30 minutes

Topping:
2 pkgs	Gelatin
½ cup	cold Water
2 cups	White Sugar
½ cup	Hot Water
½ cup	drained chopped cherries
½ cup	chopped Walnuts
¼ to ½ teaspoon	Lemon flavouring
¼ to ½ teaspoon	Almond flavouring
	Food colouring according to the colour you want

Sprinkle gelatin over cold water let stand
Combine sugar and hot water
Place over high heat and boil 2 minutes
Remove from heat and add gelatin
Beat until thick
Then add cherries & nuts
Spread over crust
Cut with a knife dipped in water
When you get it finished you can sprinkle a little coconut on top

Be sure you time your sugar if it is cooked to much it will grain

Pistachio Cranberry Icebox Cookies

Contributed by: Liane Desmarais-Cavanagh
Source: Laura Press, Toronto, 1981
Yield: 3 dozen
Note: Pretty and yummy. Dough logs can be chilled up to 3 days, or frozen for about a month.

Ingredients

1½ cups	all-purpose Flour
½ teaspoon	Cinnamon (I prefer nutmeg)
¼ teaspoon	Salt
¾ cup	unsalted Butter, softened
¼ cup + 2 tablespoons	granulated Sugar
½ teaspoon	finely grated fresh Orange zest
½ cup	shelled Pistachios (not dyed red)
1/3 cup	dried Cranberries
1 large	Egg, lightly beaten
¼ cup	coarse Decorative Sugar

Directions

Stir together flour, cinnamon, and salt in a bowl.

Beat together butter, granulated sugar, and zest in a large bowl with an electric mixer at medium-high speed until pale and fluffy, about 3 minutes.
Reduce speed to low and add flour mixture in 3 batches, mixing until dough just comes together in clumps, then mix in pistachios and cranberries.
Gather and press dough together, then divide into 2 equal pieces.

Using a sheet of plastic wrap or wax paper as an aid, form each piece of dough into a log about 1½" in diameter.
Square off long sides of each log to form a bar, then chill, wrapped in plastic wrap, until very firm, at least 2 hours.

Slice and bake cookies:
Put oven racks in upper and lower thirds of oven and preheat oven to 350°F.
Line 2 large baking sheets with parchment paper.
Brush egg over all 4 long sides of bars (but not ends).
Sprinkle decorative sugar on a separate sheet of parchment or wax paper and press bars into sugar, coating well.
Cut each bar crosswise into ¼ inch thick slices, rotating bar after cutting each slice to help keep square shape. (If dough gets too soft to slice, freeze bars briefly until firm.)
Arrange cookies about a ½ inch apart on lined baking sheets.

Bake cookies, switching position of sheets halfway through baking, until edges are pale golden, 15 to 18 minutes total.
Transfer cookies from parchment to racks using a slotted spatula and cool completely

Porcupines

Contributed by:	Judy Ross and Ellen Desmarais
Source:	Christina Henderson 1974
Yield:	3 doz.
Note:	"A Christmas favourite in the Henderson family as long as I can remember!"

Ingredients

1 tablespoon	Butter (don't be generous with your measure. Grama's note)
1 cup	Sugar
½ teaspoon	Vanilla
1 cup	Dates, chopped
1 cup	Walnuts, chopped
2	Egg yolks, beaten
1	Egg white, beaten stiff
	Coconut

Directions

Cream butter and sugar, add walnuts, dates, vanilla; mix well.
Add egg yolks, blend.
Fold in egg white.

"I let them set in fridge for a while, makes them easier to handle" (Grama's note)

Roll spoonful sized balls in coconut.

Bake at 325° – 350 °F for 15 minutes.

Shape into balls while still warm.

Store in wax paper lined air tight tin

Pudding au Chomeur

Contributed by: Liane Desmarais-Cavanagh
Source: Chef Anna March, Au Pied du Chochon, Montreal, 1995
Note: I was lucky enough to get this recipe while doing an event for Canada Post.

Ingredients
4	Eggs
1¼ cups	Butter (room temperature)
1¾ cups	granulated white Sugar
2½ cups	all-purpose flour
2 teaspoons	Baking Powder
½ teaspoon	Salt
½ teaspoon	Cinnamon (I use Nutmeg)
4 cups	Maple syrup
4 cups	Whipping Cream (35%)
1	Vanilla bean (or 1 teaspoon vanilla)

* butter ramekins ahead of time

Directions:
In a medium sized pan, bring the maple syrup, vanilla and cream to a boil and set aside.
In a mixer with a paddle attachment, combine the room temperature butter and sugar together.
Mix at medium speed until it becomes light and fluffy.
Add the eggs one at a time while mixing on low and scrape the bottom of the mixer bowl with a spatula to prevent lumps from forming.
In a separate bowl, combine the salt, cinnamon, baking powder and flour and whisk together.
Slowly add in the flour mixture into the butter mixture on low speed, scraping the bottom of the mixer bowl to prevent flour lumps from forming.
Put about 1 oz of dough in each ramekin and pour the maple cream mixture over each dough to fill the ramekin about ¾ of the way up.
Bake at 450°F for 20 minutes or until a toothpick can come out relatively clean from the center of the cake.

Tip: bake these 20 minutes before you are ready to serve.
 This dessert does not sit well or store overnight.
 It's best served while it is really hot!

Pumpkin Pie

Contributed by: Ellen Desmarais
Source: Christina Henderson
Yield: Makes three 8 inch pies.
Note: This is Teeny's recipe; the best ever pumpkin pie recipe, but then our family has never had any other!

Ingredients

4	Eggs, beaten slightly
1 large can	Pumpkin (3 cups)
1 cup	Sugar
2 cup	Scalded Milk
1 cup	Brown Sugar
2 tablespoons	Molasses
1½ teaspoons	Cinnamon
1½ teaspoons	Cloves
1 teaspoon	Salt

Directions

Mix well with electric mixer and pour into uncooked pie shells.
Sprinkle grated nutmeg over top before placing in oven.
Bake slowly at 350°F for 30-30 minutes.

Queen Elizabeth Cake

Contributed by: Liane Desmarais-Cavanagh
Source: Gary Rhodes
Yield: 10 servings
Note: This is Larry's favourite cake. Apparently this recipe originated in Buckingham Palace shortly after the coronation of Queen Elizabeth II. It is supposed to be the only cake that Queen Elizabeth (II) makes herself. At the Queen's request this cake it to be sold for CHURCH purposes only. However each piece of the cake is to be sold with a RECIPE so that more cake can be made and more money can go to the church.

Ingredients

½ cup	Water, boiling
½ cup	Dates, pitted and chopped
2 tablespoons	Butter, softened
½ cup	White sugar
1	Egg
½ teaspoon	Vanilla extract
¾ cup	all-purpose flour
½ teaspoon	Baking Soda
½ teaspoon	Baking powder
¼ teaspoon	Salt
¼ cup + 2 tablespoons	Walnuts, chopped (I use Pecans)
½ cup	Coconut, shredded
1/3 cup	Brown sugar
3 tablespoons	Butter
2 tablespoons	Cream

Directions

Pour boiling water over dates in a small bowl, and let stand until cool.
Measure: flour, baking powder, soda, salt, and nuts into a small bowl.
Stir to mix.
Cream ¼ cup butter or margarine and white sugar together in a mixing bowl;
beat in egg and vanilla.
Add flour mixture to creamed mixture in three parts alternately with date mixture in two parts, beginning and ending with dry mixture.
Spread batter into a greased 8" x 8" (or 9" x 9") inch pan.
Bake at 350°F (175°C) for 30 to 40 minutes, or until an inserted wooden pick comes out clean.

    To Make Topping:

Mix coconut, brown sugar, 6 tablespoons butter and cream in a small saucepan over medium heat.
Boil for three minutes.
Spread over warm cake, and
Brown under broiler.

Raspberry Dessert

Contributed by: Valerie Healy
Source: Christina Henderson
Note: I use about 1/3 of a Chapman's brick of ice cream & ½ bag of President's Choice raspberries. I drain some of the juice off otherwise it doesn't set. This is Marshall's absolute favourite dessert.

Ingredients
1 pkg (3 oz) Jell-O
1 pint Vanilla Ice Cream
1 pkg frozen Raspberries

Directions
Dissolve Jell-O in 1 cup boiling water
Add Ice cream and let dissolve
Add Berries
Let set in fridge

Raisin Pie Filling

Contributed by: Valerie Healy
Source: Aunt Chattie
Note: This was the first pie I ever made for Allan. I knew it was really good when he said "It's better than my mother's."!

Ingredients
2 cups   Raisins
2 cups   Water
2½ tablespoons   Lemon juice
¾ cup   Brown Sugar, packed

1/3 cup   Flour
½ teaspoon   Nutmeg
¼ teaspoon   Cinnamon
3 tablespoons   Sugar
2/3 cup   Water

Directions
Combine raisins, 2 cups water, lemon juice & brown sugar in a sauce pan.
Bring to a boil, turn down heat and simmer for 3 minutes.

Combine flour, nutmeg, cinnamon, & sugar
Slowly stir in 2/3 cup water until smooth
Add this to the raisins and bring to a boil, let simmer

Pour into unbaked pie pastry, and add top crust.

Bake in 450°F oven for 15 minutes, turn down oven to 350°F and bake for a further 45 minutes.

Rhubarb Cake

Contributed by: Mireille Desmarais
Source: Violet Eggleston

Ingredients

1½ cups	Brown sugar
1	Egg
½ cup	Shortening or margarine
1 teaspoon	Baking Soda dissolved in
1 cup	Sour milk (or buttermilk +1 tablespoon lemon juice or vinegar to make it sour)
2 cups	Flour
1½ cups	Rhubarb, chopped
1 teaspoon	Vanilla
½ cup	Sugar + 1 teaspoon cinnamon

Directions

Mix together: brown sugar, egg, shortening.

Add baking soda dissolved in 1 cup sour milk or buttermilk

Add 1 cup flour, rhubarb coated with 1 cup flour and vanilla.

Put mixture into a 9 X 11 inch pan

Bake in 350°F oven for 35 minutes.

When cooked, sprinkle with sugar and cinnamon mixed together.

Rice Krispies Squares

Contributed by: Mireille Desmarais

Ingredients
¼ cup	Butter or you can use 1 - 1/4 butter stick.
40	Marshmallows (2/3rds of the bag)
1 teaspoon	Vanilla Extract
4 cups	Rice Krispies cereal.

Directions
Using Wax paper butter the sides and bottom of a long rectangular baking pan well and set aside.

Use a spaghetti pot, melt your butter on very low heat
When the butter is melted add the Vanilla Extract,

Add your 40 marshmallows and let all of the marshmallows melt,

Once all of the marshmallows have melted add your 4 cups of the Rice Krispies.

Take the pot with the mixture off the heat and mix well.

Pour the mixture into the buttered baking pan and flatten out the sticky Rice Krispies with a spatula one side buttered.

Let it cool, before cutting it into squares

Sierra Trail Mix Krispies Squares
Add 2 cups Sierra Trail mix and
2 cups Rice Krispies and follow the recipe from above. It makes a nice treat.

Rice Pudding (Christina Henderson's)

Contributed by: Judy Ross
Source: Christina Henderson - 1969
Background: A frequent dessert at home and one of my comfort foods. Served hot from the oven with a bit of milk or cream. Most often served after meat loaf, baked potatoes, and carrots."

Ingredients

¾ cup	Rice, cooked
2	Eggs
3 tablespoons	Sugar
1 teaspoon	Vanilla
S cup	Raisins
¼ teaspoon	Cinnamon
¼ teaspoon	Nutmeg

Directions

Into casserole, break eggs and stir slightly with a fork.
Stir in sugar, spices, vanilla and raisins.
Stir in 2+ cups warm/scalded milk into rice, then add to egg mixture.
Set casserole in baking pan and fill pan with hot water.
Bake uncovered 1 to 1½ hours at 325° - 350°F, stirring after the first half hour.

Rice Pudding – (Doris Desmarais')

Contributed by: Ellen Desmarais
Source: Doris Desmarais (also in Mabel Holmes handwritten cook book)
Note: This is Doris Desmarais recipe for rice pudding and John's absolute favorite. Quantity to double recipe in brackets.

Ingredients

¼ cup	Rice (½ cup)
½ cup	Raisins (1 cup)
1 cup	Milk (1½ cups)
2	Eggs well beaten (3 or 4 eggs)
½ cup	Sugar (1 cup) may substitute Splenda
½ teaspoon	Salt (1 teaspoon)
1½ cups	Milk (3 cups)

Directions

Cook first three ingredients over hot water ½ hour or until the milk has been absorbed by rice. (Use as low heat as possible.)

Mix together the eggs, sugar (Splenda), Salt and Milk

Add custard mix to the rice and mix with a fork.

Steam over very low heat 1 hour or until custard is firm, stir occasionally.
If water is rapidly boiling, the pudding will be watery, so cook slowly.
OR: put into small dishes and set into a pan of water and bake in the oven until thickened, exactly like a baked custard oven at low heat approx 300°F.

Rum Balls

Contributed by: Ellen (Henderson) Desmarais
Source: Cathy Craig-Bullen
Yield: Makes about 30 balls.
Note: From Cathy Craig-Bullen, a colleague at the National Archives. She always made these for the Christmas Breakfast.

Ingredients

2 squares	Semi-sweet chocolate (melted)
¼ cup	Corn syrup
¼ cup	Icing sugar
1/3 cup	Dark Rum
2 cups	vanilla or chocolate Wafer Crumbs
1 cup	Pecans, finely chopped
1	Egg white, slightly beaten
	Chocolate Jimmys/sprinkles (about 4 oz.)

Directions

Combine melted chocolate, corn syrup, rum, wafer crumbs, sugar and nuts; mix well.

Chill until firm (approx. 1 hour).

Shape into 1 inch balls.

Dip in egg white and roll in Jimmys.

Store in air tight container in refrigerator.

Chill at least one week to mature.

Sherry Ton Torte

Contributed by: Liane Desmarais-Cavangh
Source: Mary (May) MacNamee via Doris Desmarais
Note: This recipe was given to Grama Desmarais by her sister. It is reputed that May learned to make it from Great Grand-Mother McNamee. I have never found this recipe in any cookbook. NB: should be eaten after a light meal because it is so rich!

Ingredients

½ cup	Butter
3	Egg, yolks
½ pound box	Vanilla Wafers (broken up into very small pieces)
1 cup	Fruit Sugar
3	Egg Whites, beaten stiff
¼ cup	Sherry

Directions

Cream butter, mix in sugar and egg yolks
Beat well
Add sherry.

Fold in beaten egg whites

Line flat dish with ½ of the vanilla crumbles,
top with ½ of the egg mixture,
top with remaining crumbs, and finally
top with remaining egg mixture.

Chill in fridge 3 hours

Decorate with Cherries or Strawberries

(I have assembled these in champagne bowls and parfait glasses with equal success)

Shortbread Cookies – Christina Henderson's

Contributed by: Ellen Desmarais
Source: Christina Henderson
Note: This is the recipe Mum used. It is a little harder to manage than Mireille's recipe and results in a harder biscuit. Either is to be avoided in excess.

Ingredients
1 pound	Soft butter
¾ cup	White Sugar
4½ cups	all-purpose Flour, sifted
	Decorations

Directions
Cream butter and white sugar together well.
Add flour and blend thoroughly, kneading and squeezing dough with hands until soft and pliable.
(It may be chilled several hours, but I prefer to use it immediately).

Heat oven to 300° F

Roll dough ¼ to 1/3 inch thick and cut in any desired shapes.

Put on ungreased cookie sheets.
Sprinkle with decorations (of cut cherries).
Bake for 20 to 25 minutes or until lightly browned on the bottom and set but still very pale on top.

Shortbread Cookies

Contributed by: Mireille Desmarais
Source: Christina Henderson

Ingredients

1 pound	Butter, soft
4½ cups	all purpose white Flour
¾ cup	White Sugar
	Assorted Decorations

Directions

Pre-heat oven to 300°F

Cream butter and white sugar together well.
Add flour and blend thoroughly.
Knead dough with hands to ensure all ingredients are well incorporated.
Ensure dough is soft and pliable.

Roll dough to a thickness of ¼ to ⅜ thick
Cut with flour dusted cookie cutter

Put on an ungreased cookie sheets and sprinkle with decorations

Bake at 300°F for 20 to 25 minutes or until lightly browned on the bottom and set but still very pale on top.

Note from Mireille: "Grandmother Henderson and my Mother (Ellen Desmarais) would use this recipe at Christmas time."

Shortbread Cookie - variations

Contributed by: Mireille Desmarais
Source: Canada Corn Starch

Ingredients
½ cup   Corn Starch
½ cup   Icing Sugar
1 cup   Flour (all purpose)
¾ cup   Butter, softened to room temperature.

Directions
Preheat oven to 300°F

Sift together: Corn starch, Icing sugar and Flour
With a large spoon, thoroughly blend in butter,
Work with hands until soft and smooth dough forms.
(If dough becomes too warm and greasy refrigerate 1 hour until easier to handle.)

Flour your board,
Put the cookie dough on the board and roll out to thickness of ¼ to S

Flour your cookie cutters to make it easier to cut through the cookie dough.
Cut out cookies. (Flouring the cookie cutters whether the cutters are plastic or metal helps prevent them sticking to the dough.)

Place cookies on an un-greased cookie sheet
Decorate with coloured sugar crystals and with Red and Green cherries
Bake for 15 to 20 minutes.

Variations: (don't forget to flour any additions to the dough to prevent it from clumping.)
- **Jewel or Stained-glass Cookies:** Add 2 tablespoons ([cup) of candied fruit

- **Santa Whiskers**: Press the tines of a fork onto the cookie dough and use a ½ of a maraschino cherry for his nose.

- **Santa's Beard**: Cut cookies in circles, press shredded coconut into bottom half, add a maraschino cherry in the centre for his nose, and to currents for eyes.

- **Squirrels:** add 2/3 cup chopped pecans, hazelnuts, almonds, or walnuts to recipe.

- **Orange Sandies:** add 1 tablespoon orange zest to the flour mixture, shape into logs or crescents, and decorate with melted chocolate.

- **Peanut Butter** decrease butter to ½ cup and add 2/3 cup peanut butter (crunchy or creamy)

Sour Cream Lemon Pound Cake

Contributed by: Liane Desmarais-Cavanagh
Yield: Serves 12
Note: This was our wedding cake (L2). Can be prepared up to 2 days ahead. Wrap in foil and let stand at room temperature.)

Ingredients

3 cups	Cake Flour
½ teaspoon	Baking Soda
½ teaspoon	Salt
1 cup (2 sticks)	unsalted Butter, room temperature
3 cups	Sugar
6	Eggs, room temperature
¼ cup	Lemon juice, fresh
1 tablespoon	Lemon zest
1 cup	Sour cream

Syrup

½ cup	Sugar
¾ cup	Lemon juice, fresh

Directions

Preheat oven to 325°F.
Grease 16-cup tube pan.
Dust pan with cake flour; tap out excess flour.

Sift flour, baking soda and salt into medium bowl.
Using electric mixer, beat butter in large bowl at medium speed until fluffy.
Gradually add sugar and beat 5 minutes.
Add eggs, 1 at a time, beating just until combined after each addition.
Beat in lemon juice and peel.
Using rubber spatula, mix in dry ingredients.
Mix in sour cream.
Transfer batter to prepared pan.

Bake cake until tester inserted near center comes out clean, about 1 hour 30 minutes.
Let cake cool in pan on rack 15 minutes.
Using slender wooden skewer, poke holes all over top of cake.
Spoon syrup over cake in several additions, allowing syrup to be absorbed each time.
Cool cake completely
Cut around cake in pan.
Turn out cake.

Spice Cake Mix

Contributed by: Ellen Desmarais
Background: This is a very handy preparation to have on hand for a quick cake and it's very good, too.

Ingredients
8 cups	All-purpose flour, sifted
2¼ cups	white Sugar
2½ teaspoons	Baking Soda
2 tablespoons	Baking Powder
3 tablespoons	Ginger, ground
3 tablespoons	Cinnamon, ground
1 teaspoons	Cloves, ground
1 tablespoon	Salt
2¼ cup	Shortening

Directions
Sift sugar, baking soda and powder, ginger, cinnamon, cloves and salt together twice.
Cut in shortening with 2 knives or a pastry cutter until mixture is finely blended.
Store in a tightly sealed container or thick plastic bag.
The mix will keep up to 3 months at room temperature.

To make a one-layer cake, measure two cups of mix into a bowl.
Combine one beaten egg, a half-cup molasses, and a half-cup boiling water.
Add to dry mix and beat until well blended.
Add remaining liquid mixture and beat again.
Pour into greased and floured 8 inch square pan.
Bake at 350°F for 30 to 35 minutes.

This recipe will make enough dry mix for 4 cakes.

If an icing is desired, use either a cream cheese icing (as for a carrot cake) or plain butter icing.

Standard One Egg Sugar Cookie

Contributed by: Liane Desmarais-Cavanagh
Source: Christina Henderson, autumn 1997 (?)
Note: My favourite Sugar Cookies – makes the house smell like Christmas.

Ingredients

½ cup	Butter or other shortening (Grama's note "I like butter best")
½ cup	Sugar
1	Egg, beaten
3 teaspoons	Milk
1½ cup	Flour
1½ teaspoon	Baking Powder
1/8 teaspoon	Salt
½ teaspoon	Vanilla

Directions

Make rolled or ice box cookies

Bake at 375°F or 400°F

Summer Fruit Terrine

Contributed by: Liane Desmarais-Cavanagh
Source: Joan (Siobhan) Daly, Dublin May 2005
Yield: 8 people
Note: Best if made a day in advance
(Can be made 3 days in advance)

Ingredients

4 cups	mixed Fruit (I use berries)
2¾ teaspoons	unflavoured Gelatin* (1 envelope of Knox gelatin)
2 cups	Wine **
½ cup	Sugar
2 teaspoons	fresh Lemon juice

Directions

Arrange fruit in a 1½-quart glass, ceramic, or non-stick terrine or loaf pan.*** (Do not use metal as it sometimes discolours the gelatin)
Pour ¼ cup wine in a small bowl and sprinkle with gelatin.
Let stand 1 minute to gel.

In medium saucepan bring 1 cup wine and the ½ cup sugar to a boil, stirring until sugar is dissolved.
Remove from heat
Add gelatin mixture to warm wine, stirring until dissolved.

To saucepan: stir in remaining ¾ cup wine and lemon juice.
Transfer wine mixture to a metal bowl, and set in an iced bain-marie. (To chill quickly)
Cool mixture, stirring occasionally, just to room temperature.

Slowly pour liquid mixture over fruit.
Transfer covered loaf pan to the fridge and chill at least 6 hours. (A full 24 hours is better)

To unmold, dip loaf pan into hot water 3 to 5 seconds to loosen.
And invert terrine onto a serving plate.
NB:
    * In very hot weather add another 1 teaspoon of gelatin to help jelly set
    ** I use Rosé from Provence, but Claret de Die might be nice too!
    *** might be nice served in wine glasses
    Always unmold just before serving.

I use thinly sliced strawberries, raspberries, blueberries, blackberries. Also nice would be peeled and thinly sliced peaches or apricots, peeled and thinly sliced peaches, and halved seedless grapes
Not recommended are: sliced pineapple, citrus fruit, and kiwi (these fruits prevent gelatin from setting)

Sweet Marie Bars

Contributed by: Valerie Healy
Source: Louise Mader
Yield: 2 doz.
Note: Another recipe from Louise Mader. Children love these squares and they are not messy.

Ingredients & Directions

1 cup	Peanut Butter
1 cup	Brown Sugar
1 cup	Corn Syrup

Warm the above just enough to mix well

Add:
5 cups	Rice Crispies
1 cup	Salted Peanuts (optional)
2 Tablespoons	Butter

Pat into a 9 x 13 pan
Top with Chocolate icing

Thimble Cookies

Contributed by:	Liane Desmarais-Cavanagh
Source:	Connie Cavanagh-Spicer
Yield:	2 doz.
Note:	These are particularly good filled with homemade jam or lemon curd. We've shared this recipe with many of our friends and each person personalizes it with the addition of their favourite jam.

Ingredients

½ cup	Butter or Margarine
¼ cup	Sugar
1	Egg, separated
2 teaspoons	Lemon juice
1 cup	Flour, pre-sifted
1 cup	Nuts, finely chopped
	Jam or Jelly

Directions

Preheat oven to 350°F

Cream together: ½ cup Butter or Margarine & ¼ cup Sugar
Add: 1 Egg yolk, well beaten & 2 teaspoons Lemon juice

Beat well

Add: 1 cup flour, pre-sifted
Combine until well blended

Shape into balls which are about 1" in diameter

Dip balls in 1 slightly beaten egg white
Then roll in 1 cup finely chopped nuts

Place on greased cooking sheets (press so that the bottoms are a little flat and they don't roll around)

Make a fairly deep indentation in the centre of each cookie (you can use a thimble for consistency)

Bake in preheated 350° F oven for 5 minutes
Remove and quickly indent the centres a second time (they will have puffed while cooking).
Bake another 10 to 12 minutes
Remove from oven and fill hot cookies with brightly coloured jam or jelly

Let cool and store in an airtight container

Tiramisu – Venice May 2012

Contributed by: Liane Desmarais-Cavanagh
Yield: 8 Servings
Note: I got this recipe while Larry and I were on vacation in Venice (May 2012). Its best if made at least the day before and left to sit somewhere cold. For a stronger alcohol flavour mix Kahlúa/Tia Maria with coffee instead of adding it to the cream. Serve with: Madeira, or wines from the Douro (Italy)

Ingredients

6 large	Egg yolks, room temperature
½ cup	Sugar
16 ounces	Mascarpone cheese
4 large	Egg whites
2 ounces	Kahlúa or Tia Maria, optional
12 to 14 (4")	Ladyfingers (and I use Amoretti cookies for the second layer)
1½ cups	brewed Espresso, room temperature
	Lemon Zest
	Unsweetened cocoa powder, for garnish

Direction

In a large bowl, whisk the egg yolks with half the sugar until pale and doubled in volume (takes 3 to 5 minutes).
Add the mascarpone in 2 or 3 additions, whisking well to combine.
Add the liquor, if using, and whisk to combine.
In a clean bowl or the bowl whip the egg whites and remaining sugar to soft peaks.
Fold the egg whites into the mascarpone mixture in two or three additions.
Pour cooled espresso into pie plate (for dipping the cookies)
Assembly in a 6" x 9" (or 8" x 8") serving dish,:
- Spread ⅓ of the mascarpone cream in an even layer on the bottom of the serving dish.
- Dip each Ladyfinger cookie (both sides) in the coffee and then arrange them close together on top of the layer of mascarpone cream (the cookies should completely cover it).
- Grate zest of ½ a lemon evenly over the cookies.
- Spoon another ⅓ of the mascarpone cream over the cookies in the pan (make sure that the cream makes contact with the sides of the serving dish). Spread cream evenly.
- Dip each Amoretti cookie (both sides) in the coffee and then arrange them close together on top of the middle layer of mascarpone cream (the cookies should completely cover it).
- Grate remaining zest of ½ a lemon evenly over the cookies.
- Spoon the last ⅓ of the mascarpone cream over the cookies in the pan (make sure that the cream makes contact with the sides of the serving dish). Spread cream in an even layer.

Cover top of serving dish with wax paper (trying not to touch the top of the cream) and wrap with plastic wrap to seal out the air.
Refrigerate for at least 1 hour or up to 2 days to set the cream.

Just before serving, dust the top with cocoa powder (Optional)

Toffee

Contributed by: Valerie Healy
Source: Nannie Barrie

Ingredients

1 cup	Corn Syrup
½ pound	Butter
1 can	Eagle Brand Sweetened Condensed Milk
3 cups	Brown Sugar

Directions

Boil until strings in cold water
Stir constantly as it will stick & burn to the bottom of the pan

Pour into buttered pan

Wedding Cake (Grandma's)

Contributed by: Valerie Healy
Source: Mrs. Healy
Yield: This makes 3 wedding cake tins & 1 more large cake. Half the recipe makes a big cake (1 large square & 1 small square)
Note: Allan's mother made the best and most moist dark fruitcake. This was my wedding cake – the cake was delicious but the decorating was god awful!

Ingredients

Full

Full	Ingredient	Half
1 pound	Butter	½ pound
1 pound	Sugar	½ pound
10	Eggs, separate and beat	5
1 cup	Rum	½ cup
1 cup	Fruit juice (I use maraschino cherry juice)	½ cup
½ cup	Molasses	¼ cup
4 cups	Flour	2 cups
2 teaspoons	Baking Soda	1 teaspoon
3 teaspoons	Nutmeg	1½ teaspoons
3 teaspoons	Allspice	1 ½ teaspoons
3 teaspoons	Cinnamon	1 ½ teaspoons
2 tablespoons	Almond extract	1 tablespoon
4 pounds	Raisins	2 pounds
2 pounds	Dates	1 pound s
2 pounds	Cherries	1 pound s
2 pounds	Pineapple	1 pound s
1 pound	Peel	½ pound
1 pint	Strawberry preserves	½ pint
1 pound	sliced Almonds	½ pound

Directions

Soak fruit overnight
In morning add nuts, set aside

Cream butter and sugar
Beat yolks and add to butter & sugar with molasses, jam & fruit juice
Add sifted flour and spices
Add fruit and nuts 1/3 at a time
Add soda & water (1 teaspoon)
Fold in whites

Bake at 300ºF for 3 to 3 hours

White Fruitcake (Jean's)

Contributed by: Valerie Healy
Source: Jean Hills
Yield: about 5 pound s
Note: This is one of the best light fruitcakes ever. The recipe comes from a quilting friend Jean Hills of Ingersall. Jean is a graduate of Guelph University and she taught Home Economics years ago. Her biscotti is to die for and maybe someday I will be lucky enough to get that recipe too.

Ingredients

4 cups	Mixed diced fruit (1¾ pounds total)
8 oz	Peel
½ pkg	Cherries
8 oz	Mixed Fruit
4 rings	Pineapple
1 cup	Dates, pitted, cut up
½ cup	dried Apricots, cut up
1¼ cups	Light seedless Raisins
2 cups (8 oz)	blanched almonds, slivered
2 cups	flaked Coconut
2 cups	sifted enriched Flour
1½ teaspoons	Baking Powder
1 teaspoon	Salt
½ cup	Butter
½ cup	Shortening
1 cup	Sugar
1 teaspoon	Rum flavouring
5	large Eggs
½ cup	unsweetened Pineapple juice

Directions

Mix fruits, peels, dates, apricots, raisins, almonds & coconut
Sift together flour, baking powder, & salt
Sprinkle ½ cup over fruit mixture, mixing well.
Thoroughly cream shortening, sugar and flavouring
Add eggs (one at a time), beating well after each addition.
Add dry ingredients to creamed mixture alternately with pineapple jouice, beating after each addition.
Add fruit mixture, stiring until mixed

Line two 8½ x 4½ x 2" loaf pans with paper, allowing ½ inch to extend above all sides of the pan
Pour the batter into the pans filling to ¾ full
Bake very slowly in 275ºF oven for 2 ½ hours – 3 ½ hours (or 'till done)
Remember to put a pan of water in the oven

Jean uses brown paper & two layers of tin foil (shiny side out). Can use a ring pan – line it etc

~Preserves~

Notes on Judy's pickle recipes.

When we moved from Schefferville to Port Daniel in 1974, we were very anxious to plant a garden to have **fresh vegetables** (for the first time in 5 years!). As neophytes, there's a whole story about getting the land broken and prepared for a garden, Lynn's extensive research, ordering seeds from Vesey's in PEI, and drawing up a detailed plan for planting, etc.

The garden was solely Lynn's project; I was kept busy enough with Tim, born in May, and Heather, then three years old.

Donald Sullivan' our next door neighbour was in invaluable coach – although very reluctant at first. He taught Lynn to "thin" the plants (Lynn couldn't throw any wee plants away so they simply got moved and replanted!) One day he came into the kitchen and said, "Don't you think it's about time you picked the cucumbers?" Lynn's reply "We don't have any cucumbers yet." With this, Don laughed and invited Lynn to join him; on the way out through the back shed, he grabbed the big square galvanized laundry tub and they headed for the garden.

A short time later they returned to the shed with 100 cucumbers (!) that had been well hidden by the vines, and this was just the first picking of the season.

Mum, Ellen, Alice Ross (Lynn's Mum) and parishioners gave me "must have" pickling recipes; **many pints** of pickles were laid away that fall. It was all quite fun because a group of ladies in Port Daniel West would get together and have a "pickling bee"; I attended one of these all day affairs with lots of laughter and then another day they all landed at the rectory and about 90% of our pickles got made. The extra (large) pots the ladies brought were very helpful!

I entered Sandy West's "Bread and Butter" pickles in the Shigawake Agricultural Fair that year and **much** to my surprise, won first prize!

The few recipes I have included were our favourites.

Other notes on the garden
Don was a wonderful helper when it came to freezing the vegetables. May days, after supper, he would arrive in the kitchen with huge amounts of vegetables from the garden. While I got H & T ready for bed, he and Lynn would clean and cut the vegetables and put the blanching pot on to heat. When possible. I would help with the blanching but if I wasn't available, Don would tend to that, as well. We put away enough vegetables to last us until the next March and when we ran out, we traded with the Sullivans: they had too many vegetables and we had too much frozen fish. The next year (1975) the garden was bigger and we have sufficient vegetables until the next harvest.

The Boudoin family were wonderful neighbours across the road and Rolland enjoyed the fact we had a garden behind our garage, out of sight. Many, many evenings while Lynn was watering, he would arrive with a brown paper bag containing two bottles of beer. He and Lynn would enjoy the beer and Lynn sometimes smoked a cigar – all out of sight of Mrs. (Francine) Boudoin!

Heather's Notes on Preserves

Preserves

I started to experiment with jam making in the late '90's. I received the following sage advice from Ellen in May 1997:

I do like making jam, and you would think that after 35 years it would be perfect, but that is not always the case. I think a lot depends on the kind and quality of berries you have, and how ripe they are. These are a few tricks I have found help sometimes:

1. Try to get a mix of berry types – the very dark red ones and the lighter coloured ones, and if possible, use ½ cup of totally green ones. The unripe berries seem to have more pectin and contribute to the "set" of the jam.

2. Keep to the proportions of berries to sugar in the recipe. John has often tried to reduce the amount of sugar, but the less sugar, the thinner the set and you end up with taffy.

I try to get nice clean berries so I don't have to wash them, thus adding water that makes the jam thinner.

(HGR note: given the amount of pesticides used on conventionally grown strawberries these days, I try to get local organic berries, or local no-spray or low-spray (spray applied before berries form on the plants) berries.

3. Add the sugar gradually, stirring it in well.
4. Be sure your jars are sterilized (put them in the oven at 200 degrees F. for about 10 minutes). And that the tops too are sterilized. I like Mason jars best, and I use the small (1 cup) size because it suits our eating pattern best.

5. Final temperatures of jams vary considerably, depending on fruits used, and as recommended boiling times can be only approximate, the jam should be tested for consistency. To test jam, remove kettle from heat, place a teaspoon of jam on a cold saucer (I cool the saucer in the freezer). Jam may move slightly, but not be runny. [If you put a large metal spoon in the jam, stir around a couple of times, then lift it out with a little of the juice, and turn the spoon so the juice runs off the spoon, you will see that the stream will at first just run off, but as it cooks and gets thicker, it may separate into two streams which then join together to form one thick one. This usually indicates that it is done.]

If jam does not set to proper thickness, cook a few minutes longer and test again. If a candy thermometer is available it will help to indicate when the jam is done. Most fruits reach the jam stage at 220 degrees F.

6. Carefully pour hot jam into hot sterilized jars leaving at least ¼ inch space at the top. To ensure a perfect seal and to prevent "weeping" or oozing of liquid, avoid any dribbling of jam on inside of jar above jam level. (I use a plastic funnel designed for Mason jars, and pour from a measuring cup with a good spout.)

This is my most successful recipe, from "Jams Jellies and Pickles," Canada Department of Agriculture, 1956 (we refer to it as Mrs Pearson's because Lester Pearson with the PM at the time!)

Mrs Pearson's Strawberry Jam

Source: Ellen Desmarais
Contributed by: Heather Ross

Ingredients
8 cups	clean, hulled Strawberries
8 cups	White Sugar
½ cup	Lemon juice

Directions
Place berries and sugar in alternate layers in preserving kettle or bowl. Let stand 2 to 3 hours.

Bring to boil, and boil uncovered for 5 minutes. Add lemon juice and boil to jam stage, about 5 minutes.

Remove from heat. Skim and stir for 5 minutes to prevent fruit from floating.

Pour into hot sterilized jars. Cool slightly and seal.

Yield: about 7 cups

Ellen's Notes
I place the kettle in the sink and use a metal spoon to lift off the scum which is on top, being careful not to also discard any berries with the scum!

I use a large wooden spoon to stir pretty constantly through the cooking to be sure the jam doesn't stick to the bottom of the kettle, but a metal spoon for testing and for skimming. I think I like the longer handle on the wooden one!

You will have to judge how much heat you need for the cooking. Most recipes say to cook it at a rapid boil, and you do have to keep it boiling vigorously and steadily. You should know, too, that as it boils it rises in the pot considerably and that's why you need a big pot. But I have a couple of different pots and some hold the heat better than others. If the heat is too high you risk burning the stuff on the bottom. Better to take a little longer to cook it than to cook it on too high heat. I had to make a complete adjustment to my cooking times when I changed from the electric to the gas stove.

Bread & Butter Pickles

Contributed by: Ellen Desmarais
Source: Sandy West, 1970
Yield: 8 pints
Note: I think this recipe has already been shared in the family, but it is worth preserving (no pun intended).

Ingredients

4 quarts	sliced medium Cucumbers (about 14 medium)
6 medium	white Onions, sliced
2	Green Peppers, chopped
6 cloves	Garlic
1/3 cups	coarse medium Salt
5 cups	Sugar
3 cups	Cider Vinegar
1½ teaspoons	Turmeric
1½ teaspoons	Celery seed
2 tablespoons	Mustard seed

Directions

Do not pare cucumbers; slice very thin.
Add onions, peppers & whole garlic cloves.
Add salt; cover with cracked ice; mix thoroughly.
Let stand 3 hours – drain well.

Combine remaining ingredients; pour over cucumber mixture.
Heat just to a boil.

Seal in hot sterilized jars.

Barbeque Glaze

Contributed by:	Liane Desmarais-Cavanagh
Source:	Gourmet Magazine, June 2002
Yield:	Makes 2½ cups sauce.
NB:	This not only tastes great but it keeps for several weeks in the 'fridge. Great on chicken as marinade and glaze. We like to serve it on the side with pork or burgers

Ingredients

1 pound	Shallots, finely chopped (2¾ cups)
¼ cup	Olive Oil
1 cup	distilled White Vinegar (or ½ cup white Balsamic vinegar)
1 cup	Tomato purée
½ cup	mild Honey
¼ cup	Steak Sauce (such as A1.)
1 tablespoon	Worcestershire sauce
¾ teaspoon	Salt
¼ teaspoon	Pepper

Directions

Cook shallots in oil in a 4 quart heavy pot over moderately low heat, covered, stirring occasionally, until soft, 12 to 14 minutes (reduce heat to low if shallots begin to brown).

Stir in vinegar, tomato purée, honey, steak sauce, Worcestershire, salt, and pepper and bring to a boil.

Remove sauce from heat and reserve 1½ cups for basting and 1 cup for serving.

Cool sauce to room temperature, (sauce will thicken as it cools).

Caramelized Red Onion Relish

Contributed by:	Heather Ross
Source:	"The Complete Book of Year-Round Small-Batch Perserving" by Ellie Topp & Margaret Howard
Yield:	2 cups
Note:	This relish is a great accompaniment to grilled meats. It's so tasty, it might not last long once you make it – you can skip the processing and keep it in the refrigerator for up to 3 weeks, or freeze it for longer storage.

Ingredients

2 cups	large Red Onions, peeled
¼ cup	firmly packed Brown Sugar
1 cup	dry Red Wine
3 tablespoon	Balsamic Vinegar
1/8 teaspoon	Salt
1/8 teaspoon	freshly ground Pepper

Directions

Slice onions into very thin slices.
Combine onions and sugar in a heavy non-stick skillet.
Cook, uncovered, over medium-high heat for about 25 minutes or until onions turn golden and start to caramelize, stirring frequently.

Stir in wine and vinegar.
Bring to a boil over medium-high heat, reduce heat to low and cook for about 15 minutes or until most of the liquid has evaporated, stirring frequently.

Season to taste with salt and pepper.

Ladle relish into sterilized jars to within ½ inch of rim.
Process 10 minutes for half-pint (1 cup/250 mL) jars.

'Dem Bones BBQ Sauce

Contributed by: Liane Desmarais-Cavanagh
Source: Mike Cain
Yeild: LOTS
Note: See notes from Mike below

Ingredients

Four 32 oz. bottles	Ketchup (store bought)
1 pound	blackstrap Molasses
1 cup	Blackberry jelly
2 cups	Vinegar
3 tablespoons	ground Red Pepper
2	white Onions, chopped
2 medium	Bell Peppers, chopped
2 cloves	Garlic, minced
1 pound	light Brown Sugar
½ cup	Pickling Spice
1	white cotton baby's sock (preferably unused)
2 teaspoons	Celery salt

Directions

Put the ketchup and vinegar on a medium-low heat until good and hot, then slowly add molasses, brown sugar and jelly, stirring all the time until they liquefy with the hot mixture.

Add chopped onions, peppers, garlic and spices.

Put pickling spice into baby's sock and tie sock closed at top making spice pouch.

Add pouch to mixture, holding under surface with wooden spoon until saturated with hot mixture.

Allow mixture to SLOWLY boil or "burble."
Keep stirring of bottom to prevent sticking.

Note from Mike: From time to time I like to "mop" the bottom of the pot with the spice pouch to release goodies in pouch and clean bottom at the same time. Allow to "burble" for about an hour and a half, until fresh peppers are soft. Don't leave out the pickling spice from this stuff. It's the key to giving this sauce its own distinctive flavour. It's a pretty sweet sauce, but ground red pepper gives it a "sneaky pete" quality that slips up behind the sweet and grabs your attention!

Dill Tartar Sauce

Contributed by: Liane Desmarais-Cavanagh
Source: Fern Radmore
Yeild: ½ cup
Note: Wonderful with any BBQ'd fish or chicken. Also yummy on Tuna Sandwiches.

Ingredients

½ cup	Tartar sauce (can be purchased)
2 tablespoons	Dill, fresh & chopped
1 teaspoon	Lemon zest (about ½ a lemon)
¼ teaspoon	Salt
¼ teaspoon	Pepper

Directions

Whisk ½ cup tartar sauce, 1 tablespoon dill, and lemon peel in medium bowl to blend.

Salt and pepper to taste

Let stand, in fridge for 1 hour for tastes to "marry"

Fresh Fig and Strawberry Jam

Contributed by: Heather Ross
Source: "The Complete Book of Year-Round Small-Batch Perserving" by
   Ellie Topp & Margaret Howard
Yield: About 4 cups
Background: After having success with Mrs Pearson's Strawberry Jam, I decided to branch out. The following recipes are from the book noted above The book contains a wide range of different recipes. The small batch nature of the recipes works well for my limited storage space.

Ingredients
1 pound	fresh Green Figs, stemmed and cut into small pieces
2 cups	quartered Strawberries
2 cups	granulated Sugar
3 tablespoons	Lemon juice

Directions

Place figs, strawberries, sugar and lemon juice in a medium stainless steel or enamel saucepan. Cover and let stand for 1 hour, stirring occasionally.

Bring to a boil over high heat, reduce heat to medium and boil rapidly, uncovered, until mixture will form a gel (Testing as per Ellen's notes - #5 on page 283), about 15 minutes, stirring frequently. Remove from heat.

Ladle into sterilized 1 cup jars leaving ½ inch of space at the top. Wipe jar rim to remove any stickiness before applying lid. Process in a hot water bath for 5 minutes.

Notes:
The figs add a lovely depth to this jam. Fresh black figs work just as well as the green figs. This year I didn't have time to make jam during strawberry season, but I did clean, quarter and freeze some berries. That was fortunate, as I noticed that there were fresh figs available in stores at the end of August, and they were a much better price than the ones available during strawberry season.
 Things have changed since the days of Mrs Pearson, and hot water processing is included in most modern recipes. To process jars, you need a canner, which includes a rack for the jars, or a large pot with a rack (i.e., a round cooling rack) to hold jars off the bottom of the pot. Bring the water in the pot to a boil while your jam is cooking so that the jars can go in as soon as possible after being filled.
 Place the jars in the canner, making sure they are covered by 1 to 2 inches of water. Cover canner and return water to boil. Begin timing once the water returns to the boil.
Current canning recipes also instruct you to sterilize jars in the canner by boiling them for 10 minutes. While I have tried canner sterilization, I find it awkward, and still use the oven method. Lids should be boiled for 5 minutes. This sterilizes them, but also softens the rubber, which helps ensure a good seal.

Hot Dog Relish

Contributed by: Judy Ross
Source: Evelyn (Prince) Major, Port Daniel – 1975
Yield: 4 pts

Ingredients & Method

Chop finely in blender or food processor:
- 8 cups unpeeled, Cucumber (approx 6 large)
- 3 cups Onions (approx. 1½ pound s)
- 1 small Green Pepper (&/or red for colour)

Soak overnight with: ½ cup coarse salt
3 Cups water

Drain very well.

Add:
- 2 cups white Vinegar
- 1½ cups white Sugar
- 1 teaspoon Mustard seed
- 1 teaspoon Celery seed
- 1 teaspoon Tumeric

Bring to a boil and cook approximately 15 minutes.
Stir in a few drops of green food colouring, if desired.
Place in sterilized jars and seal.

Note: This is one half the original recipe.

Jezebel Sauce

Contributed by: Liane Desmarais-Cavanagh
Source: Connie (Cavanagh) Spicer, June 1996
Note: Love the name, and the taste.

Ingredients

One 5 oz jar	Horseradish sauce
One 1.5 oz can	dry Mustard
One 18 oz jar	Pineapple preserves
One 18 oz. jar	Apple Jelly
1 tablespoon	coarsely ground Pepper

Directions

Mix the horseradish and dry mustard well.
Combine with remaining ingredients.

Will keep in refrigerator for months.

Especially good on sliced ham, or as a dunking sauce for chicken or ham chunks as an appetizer.

Marvelous Mustard

Contributed by: Judy Ross
Source: Evelyn Jackson, Magog – 1990
Note: Evelyn kept Mum, Lynn's parents and our household (as well as others) supplied with this as long as she was able. Mum really liked it.

Ingredients & Method

Mixture #1: Let stand for several hours
    3½ oz   "Keen's" dry Mustard
    1 cup   Wine Vinegar

Mixture #2:
    2   Eggs, slightly beaten
    1 cup   Sugar

Combine Mixtures #1 and #2.

Cook over low heat until thick, giving it an occasional stir.

Cool.

Add:
    1½ cups   Mayonnaise

Message from source: "This mustard is addictive; makes husbands grouchy when you run out."
                    EVELYN JACKSON - 1990

Mustard Relish

Contributed by: Judy Ross
Source: Ada Prince (Port Daniel) via Joyce Prince MacKenzie, (Shigawake) 1974
Yield: Yield: 4-5 pts
Note: This started out "chunky" as "Grace's Pickles" from either Ada Prince (Port Daniel) or her daughter; Joyce Mackenzie (Shigawake) in 1974 and by 1984 had been altered to make this as a relish. You can choose chunky or fine!

Ingredients & Method

Chop very fine in blender or food processor

5 large	Cucumbers
4 medium	Onions
1 small	Green Pepper
1 small clove	Garlic

Let stand 3 hours, using 3 tablespoon coarse salt.

Rinse slightly and add:

2 cups	Water
1 cup	Cider Vinegar
1 cup	White Vinegar

Cook 10 minutes, then add:

3 cups	white Sugar
½ cup	Flour
3 tablespoons	dry Mustard
1 tablespoon	Ginger (powdered)
2 teaspoons	Tumeric
1 tablespoon	Celery seed
½ teaspoon	Pepper

Cook 10 minutes.

Place in sterilized jars and seal.

Onion Confit

Contributed by: Liane Desmarais-Cavanagh
Source: Mireille Groseiller, October 2006
Yield: Makes about 4 cups
Note: Larry and I had just come back from a trip in the Loire Valley and I asked Mireille if she had ever had Onion Confit, when she asked if I wanted the recipe I jumped at the opportunity.

Ingredients

2 tablespoons	unsalted Butter
2 tablespoons	Olive Oil
3 pounds	yellow Onions*, thinly sliced
1 tablespoon	Sugar
1 teaspoon	Salt
½ teaspoon	freshly ground Pepper
½ cup	Wine**
2 teaspoons	chopped Thyme

Directions

Heat the butter and olive oil in a large skillet over medium heat.
Add onions and sugar.
Season with salt and pepper.
Cook, stirring occasionally, until onions are soft, 15 to 20 minutes.

Increase heat to medium-high.

Add wine and cook, stirring occasionally, until wine is reduced and onions are deep golden brown, 15 to 20 minutes more.

Add thyme; taste and adjust for seasoning.

Transfer onions to a bowl and serve immediately. (You can also put in glass jars and freeze until ready to use.)

* Vidalia's are best

** I prefer Vouvray (white from the Loire valley) but you can a red Merlot it just depends on how strong you want it to taste. (Remember only cook with wine that's good enough to drink.)

Pear and Currant Chutney

Contributed by:	Liane Desmarais-Cavanagh
Source:	Ellen Desmarais
Yield:	2 to 3 cups
Note:	Allow this Chutney to ripen in the refrigerator for up to four weeks; it improves with age.

Ingredients

1 cup	dried Currants
6 tablespoons	Pear Brandy
4	Bosc Pears, cored and cut into ½" pieces
2 ribs	Celery, cut into ¼ " pieces
½ cup	Sugar
1/3 to ½ cup	Lemon juice, fresh is best
3½" piece	Ginger, peeled and grated
	Pinch cayenne

Directions

Put currants and brandy into a medium saucepan and simmer over medium heat until currants are plump and have absorbed most of the liquor, about 7 minutes.

Add pears, celery, sugar, lemon juice, ginger, and cayenne and stir well.

Return to a simmer, reduce heat to medium-low, and simmer until pears are very soft and translucent and juices are thick and syrupy, about 1 hour.

Put chutney into a clean jar with a tight-fitting lid; set aside to let cool.

Cover and refrigerate until ready to serve.

Serve at room temperature.

Rhubarb, Date and Apricot Chutney

Contributed by: Heather Ross
Source: "The Complete Book of Year-Round Small-Batch Perserving"
    by Ellie Topp & Margaret Howard
Yield: about 3 cups
Note: This recipe works well with frozen rhubarb. I prefer to make it in the fall or winter, after I've done all my fresh-produce preserves. This pairs well with cheese, especially in a grilled cheese sandwich. It's also great with meat

Ingredients

4 cups	sliced Rhubarb
1 cup	chopped dried Dates
1 cup	lightly packed Brown Sugar
½ cup	chopped dried Apricots
½ cup	Cider Vinegar
¼ cup	finely chopped Onion
¼ cup	finely chopped candied or crystallized Ginger
1 teaspoon	Curry powder
¼ teaspoon	ground Nutmeg
¼ teaspoon	Pickling Salt

Directions

Combine rhubarb, dates, sugar, apricots, vinegar, onion, ginger, curry powder, nutmeg and salt in a medium stainless steel or enamel saucepan.

Bring to a boil over medium-high heat; reduce heat and cook, uncovered, for 8 minutes, or until thickened and fruit is soft, stirring frequently.

Remove hot jars from canner and ladle chutney into jars to within ½ inch of rim.

Process 10 minutes for half-pint (1 cup/250 mL) jars and 15 minutes for pint (2 cup/500 mL) jars.

Makes about 3 cups.

Sauce for Ham - Thelma's

Contributed by: Ellen Desmarais
Source: Thelma Bolter-Swinford
Yield: 1 cup
Note: This sauce was often made by Thelma (Bolter-Swinford) when ham was served at 3622 Northcliffe Avenue.

Ingredients

¼ cup	Brown Sugar
1 teaspoon	prepared Mustard (Dijon)
1 teaspoon	Flour
2 tablespoons	Raisins
2 tablespoons	Vinegar
¾ cup	Water

Directions

Mix dry ingredients.
Add raisins, vinegar.
Cook to a syrup.
(Pineapple, peach slices or maraschino cherries may be added)
Serve hot or cold.

Sauce for Ham - Judy's Lemon Raisin

Contributed by: Ellen Desmarais
Source: Judy Ross
Yield: 1 cup

Ingredients

½ cup	Brown Sugar
¼ teaspoon	Salt
Pinch	Cloves, ground
½ cup	Raisins
1 tablespoon	Lemon juice
2 teaspoons	Cornstarch
½ cup	Water, hot
1 tablespoon	Butter
1 teaspoon	Lemon zest

Directions

Combine Sugar, starch, salt and cloves in saucepan
Gradually add hot water and cook until thickened, stirring occasionally
Add raisins & continue cooking 1 – 2 minutes
Remove from heat and blend in butter, lemon juice & zest
Serve hot

Spiced Onion Marmalade

Contributed by: Liane Desmarais-Cavanagh
Source: Ellen Desmarais, October 2007
Yeild: Makes About 1½ cups
Note: This marmalade is delicious with: pork or roast Cornish game hens. Can be made 5 days ahead.

Ingredients

¼ cup	Olive oil
1 pound	Vidalia Onions, diced
3 cloves	Garlic, chopped
¼ cup	Balsamic Vinegar
¼ cup	Golden Brown Sugar (I use Splenda Brown Sugar)
2 tablespoons	Tomato paste
½ teaspoon	Ginger, ground
¼ teaspoon	Cloves, ground
¼ teaspoon	Nutmeg, ground

Directions

Heat oil in heavy medium skillet over medium-high heat.

Add onions and garlic; sauté until onions just begin to brown, about 10 minutes.

Add vinegar and sugar and cook 5 minutes, stirring often.

Stir in tomato paste, ginger, cloves and nutmeg.

Reduce heat to low and simmer until marmalade is thick, stirring often, about 1 minute.

Season with salt and pepper.

Cover and chill.

Rewarm before serving

Sun Relish

Contributed by:	Heather Ross
Source:	"The Complete Book of Year-Round Small-Batch Preserving" by Ellie Topp & Margaret Howard
Yield:	4 cups
Notes:	This relish makes a lovely addition to a cheese plate. It's also lovely with warm biscuits or omelets.

Ingredients

6	Peaches, peeled, pitted and chopped
6	Sweet Yellow Peppers, seeded and chopped
1	Hot Yellow Pepper, seeded and chopped
1	Lemon, halved
½ cup	White Wine Vinegar
2½ cups	granulated Sugar
1½ teaspoons	Pickling Salt

Directions

Place peaches, peppers, lemon and vinegar in a large stainless steel or enamel saucepan.
Bring to a boil over medium-high heat, reduce heat and boil gently, uncovered, for 30 minutes or until softened.
Remove and discard lemon, add sugar and salt; return to a boil.
Cook, uncovered, for about 20 minutes or until mixture thickens, stirring frequently.

Ladle relish into sterilized jars to within ½ inch of rim.
Process 10 minutes for half-pint (1 cup/250 mL) jars and 15 minutes for pint (2 cup/500 mL) jars.

Sweet Cucumber Pickles (aka "Tongue Pickles")

Contributed by: Judy Ross
Source: Christina Henderson
Yield: 4 to 5 pints

Ingredients & Method

Peel, quarter, remove seeds and cut into 2 inch lengths:
12 large, over-ripe Cucumbers

Prepare brine of:
¼ cup   Coarse Salt
8 cups   cold Water

Cover cucumber pieces with brine and soak overnight.
Make sure cucumber pieces remain submerged by placing a plate on top of them.

Drain the cucumbers well.

Syrup:
4 cups   White Vinegar
1½ cups   White Sugar
2½ cups   Brown Sugar
¼ cup   mixed Pickling Spice

Prepare syrup of sugar and vinegar; tie spices in a cloth bag (or place in large tea egg) and add to syrup. When syrup boils hard, add cucumbers and cook over medium heat.

As pieces of cucumber become transparent, place them in sterilized jars.
Thick pieces may need approximately 1 hour of cooking but you can usually start removing the smaller/thinner pieces after 20-30 minutes of cooking.

Cover with hot syrup.

Remove air bubbles and seal.

~ Drinks ~

Anniversary Punch

Contributed by: Liane Desmarais-Cavanagh
Source: James Roger

Ingredients
1 package (15 oz) frozen Strawberries, thawed
2 teaspoons Lime zest
Juice of 1 Lime
1 (750-ml) bottle Pinot Noir
1 (750-ml) dry White Wine
1 (750-ml) bottle diet Gingerale / Club Soda

Directions
Combine strawberries, lime peel, and lime juice in saucepan.
Simmer together 10 minutes; put through food mill or sieve.
Cool. Pour fruit mixture over block of ice in punch bowl.
Add wines just before serving.
Garnish with whole strawberries or lime slices, if desired.

Bellini Cocktail

Contributed by: Liane Desmarais-Cavanagh
Source: originated: Harry's Bar, Venice, in 1934.
Yield: 2 people
Note: Dangerous as you don't feel the effect of the alcohol until you try to stand up.

Ingredients
2 ripe	Peaches, peeled, halved and stone removed
1 bottle	chilled Champagne (I have used Prosecco)
2 chilled	champagne glasses

Directions
Place the peaches in a small blender and purée until totally smooth.
This can be done well in advance and kept in the fridge.
Spoon half into the chilled champagne glasses and slowly top up with champagne, stirring as you pour.
You should ideally have one third peach purée to two thirds champagne.
Serve straight away as a pre-dinner drink, leaving plenty of time for a second glass each.

Champagne Cassis Punch

Contributed by: Liane Desmarais-Cavanagh
Source: Chef at the Chateau Lake Louise, Fall 1990
Note: This was the punch served at a friend's wedding reception.

Ingredients
3 bottles   chilled dry Champagne (I've used 2 bottles Prosecco + 1 bottle Club Soda)
¼ to ½ cup   Chambord (or Ribena), or to taste
     Fresh black raspberries
     Garnish: thin Lemon slices

Directions
In a punch bowl set in a hollowed-out block of ice, combine the champagne with the Chambord (Ribena).
Garnish the punch with the raspberries and the lemon slices.
(Beware if there are any berries left at the bottom of the bowl they pack a punch!!!)

Christmas Pudding

Contributed by: Liane Desmarais-Cavanagh
Source: LCBO Magazine, Holiday edition 2011

Ingredients
1½ oz	Grey Goose Vodka
¼ cup	Golden raisins
½ oz	Christmas Syrup (see below)
3 oz	Apricot juice
	Pinch of nutmeg
	Toasted and crushed almonds mixed

Christmas Syrup
1 cup   Brown Sugar + 3 Cloves + 1 cup boiling Water

Combine all and stir to dissolve sugar. Allow to cool
Remove cloves, cover and refrigerate
Keeps for 1 to 2 weeks.

Directions for drink
To a cocktail shaker add raisins and Christmas Syrup, Muddle
Fill shaker with ice and pour in Vodka and apricot juice.
Shake and strain into a stemmed Margarita-style glass rimmed with crushed almonds and lemon zest.
Sprinkle with a touch of nutmeg.

Diabetic Friendly Eggnog

Contributed by: Liane Desmarais-Cavanagh
Source: Splenda pamphlet via Ellen Desmarais
Yield: 2 liters (Serving size: ½ cup)

Ingredients

1 cup	SPLENDA® No Calorie Sweetener, Granulated
1 tablespoon	Cornstarch
1 teaspoon	ground Nutmeg
7	Egg yolks
4 cups	Milk
2 cups	fat-free Half and Half
2 tablespoons	Vanilla extract*

Directions

Mix together first 3 ingredients in a large heavy saucepan. Set aside.

Whisk egg yolks. Add to SPLENDA® Granulated Sweetener mixture whisking until blended. Gradually whisk in milk.
Cook over low heat, whisking constantly until the temperature reaches 175 degrees approximately (5 to 8 minutes).
Remove from heat and whisk in half and half; cool.
Cover and chill 3 hours or up to 3 days.
Stir in vanilla extract just before serving.

Note

If desired, 2 tablespoons of vanilla extract can be replaced with 1 cup dark rum.

Nutrition info (per 1/2 cup): Fat: 4 gr., Carbs: 7 gr., Fibre: 0 gr., Sugar: 5 gr.

Garnet Punch

Contributed by: Liane Desmarais-Cavanagh
Source: James Roger
Yield: 2 liters (Serving size: ½ cup)

Ingredients

1½ pounds	fresh or frozen Cranberries (6 cups; thawed if frozen)
2 cups	Splenda
1 tablespoon	finely chopped fresh Rosemary
4½ cups	Water
1 (750-ml) bottle	Vodka (3 cups) (I use Club Soda)
	Garnish: fresh rosemary sprigs (leaves stripped except for top 1 inch)

Directions

Simmer: cranberries, Splenda, rosemary, and water in a 4-quart heavy saucepan over moderately low heat, uncovered, stirring occasionally, until cranberries have burst and are very soft and liquid is slightly syrupy, about 30 minutes.
Pour syrup through a fine-mesh sieve into a bowl, gently stirring cranberries but not pressing on them, then discard berries.
Chill syrup, uncovered, until cold, at least 3½ hours.
Just before serving, stir together vodka and syrup in a pitcher.
Serve over ice in 6- to 8-ounce glasses.
(Syrup can be chilled, covered, up to 3 days.)

Happy Apple Rum Twist

Contributed by: Liane Desmarais-Cavanagh
Source: James Roger, 1982
Yield: 1 person (multiply as necessary)
Note: This recipe (and the one below) is frequently served at James' house.

Ingredients
1½ oz	light or dark Rum
3 oz	Apple Juice or cider
1½ tablespoons	Lime juice
½ cup	crushed Ice
	Twist Lime peel

Directions
Combine all ingredients except the peel in a cocktail shaker and shake vigorously.

Strain into a cocktail glass and drop in the peel.

Jackie's Irish Cream

Contributed by: Liane Desmarais-Cavanagh
Source: Jackie Sampson, NRCan
Yield: 1 good party
Note: Yummy, keeps for weeks in the fridge

Ingredients

1 can	Eagle Brancd Codensed Milk
1½ cup	Whisky
1 cup	Cream (35%)
3	Eggs
	Chocolate Syrup (to taste)

Directions

Mix with hand blender
Let stand a few minutes
Refrigerate

Napoleon Champagne Cocktail

Contributed by: Liane Desmarais-Cavanagh
Source: Dick Pound, 1992
Yield: Makes 6

Ingredients

6	Sugar cubes
	Bitters
6 teaspoons	Cognac
6 tablespoons	Grand Marnier or other orange liqueur
1 750-ml bottle	chilled Champagne (preferably extra dry)
6	Orange peel strips

Directions

Sprinkle each sugar cube with 2 dashes of bitters.

Place 1 sugar cube in each of 6 champagne flutes.

Pour 1 teaspoon Cognac over each sugar cube.

Add 1 tablespoon Grand Marnier to each glass.

Fill glasses with champagne.
Garnish glasses with orange peel strips and serve.

Pimm's Cup

Contributed by:	Liane Desmarais-Cavanagh
Source:	Keith Angus-Whiting, Summer 1993
Yield:	Serves 4.
Note:	Refreshing, tart, citrusy, this old fashioned drink served in a highball glass is perfect by itself or as an accompaniment to grilled meats, fried chicken, or spicy salsas.

Ingredients

4	Lemon slices
4	Apple slices
4	Orange slices
4	Cucumber slices
3 cups	Pimm's No. 1 Cup
2 cups	Lemonade soda
4	fresh Mint sprigs
	Ice cubes

Directions

Fill four 8- to 10-ounce highball glasses with ice cubes.
Divide the fruit slices among the glasses.
Pour ½ cup of lemonade and 3 tablespoons of Pimm's into each glass.

Garnish with the mint and serve.

Planters' Fruit Punch

Contributed by: Ellen Desmarais
Source: This recipe is from Bermuda (Christmas 1967) and is super good.
Yield: 16 servings

Ingredients

1 cup	Roses Lemon Squash
2 cups	Roses Orange Squash
½ cup	Pineapple juice
16 drops	Angusta Bitters
	Sugar to taste (maybe ½ cup)
	Cherries
½ cup	Rum
12 cans	Ginger ale

Directions

Mix the first 5 ingredients & chill. Just before serving, put ice in punch bowl or glasses, with a cherry. Add ginger ale to fruit mix and stir.

Pour.

Quarante quatre (44)

Contributed by: Liane Desmarais-Cavanagh
Source: Laura Calder

Ingredients
1 large	organic Orange, well washed
44	Coffee beans
44	Sugar cubes
4 cups	Vodka

Directions
For each coffee bean cut small slit the orange with a skewer or knitting needle.
Insert the coffee bean through the slits in the skin into the orange flesh.
Repeat all over the orange until all 44 of the coffee beans are evenly distributed.

Put the whole orange in a sterilized preserving jar (do not cut open the orange to make it fit, it must remain whole).
Add the cubes of sugar,
Pour in the alcohol, seal, and shake.

Store in a cool, dark place, giving the jar a shake every day for 44 days.

Filter the liqueur through a coffee filter into a serving bottle.

Summer Sangria

Contributed by:	Liane Desmarais-Cavanagh
Source:	LCBO recipe site
Yield:	Serves: 8 pitchers
Note:	This is a great 'make-ahead' summertime drink for the cottage; easy to make, serves a crowd, and goes well with BBQ meat.

Ingredients:

1	Granny Smith Apple, cored and sliced ¼ inch thick
1	Pear, cored and sliced ¼ inch thick
A third of a	fresh pineapple, unpeeled, then sliced into wedges ¼ inch thick
2	Oranges, flesh and zest
2	Lemons, flesh and zest
1 cup	Sugar
4 bottles	Red Wine (inexpensive, robust).
8 oz	Brandy
6 oz	Orange liqueur, such as Triple Sec
6 oz	off-dry Spanish Sherry, such as Amontillado
	7Up / Club Soda

Directions:

Prepare the citrus fruit. Use a vegetable peeler to peel off the zest of the lemons and oranges.
With a sharp pairing knife, trim off the bitter white pith of the fruit and discard.
Slice the flesh.
In a clean vessel, large enough to accommodate 5 litres of liquid and fruit, add the cut fruit and the sugar.
Put a lid on the jar and shake it around to coat the fruit with the sugar.
Add the remaining ingredients.
Stir to combine and cover.
Store in a cool place for at least a week to allow flavours to combine.
To Serve:
Fill a pitcher half full with ice.
Add enough of the wine mixture to fill about ¾ full. Add a few slices of the marinated fruit (WARNING: the marinated fruit packs a serious punch), along with some fresh berries.
Top with either Club Soda or 7Up (depending on your preference).
Serve immediately.

Summer Sangria 2

To serve a single pitcher right away, use the following method:
Fill a pitcher half full with ice.
Add fresh slices of apple, pineapple, lemon and orange.
Add 4 tablespoons sugar and muddle slightly with a wooden spoon.
Pour over enough red wine to fill halfway.
Add 3 oz brandy and 2 oz each of the orange liqueur and sherry.
Top with 7Up, Stir, and serve immediately.

Sgroppino (limone)

Contributed by:	Liane Desmarais-Cavanagh
Source:	Bartender @ Cipriani Hotel, Venice - 2012
Yield:	4-6 servings
Note:	NB: Do <u>not</u> use a blender, while it is fast it makes everything to "runny" I make this at the table using a chilled metal bowl and whisk.

Ingredients
1 liter	Lemon Gelato
1 bottle	Prosecco
2 jiggers (oz)	Vodka
	Zest of 1 Lemon

Directions
Chill champagne flutes.

In a bowl whisk lemon gelato until it is smooth (consistency of dairy Queen ice cream).

Gradually whisk (do not use a blender) in the vodka and finally the Prosecco.

Don't whisk too much or it will become too liquid. (You must whisk the sparkling wine in by hand because a machine will melt the ingredients. You don't want it too thick, but you don't want it real thin, either.)

Pour mixture into glasses, sprinkle lemon zest on top

Serve immediately with straw-spoons

NOTE: The drinks will separate rapidly if left standing.

Toasted Crown

Contributed by: Liane Desmarais-Cavanagh
Source: LCBO Magazine, Christmas 2011

Ingredients
1½ oz	Crown Royal (Black)
2 oz	Cloudy Apple Juice
1 tablespoon	Pumpkin Pie filling
2 oz.	Cream

Garnish: Whipped Cream and toasted Pumpkin Seeds

Directions
In a cocktail shaker filled with ice add all the ingredients and shake to blend thoroughly.
Strain into a stemmed margarita-style glass
Top with whipped cream and dust with seeds.

The Grand 75

Contributed by: Liane Desmarais-Cavanagh
Source: LCBO Magazine, Christmas 2011
Yield: Serves 1.

Ingredients
1 oz.	Grand Marnier
½ oz	Lemon Juice
1 oz.	Fresh Cranberry juice
	Splash of sparkling white wine
	Orange slice and a cranberry on a skewer

Directions
In a cocktail shaker filled with ice add Grand Marnier, Lemon juice, and Cranberry juice
Shake well and strain into a chilled flute glass
Top with white wine and garnish

www.ingramcontent.com/pod-product-compliance
Lightning Source LLC
Chambersburg PA
CBHW081440070526
44586CB00019B/2183